Active Learning for Threes

Debby Cryer

Thelma Harms

Beth Bourland

Frank Porter Graham Child Development Center
University of North Carolina, Chapel Hill, North Carolina

Dale Seymour Publications

Dale Seymour Publications®
An imprint of Pearson Learning
299 Jefferson Road, P.O. Box 480
Parsippany, New Jersey 07054-0480
www.pearsonlearning.com
1-800-321-3106

Developed with the partial support of the North Carolina Department of Human Resources, Office of Day Care Services, with funds provided by the Social Services Block Grant.

Design: Paula Shuhert
Cover Design: Lydia D'moch
Illustrations: Cynthia Swann Brodie
          Jane McCreary

ISBN 0-201-21337-0

17   03

Acknowledgments

These materials for three-year-olds could not have been developed without the time and talent of a large number of day care and materials production professionals.

The idea and the funding for the project originated from the Office of Day Care Services of the North Carolina Department of Human Resources, directed by Rachel Fesmire. Continuous contact with this agency was provided through the very supportive project officer, Beth May, whose careful and timely reviews of the materials were sincerely appreciated. We were fortunate to receive additional feedback on the materials from Mary Holroyd, also of the Office of Day Care Services.

The Advisory Board, listed below, was a hard-working, knowledgeable group. They reviewed all the materials and offered excellent suggestions. Members who had access to groups of Threes helped us try out the activities.

Roberta Barrett
Sycamore Preschool
Chapel Hill

Sue Baynes
Baynes Happy Day Nursery and
    Kindergarten, Inc.
Greensboro

Helen Canaday
School of Home Economics
University of North Carolina
Greensboro

Bonnie Craig
Developmental Day Care and Child Care
    Resources and Referral of High Point
High Point

Dorothy Graham
Durham Day Care Council
Durham

Sylvia Hall
Winterpark Preschool
Wilmington

Juliette McKoy
Office of Child Day Care Licensing
Raleigh

Donna McNeill
Wilkes Community College
Wilkesboro

Sarah Mansfield
Frank Porter Graham Child Care Center
Chapel Hill

Beth May
Office of Day Care Services
Raleigh

Selma Smith
Office of Day Care Services
Wilmington

Brenda Walker
Office of Day Care Services
Gastonia

Holly Willett
Frank Porter Graham Child Development
    Center
Chapel Hill

Pilot testing of the activities with groups of three-year-olds was done by teachers and directors in 15 North Carolina centers. Their feedback assured us that the activities do work in the real world of day care.

Children's World Day School
Wilkesboro

Clara Cox Day Care Center
Developmental Day Care
High Point

Daniel Brooks Day Care Center
Developmental Day Care
High Point

Fairplains Elementary Day Care
Wilkesboro

First Baptist Child Development Center
Gastonia

Frank Porter Graham Child Development
    Center
Child Care Center
Chapel Hill

Gaston College Child Care Training Center
Dallas

Joyland Nursery School
Lumberton

Miss Nancy's Early Learning Center
Morehead City

Our World Child Development Center
Jefferson

Southeastern Preschool Education Center
Wilmington

Southside Day Care Center
Development Day Care
High Point

Sycamore Preschool
Chapel Hill

Winter Park Preschool
Wilmington

Wilkesboro Day Care Center
Wilkesboro

Charlsena Stone, project secretary, competently used the word processor to print out the activities within the page design, which facilitated the enormous task of materials preparation.

We are most grateful to all these people who contributed their knowledge, energy, and enthusiasm to this project.

Contents

Planning for Threes

Quality Care for Threes 1
The Active Learning Series 2
Sharing Ideas with Parents 4
Helping Threes Feel Special 5
Giving Threes Practice with Words 5
Handling Problems 6
Making Time for Activities in the Schedule 11
Self-directed and Teacher-directed Activities 12
Activity Tips 14
Gathering or Group Time 16
Sample Schedule 16
Making Spaces Safe and Healthy for Threes 17
Making the Most of Your Space 18
Making Activity Centers 19
Stretching Space with Activity Boxes 21
Activity Box Ideas 22
Outdoor Play 25
Trips 25
Planning Activities Around Topics 27
Weekly Planning 31
Planning for Individual Children 31
Writing an Activity Plan 32
Activity Plan 33
Finding the Right Activities 36
When You Start to Use the Activities 36
Writing Your Own Activities 38
Activity Checklists 38
"Threes Can" Lists 39
Activity Guide 42
When You Want to Know More 43
Materials Index 44

Activities for Listening and Talking

Here's Why 51
Books and Pictures
    Materials and notes 52
    Activity Checklist 53
    Activities 54
    Tips for Story Times 75
    Ideas on Pictures for Threes 76
    How to Make a Peek-A-Boo Board 79
    Sequence Cards 79
    Sequence Cards to Use with Threes 81
    How to Make Stick Puppets 83
    Sunshine Note 84
    Words to "The Bear Hunt" 85
Conversation
    Materials and notes 86
    Activity checklist 87
    Activities 88
Your Own Activities: Listening and Talking 111

Activities for Physical Development

Here's Why 113
Large Muscles
    Materials and notes 114
    Activity checklist 115
    Activities 116
    Tent Ideas 135
    How to Make Broomstick Horses 135

Small Muscles
    Materials and notes 136
    Activity checklist 137
    Activities 138
    How to Make Geoboards 153
    Puzzle Place Ideas 154
    How to Make Follow-the-Path Cards 154
    Making Activity Boards 155
Your Own Activities: Physical Development 157

Creative Activities

Here's Why 159
Art
    Materials and notes 160
    Activity checklist 161
    Activities 162
    Art Area Ideas 179
    Art recipes 180
Blocks
    Materials and notes 182
    Activity checklist 183
    Activities 184
    Block Area Ideas for Threes 199
Dramatic Play
    Materials and notes 200
    Activity checklist 201
    Activities 202
    Dramatic Play Area Ideas 217
Music
    Materials and notes 218
    Activity checklist 219
    Activities 220
    Music Area Ideas 241
    Songs and Rhymes 243
Your Own Creative Activities 251

Activities for Learning from the World Around Them

Here's Why 253
Nature
    Materials and notes 254
    Activity checklist 255
    Activities 256
    Nature Area Ideas 275
    Tips for Nature Walks and Fieldtrips with Threes 275
    How to Make a Matching Game for Threes 277
    Ideas for Making Bird Feeders 278
    How to Make a Flannelboard 279
Numbers
    Materials and notes 280
    Activity checklist 281
    Activities 282
    Felt Flower and Flower Pot Patterns 301
    How to Make Sand-Dot Number Cards 302
    Counting Songs and Rhymes 303
Five Senses
    Materials and notes 306
    Activity checklist 307
    Activities 308
    Sample Fruit Salad Picture Word Recipe 325
    Recipes to Cook with Children 326
Shape, Size and Color
    Materials and notes 328
    Activity checklist 329
    Activities 330
    Homemade Shape-Sorting Boxes 347
    How to Make Sorting Boards 348
    How to Make Picture Card Sets for Sorting Boards 350
    Sample Pictures for Color Sorting Board 350
    Inch Cube Patterns 351
    Sample Bead Patterns 352
    Sample Parquetry Patterns 352
Your Own Activities: Learning from the World Around Them 353

*Active Learning
for Threes*

Activities for Learning
from the World Around Them

Index

of Activities for Learning from the World Around Them

All About Babies   308
Animal And People Body Parts   327
Animal Matching Game   322
Animals in Cages   364
Answering How Many   353
Bead Patterns   427
Big/Little Sorting Game   404
Big to Little   429
Bird Feeders   304
Blankets for Babies   339
Box Color Sort   407
Bug Search   311
Caring For Plants   306
Changing Food Flavors   382
Circle Designs   412
Circle Parts   354
Cloth Color Card Match Game   409
Clothes Colors   408
Clothes Sort   302
Color Beanbag Toss   431
Color Play   422
Color Search   406
Color Sorting Board   428
Color Surprise Game   434
Cook with Kids   402
Copying Simple Shapes   416
Count as You Cook   359
Count to Ten   352
Count with Rhythm   346
Counting Buttons   356
Counting Exercises   365
Counting Small Toys   337
Counting with Animal Toys   338
Cozy Corner   369
Eyes-Closed Walk   395
Far/Near Running Game   366
Feel-It Box   386
Feelie Books   371
Flannelboard One-To-One
    Game   341
Flashlight Play   389
Flower Hunt   298
Flower Picture Matching Game   299
Freeze and Melt   310
From Lemon to Lemonade   377
Grasshopper Pets   315
Heavy-Light Cans   374
Help to Feed Pets   318
Hop Once, Hop Twice   367

Hot Foods/Cold Foods   392
How Many Does It Take?   355
How Old Are You?   343
How Tall Body Outlines   420
Inch Cube Match Game   410
Inside Number Hunt   335
Leaf Match Game   320
Leaf Prints   319
Light, Dark, and Medium
    Colors   380
Long Path/Short Path Game   424
Looking at a Colored World   375
Looking for Shadows   312
Looking Inside a Seed   323
Magnet Fun   300
Magnetic Numbers   363
Magnifying Glasses   307
Make Number Posters   348
Make Sounds Softer   397
Making Number Books   358
Matching Textures   400
Measuring Sand or Water   344
Melody Bell Match Game   385
Mixing Juices   388
Name Plant Parts   314
Naming Shapes   435
Nature Area   293
Nature Collections   305
Nature Feelie Bag   313
Nice Smelling Plants   390
Number Books   334
Number Feelie Bag   357
Number Grocery Bags   362
Number Picture Sorting Game   361
Number Picture Match Game   360
Number Songs and Rhymes   331
Number Sort Game   351
Numbers at Meals   333
One-Many Listening Game   349
One-to-One Table Setting   342
Outdoor Number Hunt   350
Outline Game   405
Paint on Shapes   413
Parquetry Patterns   433
Parquetry Block Party   423
Pattern Match Game   432
Pegboard Birthday Cake   332
Pegboard Match Game   414
Pet Store Trip   330

Petting Time for Pets   316
Popping Corn   383
Put Together Circles and
    Squares   403
Ring Around the Rosey Count   365
Sand Play   295
Sand-Dot Number Cards   336
Scratch and Sniff Books   381
Shape Potato Prints   430
Shape Sorting Board   425
Shape Stencils   421
Shape, Color, and Size Books   415
Shape-Sorting Boxes   418
Shapes Feelie Bag   426
Shapes in the Room   417
Sharing Food   345
Sink or Float Sorting Game   321
Size Puzzles   419
Sky Flannelboards   326
Slugs and Snails   309
Smell-Taste Surprises   373
Soft, Harder, Hardest Game   396
Sorting Feelie Shapes   411
Sorting Nature Picture Cards   329
Sorting Number Pictures   340
Sorting Soft and Hard   387
Sound Tubs   376
Sounds of Real Things   391
Spice Packets   370
Sprouting Seeds   324
Surprise Packages   393
Sweet, Sour, and Salty Tastes   398
Talk About Seasons   317
Texture Hunt   401
Things in the Sky   325
Thirsty, Sleepy, Hungry   328
Tickle Things   378
Time Talk   368
Tracing Shapes   436
Upside-Down World   372
Water Play   296
Weather Pictures   294
Weather Walks   301
Wet Sand/Dry Sand   297
What Makes This Noise?   394
What's in the Sand Table?   303
What's It Made Of?   399
Which Holds Most?   384
Whispering Directions Game   379

Quality Care for Threes

Three-year-olds are usually easier to deal with in a group setting than either Twos or Fours. Most Threes are over the tantrums of two-year-olds and are not yet showing the rebellion of four-year-olds. They are interested in pleasing the important grownups in their lives, their parents and teachers, and they try to do what adults ask.

Children develop many skills during the third year. Most Threes are completely toilet trained, at least during the day. They can use words well to explain what they want and describe what they see. Threes also enjoy saying nursery rhymes and learning the words to songs. They can dress and undress themselves with a little help, if their clothes are easy to handle. They can serve themselves at mealtimes and use a spoon and fork well. A program for Threes should provide lots of activities so that children can practice all these skills that they are proud of doing by themselves.

Threes need quality child care. Quality care means developmental care that helps children develop both their minds and bodies in a safe and healthy place. Providing quality care is not an easy job. That is why caregivers have to use everything they do during the day to help children feel good about themselves and to learn social and thinking skills. It is not enough in child care to see that children are fed, clean, and safe from harm. That is only custodial care, meeting the child's basic needs for health and safety. Developmental care tries to meet *all* the needs of the growing child, including love, guidance, and learning as well as basic care.

Threes have much to learn. They need to learn to get along with others and take care of themselves independently. Just as importantly, they need to learn many new skills in thinking and talking. The key to working with Threes is to remember that they are learning all the time. They will learn more if we give them safe ways to explore and help them think and talk about what they are doing.

The Active Learning Series

The Active Learning Series is made up of activity books for infants, one-, two-, and three-year-olds. In each of these books there are a planning guide and four activity sections.

Active Learning for Threes has many ideas for children whose abilities are between 36 and 48 months of age. The book is divided into five sections, which are listed on the following page.

Planning for Threes

This section has ideas for setting up your room and schedule to provide good care and avoid problems. It includes ways of handling Threes that help them develop self-discipline. It shows how to plan activities so that things will run smoothly.

Activities for Listening and Talking

This section has ideas to help you make the best use of talking with and listening to Threes all through the day. It also has play ideas using books, pictures, and puppets. Activities are numbered 1 through 88.

Activities for Physical Development

This section has ideas to develop the large muscles, such as those in the legs, arms, and back. These muscles help children run, balance, and climb. It also has ideas to develop the small muscles in the hands and fingers. Activities are numbered 89 through 156.

Creative Activities

This section has activities with art, blocks, dramatic play, and music. These activities help to develop the senses, the imagination, and the skills to enjoy the arts. Activities are numbered 157 through 292.

Activities for Learning from the World Around Them

This section has activities that focus on nature, the senses, size, shape, color, and numbers. These activities help children enjoy and learn about the world around them. Activities are numbered 293 through 436.

Sharing Ideas with Parents

Parents are interested in what you do with their children. It makes a parent feel good to know that you have been doing special things just for his or her child. You can share the ideas in this book with parents.

- Tell parents about an activity their child likes.

- Have things on hand for parents to borrow and read. Cut out articles from magazines and put them in folders. Let parents know that you have materials they can borrow.

- Call state offices and agencies for free materials on child care topics. They may have materials on feeding children, growth of children, or ways parents can spot problems.

- Have a meeting for parents. Show a film or slides and talk about helpful ideas for raising children. Topics such as handling behavior problems or activities for Threes are good ones to start with. Your local community college may be able to help with speakers, films, and other resources.

- Work closely with parents so that the child benefits from the feeling of trust and warmth you share with them.

- Keep a bulletin board for parents near the entrance with current information about center activities, notices about parenting education, and fun things to do with children.

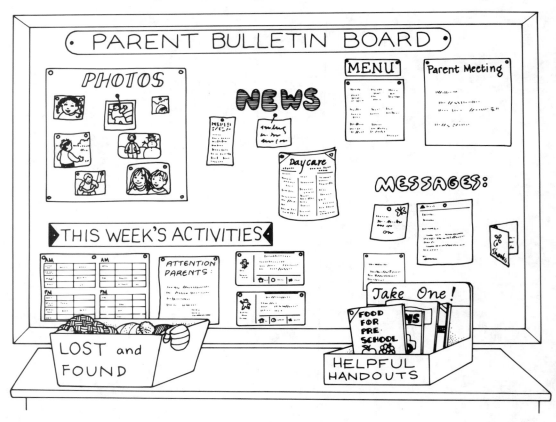

Helping Threes Feel Special

Threes need to know that you really care about them. They know this from your kind tone of voice and gentle touch. They feel good when you look into their eyes as you talk to them and really listen when they talk to you. Threes become frustrated and angry when you handle them in a rough or unfriendly way, use a loud voice, or ignore their interests. The way you relate to the children in your care is very important. It helps shape the way a child sees himself.

Developmental care means that you show children you value and like them. Throughout this book, you will find ideas to help children feel special. Although there are no separate activities for social and emotional growth, emotional support is part of all the activities. Be sure to follow these ideas and you will be helping Threes feel good about themselves.

- Talk to Threes often. It builds a happy relationship.

- Look right into the child's eyes when you and the three-year-old talk together. It helps her feel important and special.

- Use the child's name when you talk with him. It makes what you say more personal.

- Listen to your Threes because they are trying to talk to you about what interests them. Carry on conversations with them.

- Use a kind tone of voice and gentle touch. Help children when they ask. It shows you care.

- Use routines, such as meals and nap time, as times to talk to and work with the children. It gives them special attention while they get personal care.

- Give praise and show delight for the things Threes can do. It helps them feel proud of what they can do by themselves.

- Even when you have to correct your Threes or stop what they are doing, remember to handle them with respect so they will continue to feel loved.

Giving Threes Practice with Words

Threes need words for different things. They need words to *understand* what you and others are saying. They need words to *think* about things. They also need words to *talk* to others about their ideas. Your job is to help Threes get practice with words in all these different ways.

You are helping a child understand words and ideas when you read stories, talk about what is happening in a picture, describe what a child is doing, and answer a child's questions.

Often we see Threes thinking aloud as they play. They may tell about what the make-believe people are doing, or talk in the different voices of the make-believe people. They may talk about the steps they take as they solve a problem. This kind of talk guides children's action and helps them develop what will become silent thinking later on. While they are little, they need to think aloud as they play. Let them do that, even if you do remind them to use an inside voice.

You will find that it helps children to remember how to do something if you talk them through an action while you show them what to do. For example, if you are showing a child how to button, you can help him notice what to do by saying, "See, I hold the buttonhole open with these fingers and try to slip the button in with the other hand. Now I pull the button through with my fingers." By talking, you have helped the child think aloud.

Threes usually understand many more words than they can use to talk. Asking simple questions is a good way to give children practice in using more words. Try to ask your Threes questions that need more than a yes or no answer. The word you use to start a question gives you a clue to the type of answer the child will be practicing:

—*"What"* starts a question that asks for information, as do "who" and "when." Children will usually answer a "what" question with one or two words. You can encourage them to say more by repeating their answer and waiting for them to add some other ideas. "What did you make with the blocks?" "A house." If they do not add more, you can say, "Tell me more about your house."

—*"How"* starts a question that asks a child to remember step by step what happened. Children usually need to use a longer sentence to answer this kind of question. "How did we make the pancakes?" asks for a step-by-step description. "How did you build this farm with the blocks?" asks the child to remember what he used and what he did.

—*"Why"* starts a question that asks for a reason or a cause. Such questions are hard for most Threes. Start with simple "why" questions, such as "Why is the boy in this story sad?" If the child can't answer, you can remind him about what happened and turn back to the other pictures. Then ask the question again, "Now, can you tell me why he's sad?"

In the activities in this book, there are many examples of questions to use with Threes and topics to talk about with them. Try out some of these ideas and notice which ones help the children to talk most. Remember, the important thing is to make children feel free to talk. You can do that if you listen to them, discuss things with them, and show that you enjoy what they tell you.

Handling Problems

Although three-year-olds are easier to handle than Twos, they may seem more grown-up than they really are. They are not yet able to work out problems by talking and without help from grownups. They are not good at waiting, and when they get tired or hungry, nothing seems to go right. Threes can use words well and can remember much of what you say to them. They are also full of love, bounce back quickly, and become happy children when things are running smoothly.

It is important to have a few clear rules with Threes and stick to them. Too many rules can confuse them. Patience and kindness are the way to work with children. If the caregiver gets angry, the children will show anger and fear. Children who are screamed at or spanked learn to hit and scream at others. Punishment that shames or frightens a child hurts the entire adult-child relationship. Remember, Threes are copycats and are copying the way you treat them. That's how they learn. So you need to be sure that you do what you want them to copy.

The best way to handle problems with Threes is to plan ahead so that there are fewer chances for things to go wrong. Plan ahead to have enough safe space, toys, and fun activities so that children won't get frustrated and strike out. But planning ahead will not do away with all the problems. Threes have to be watched closely. You will get to know the signs before a child hits someone else, and that's the time to stop him if you can. If you stop things early by reminding the children about the words or actions they need to use, you can prevent a lot of fights. You will get to know which children need to have you close to them because they do more hurting. The child who hurts needs lots of love to help him grow. Stop what he does, and make it clear that you don't like it. Tell him what you want him to do next time. But also make it clear that you still love him.

Here are some suggestions for handling the common problems of three-year-olds.

Problems around routines

Have the three-year-old help as much as he can with routines—hanging up his own coat, helping set the table for lunch, helping serve himself, and putting toys back where they belong.

Take care of children a few at a time rather than all at the same time whenever you can. This makes it easier to prevent a rush when you're changing activities or getting them up from a nap.

Don't rush during routines such as toileting or meals. This puts pressure on the child and she might just stop and resist you.

Use songs, fingerplays, and stories to prevent waiting with nothing to do before meals or during toileting.

Treat things with a light touch. You'll get better results by using humor and neutral words, such as *rest* instead of *nap* or *sleep.*

Don't insist too much or threaten something you can't carry out. You will only back yourself into a corner. Remember, the child really has the final say about what he will eat or whether he will go to sleep.

Give children choices as often as you can. Sometimes a big problem can be helped by giving a child a choice that she can make. For example, if a child is having a problem with rest time, ask her whether she wants a soft doll or a cuddly toy to rest with.

Give children notice before a change in activity is coming: "You are having a good time building with blocks. You may play for a little while longer before it is clean-up time." Remind them again about two minutes before they have to finish up. Whenever possible, let Threes finish up what they are doing and then move on to the next activity in their own time.

Making it easier to say goodbye

Help parents feel at ease with their child care. Invite them to visit or drop in any time while the child is with you. Have the parent bring the child in for a few short visits at fun times before she leaves him. Then the child will feel at ease with you and the new place.

Visit the child in her home if she's having a hard time saying goodbye.

Have a new child bring something from home to keep with him.

Have the parent leave something that is hers, such as a book or scarf, with the child so that he can hold it till she comes back. He will be sure mommy will come back for the thing that is hers.

Tell a "goodbye to mommy/daddy" story to all the children, using little dolls or flannel board pieces. Remember to repeat that mommy or daddy is going to work and will be back.

Have a special toy or story ready for the child who finds it hard to have her parent leave.

Remember to give that child plenty of attention during the rest of the day.

Don't be surprised if problems with the parent's leaving start over again after a vacation or an illness.

Always handle these problems with kindness and lots of reminding that the parent will be coming back.

Hurting and fighting

Watch the children closely and stop things before they get out of hand. If you see things in time, you can help the child to solve the problem without hurting others. Sometimes you can avoid problems. For example, you can remind the child to get himself a toy from the shelf instead of taking another child's toy.

If a child is a fighter, be aware of him as soon as he seems angry. Tell him "talk—no hurting." Help him to use the words he needs to solve the problem.

Make sure there are enough toys of the same kind out at the same time so children don't have to fight over toys.

Remind children how to ask by saying easy words such as "please show me," or "may I." Play an asking game at group time so that your Threes can practice taking turns.

Make sure you set a good example. *Never* bite a child who has bitten. Never hit, scream, or kick things around; children will copy what you do, not what you tell them to do.

Make sure children have enough space to play. Crowding causes fights.

Tantrums

Although Threes do not have tantrums as often as Twos, they still happen. Watch out for tantrums when a child is hungry, tired, too hot, expected to do something that is too hard, or when there is too much going on.

Show the children that you still love them as you help them work through their tantrums safely. Most children don't like their own tantrums any more than you do.

Pick out a safe place to leave the child who is having a tantrum; make sure that you can see the child and that he is not a danger to himself or others. As soon as the child is calm, help him come out and join the group.

Keep yourself calm; don't let yourself get angry or aggressive.

If tantrums happen often, talk to a child development specialist, a mental health consultant, or a social worker. Some problems are too hard for you to handle alone. The agency that supervises your center can suggest someone. If possible, get the person to come in and see the child in your group. There may be something in your program or schedule that is setting off the child's tantrums.

Be sure to talk to the parents to find out if the child has tantrums at home. Ask how the parents handle those tantrums. Decide on one way to handle tantrums at home and at school.

Avoid tantrums by stopping an upsetting situation as soon as you can, before the child loses control.

"I'll do it myself"— independence

Ask parents to dress Threes in easy-to-manage clothes—elastic waist bands, big zippers and buttons, slip-on shoes—so they can dress themselves.

Explain things clearly and make things easy to remember by showing Threes as well as telling them. Pictures of the toys that go on each shelf help them remember where things go.

Give Threes as many chances to do things for themselves as you can, but keep things safe. They can set the table, wipe up spills, and put toys away.

When a three-year-old tries to do something that is too hard for him, help him, but leave the last bit for him to do so that he feels he's done it himself.

Sharing and taking turns

Have enough of the same toys so that Threes can play side by side without having to share. They are still learning how to play together.

When you get a child to share or take turns, praise her and tell her you like sharing and taking turns. Use the words often so that she remembers what you like her to do. When you share something or give someone a turn, call the children's attention to it: "Now it's Becky's turn. See, I'm sharing."

Make a game of taking turns: you take a turn, then give the children their turns.

Put up a waiting list near each activity center, or for taking turns on a popular toy. Put the waiting list down low where the children can see you print their names on the list. Check off each child's name as he finishes his turn and send him to get the next child on the list.

Growing up too fast

Remember that Threes are still very young children. Be realistic about what you expect. Also work with the parents so they don't expect too much.

Threes may need a reminder to use the toilet. Don't make a fuss or worry if a child goes back to having accidents. Use a light touch and lots of praise for success.

Talk to the parents if their child still has a bottle at home. Agree on what to do at the center. Have the child drink from a cup at meals and snacks. Try a soft record or patting a child's back instead of a bottle to get him to sleep.

Tips on handling problems

- Make a few clear rules for safety and how to treat others. Repeat the rules as you gently stop a child. Always stick to those rules.

- Tell three-year-olds what you want them to do if they are doing something you don't like.

- Encourage Threes to use words instead of hitting or fighting. Remember, you may need to tell them words to use at first.

- Get two or three of the same popular toys. Then you can show a child where to get a toy for himself instead of grabbing the toy the other child is using.

- Always have plenty of safe toys out on low shelves for children to play with by themselves. Change these toys often.

- Take Threes outdoors every day to play in a safe area. Leave enough indoor space for active play too.

- Keep groups of children small by using four or more activity centers in the room at the same time. Crowding causes fights.

- Allow Threes to choose what they want to do. They are too little to have to do things as part of a group for a long time. They will usually play alone or near another child. Keep big group activities short.

- Make sure lunch and nap are early enough so that Threes don't get too hungry or tired. If you are stuck with a fixed meal schedule, make sure they can have small, healthful snacks when they are hungry.

- Keep Threes from having to wait with nothing to do. Have some books to look at, sing a song, or do a fingerplay if they must wait.

- Use imagination, humor, and a light touch to prevent emotional upsets. Step in early, before things get out of hand. Take children outside or to another room, because a change of scene sometimes puts a new look on things.

- Keep a special eye on the child who hits, bites, or hurts others. Then you will be able to catch that child when you see he is frustrated or angry and help him *before* he hurts someone. Make sure to praise the good things he does.

- Be calm. Comfort a hurt child, but also keep loving and caring for the one who hurts others. He needs you to help him grow.

Making Time for Activities in the Schedule

The way you use the time children spend with you is called the *schedule.* Everything that is done for care and play needs its own time in the schedule. You must plan ahead to make time for both care and play.

When you are gone and someone else is taking care of the children, he or she will need to know the schedule. If you write down the main things you do and when you do them, then others who care for your children can do things at the same time. Your Threes will start to expect certain things to happen every day in the same order. If things go on as they should, it makes them feel more relaxed, even if you are not with them.

The most important thing about a schedule is that it helps you think ahead. Then you can plan many activities for both morning and afternoon and get the things that you will need ready. Any schedule should be flexible so that you can take advantage of all the interesting things that come up.

Use routines, such as nap time, meals, and snacks, as times to give a child personal attention. With a little planning, some of the activities in this book can be done during routine care and will not add much work for you. Routines are good times to talk to children, do fingerplays or nursery rhymes, and sing songs. As you use the activities, make sure to choose some that can be done during routines.

As much as you can, try to let Threes choose their own activities and play by themselves or in small groups. Try not to have all of them do things together in a large group. Expecting lots of young children to do things together is frustrating to the teacher and the children and may cause discipline problems.

You will need to have many safe things to play with in different parts of the room so that all the children don't crowd together to play with the same thing at the same time. If you share a space with another group, try to schedule different times to use the space. For example, take your children outside and arrange for the other group to be inside at that time.

Make sure your schedule has outdoor play times and indoor play times every day. Also make sure to schedule a balance of quiet play times and active play times. Plan a short time for a story, fingerplays, and nursery rhymes once or twice a day. Have music times often. Threes love to dance, play instruments, and sing easy songs with you.

Changing from one activity to another, or making transitions, can be hard for Threes. Big changes, such as the transition between lunch and nap, or between indoor and outdoor time, must be carefully planned. Try to let children finish up one or two at a time and move on to the next activity instead of all moving on at once.

If you have someone help you, it is easier to take care of the children one at a time and send them on to the next activity. For example, as each child finishes lunch, he can go to wash up and brush his teeth with your helper. Then that adult can take a small group with her to the next thing on the schedule. By that time, the rest of the children will probably be finished with lunch. You can take that small group to the bathroom and on to the next activity.

Even if you are alone, it helps to have everything ready for the next activity so that you can get the children started on the new activity quickly. It is hard for Threes to wait with nothing to do.

While you are taking care of the children, don't take the time to clean up completely. Just clear away what you have to. You can come back and do the clean-up when children are asleep or after most of them have left for the day. When the children are there, give them your attention. If they must wait, use that time to read a story, sing songs, do fingerplays, or dance to music.

Always have a few extra ideas ready that you can use in case you need them. It is better to have too many activities planned than too few. Threes can go through activities very quickly, so have the materials prepared for some extra things to do. During bad weather it helps to have some new toys to put out and some active games to play.

Self-directed and Teacher-directed Activities

Threes want to do things by themselves. They need to have many safe, easy-to-use toys out on low shelves or in open boxes. Activities children can do by themselves are called *self-directed activities*. During the day, help Threes pick up and put back toys as they finish using them. This keeps the toys ready for others to use in play. If everything is a jumble, the children soon lose interest. Also, when you keep the room in order, clean-up is easier at the end of the day. There should always be enough self-directed toys out, but not too many. Constant clutter makes children get confused and lose interest. Bringing out some toys children have not used that day can pep up their interest.

You need to be right there with the children when they do some activities. These are called *teacher-directed activities*. Teacher-directed activities need to be done at times when you are free to work with the children. Fingerpainting or cooking are examples of activities that should be teacher-directed. If you have enough self-directed toys out at all times, the children will have a lot to keep them busy. Then you can bring out the teacher-directed activities only at scheduled times.

Activity Tips

Plan ahead to make things go smoothly.

- Plan activities ahead of time and write them on a planning form.
- Choose activities to match children's skills. If an activity turns out to be too hard, try an easier one.
- Plan when and where you will do each activity.
- Include quiet and active, indoor and outdoor, small group and individual activities.
- Add new activities to old favorites.
- Always have extra activities ready in case you need them.
- Set materials out ahead of time and make sure you have enough materials for all Threes who want to take part.

Keep Threes interested and active.

- Allow three-year-olds to choose their activities much of the day.
- Divide and organize big spaces into smaller play areas with low shelves and other furniture. Be sure adults can see over the dividers.
- Some play areas to include are: a book corner, blocks, playhouse, puzzles and put-together toys, art, and a quiet corner with a rug and a few soft pillows.
- Set up the areas to help Threes learn to do things for themselves. Have plenty of safe toys on low shelves for Threes to use.
- Separate the quiet interest centers from the active interest centers. Help the children enjoy quiet play as well as active play so that they won't get too tired.
- Label shelves and other toy containers with clear pictures.
- Keep toys organized—same kind of toys in one area, toys with small pieces in dishpans or boxes.
- Help Threes learn to take out, use, and put away the toys.
- Keep Threes from having to wait with nothing to do. Have enough toys so that children don't have to wait a long time for turns. While you are gathering the children for group time, let the early birds look at books.
- Set up an indoor active play area with some safe large-muscle play things. This lets the Threes move around indoors, especially in bad weather.
- Set up a safe, fenced, outdoor play area. Check it daily before you take the children out.

Activity Tips

Slowly help Threes learn to be part of a group.

- Keep group times very short, five to fifteen minutes. Have two smaller groups instead of one big group, if you can.
- Encourage but don't force a child to be part of a group.
- If the group activity you planned isn't working, stop and try something else.

Make everything you do count twice.

- Give children practice talking about what they and others are doing. Help them think things through by asking simple questions they can answer.
- Remember to look into the child's eyes as you talk and listen. This gives each child a turn to be special.
- Use routines such as eating and getting up from naps as a time to talk with a few children. Try doing some of the activities at this time.
- Use the same materials to do more than one activity.
- Try the same activity with all the Threes who are at about the same level.
- Let the children learn to do as much as they can by themselves: setting the table, serving themselves, putting toys away.

Avoid safety problems.

- Cover electrical outlets, put safety locks on low cabinets, and get rid of the toy box with a heavy lid that can crash down.
- Have children pick things up and put things away as they go along.
- Let the Threes use toys and activities that need to be closely watched only while you are there with them. Put away fingerpaint, carpentry, and cooking when you can't watch carefully.
- Bring out two or three toys of the same kind to avoid fights. Divide toys like Lego Bricks into several small boxes. Use a waiting list to help Threes take turns.
- Make the room safe so that Threes won't hurt themselves when playing on their own.

Gathering or Group Time

Threes can be gathered together in a larger group once or twice a day to sing, do fingerplays, or listen to a story. Keep them together only as long as everybody is really interested. Usually with young Threes, that means only five to ten minutes. Older Threes might stay for 10 to 20 minutes. If you have someone working with you, divide a big group into two smaller groups. The smaller the group, the easier it is to have a good gathering time and for children to take part in what you do.

For more ideas on group times, look at Tips for Story Time at the end of the "Listening and Talking" section of this book.

Sample Schedule

You can change this schedule to fit your Threes' needs. Remember to be flexible and follow the children's needs and interests. The main purpose of the schedule is for you to think ahead and plan so the day will go smoothly and things will get done.

Children arrive:	Greet each child and parent Self-directed activities in activity centers
Midmorning:	Wash hands Breakfast or snack Planned play time: self-directed activities for some children, teacher-directed activities for others
Late morning:	Planned large-muscle play outdoors or indoors Gathering or group time: stories, music Routines before lunch (toileting, washing hands) Lunch Clean up after lunch Get ready for nap
Early afternoon:	Nap
Mid-afternoon:	Planned quiet play time: teacher-directed activities for those who are awake Napping Threes get up Routines (toileting, dressing, putting cots away) Snack Planned play time: self-directed activities for some, teacher-directed activities for others Outdoor play time
Late afternoon:	Self-directed activities in activity centers Routines (toileting, getting children's things ready to send home) Talk to parents as children leave
After most children are gone:	Clean up room Set up for next day

Making Spaces Safe and Healthy for Threes

If you do all you can to avoid health and safety problems, you will feel more relaxed and enjoy your work with the children more. Child proofing the room and the outdoor area where the children play takes a lot of thought. Think about what you can do to make it safe for your Threes at all times.

You have to be very careful with children. They get into everything around them because they are curious and forget about dangers. They can get into the same trouble again in a minute because they forget what you just told them not to do. Yet you can't always be close by. There will be times when the children are playing with toys on their own while you are busy helping a child with toileting or working with a few others. These questions will help you start thinking about child proofing your room.

How can I block off the windows, doors, hot stove, and electrical outlets so that the children can't get hurt?

Where can I lock away medicines, cleaning materials, and other harmful things?

Where can I store things I don't want Threes to use by themselves? Where can I put these things so that it's easy to get them out often for use when I can watch?

Is everything I have left out safe for Threes to use by themselves?

How can I make everything they will climb on safe?

Can I see what all the children are doing from every place in the room?

Tips on health and safety

- Never leave Threes alone. They need to be watched by an adult at all times.
- Make sure gates and doors are closed so that Threes can't go outside of safe areas. Place door knobs higher, or put on locks, if needed, to prevent children from wandering out.
- Cover all electrical outlets.
- Buy toys you can keep clean easily. Wash toys in soap and water when necessary. Use strong liquid soap called tincture of green soap, which you can buy in a drug store. Rinse well. Let toys dry in the air.
- Make sure all the materials and colors are safe for children to put in their mouths (nontoxic paints, fabrics, and dyes).
- Do not store toys in a toy chest with a heavy lid that can fall down. Use open, low shelves that are fixed so they can't fall over.
- Check indoor and outdoor toys for sharp edges, splinters, and other dangers that happen as toys get old.
- Make sure that outdoor areas are free of tall grass, weeds, and harmful insects and are fenced in for safety.

- Cover the sandbox to keep animals out.

- Put up strong fences to keep Threes away from open windows, hot stoves, and other dangers.

- Teach children to flush toilets as soon as they are used. Check on toilets yourself. Disinfect once daily.

- Wash your hands with soap after you help children go to the toilet or wipe their noses. Remind the children to wash their hands, too. Hand-washing cuts down on germs and illness.

- Be sure to read the *Notes* in the activities for more health and safety ideas.

Making the Most of Your Space

Threes need a lot of space in which to move around. There never seems to be enough usable space for play when you care for a group of young children. Planning how to best use space can help, even though it may not solve all the problems. Look around your room and ask yourself the following questions.

What can I store outside the room?

How can I move the furniture around to open up space for play?

How can I divide my space into different areas but still see all the children in a glance?

What activities are better outdoors than indoors?

Where can children do large-muscle play in rainy weather?

Tips for routine care

- Use all the space you have. Put away anything you aren't using. Try to get things that stack well.

- Make sure routine care areas take up as little space as possible. Use routine care spaces and furnishings for play whenever possible. For example, use eating tables for art and small-muscle play when it is not time to eat. Put cots out in play spaces when it is nap time instead of having cots set up all the time.

- Remember that cots should be about 18 to 24 inches apart to cut down on the spread of germs.

- Give each child a storage space for his coat, spare clothes, and art work.

Tips for play

- Set up some safe activity centers for quiet play and an open area for more active play. Remember to put some soft pillows and toys in the quiet area.

- Have plenty of safe, easy-to-use toys on low, open shelves in the activity centers so that Threes can get them by themselves. Have two or more of the same toys to cut down on fighting.

- Change the toys in the activity centers often.

- Have some very low tables in the activity centers for drawing, puzzles, and other table-top toys. Make sure chairs are small and strong, and that the children's feet rest on the floor when they sit down.

- Set up a safe, fenced-in outdoor area. Take the children out every day. Wheel toys, balls, swings, a low slide, climber, and a sandbox work well outdoors.

Making Activity Centers

An activity or interest center is a place where the toys, open storage, and play space have been set up for a special kind of play. For example, you might set up a playhouse center, a book center, a block center, an art center, or a music center.

In each activity center make sure to have these things.

- open shelves so that the children can get the toys and put them back

- the right furnishings for the children to use the toys on, such as soft pillows to sit on in the book area, a rug on the floor in the block area, an easel or art table in the art area

- any special things needed to make the center easy and safe to use, such as a large towel under the water table, plastic aprons for the children to wear, a plastic shower curtain or throw rug spread under the sand table, and a place to dry paintings

Activity centers Threes can enjoy every day are the following.

- playhouse or housekeeping center with dishes, pots and pans, play sink, play stove, small table and chairs, dolls and doll beds

- dress-up clothes near an unbreakable mirror

- block center with different kinds of blocks and things to use with blocks, such as toy animals, trucks and cars, and airplanes

- book center in a cozy, soft place to look at books

- puzzle and small-muscle toy center with many kinds of simple puzzles, beads to string, and toys with pieces that go together and pull apart

- art center with paints, paper, crayons, watercolor markers, and play dough

- sand and water center with a water table, sand area, play dishes, strainers, shovels, and pails

- large-muscle center with steps, a rocking boat, a small slide, crates or cubes for climbing or crawling, and wheel toys

Tips

- Before you make up your mind about where to put activity centers, look at your indoor and outdoor space. Decide which activity centers to have indoors and which outdoors. This will change as seasons make it harder or easier to go outdoors.

- Remember to keep pathways clear for children and adults to walk around activity centers.

- Set up quiet activities like books and art away from noisy activities like music and blocks.

- It is important to have enough safe toys out all the time, but not too many, so the centers don't get cluttered. As the Threes grow more able, you can keep more toys out.

- Threes enjoy toys that have many small pieces. Keep toys with many pieces organized in activity boxes so that it is easy to change what is out. You and the children can choose which toys to bring out in the small-muscle toy center.

- Two or three different toys with small pieces will be as much as Threes can keep in order at one time. The children can help put the pieces back in the right boxes before other boxes are taken out.

- Make sure puzzles and other put-together toys have all their pieces before they are put away. Put-together toys with missing pieces are very frustrating to Threes and should not be used.

- You can make some centers special for part of the day by adding different toys. For example, in the playhouse center where you have dolls, dishes, and some dress-up clothes, you might add some tote bags and doll strollers in the morning. That will make the children want to walk around and play "traveling" with the playhouse things. In the afternoon you might want to put those "traveling" things away and bring out lots of stuffed animals, dolls and doll clothes so that the playhouse becomes a calmer area.

Stretching Space with Activity Boxes

You will have many more toys and materials for each activity center than you can keep out all the time. In order to keep these extra toys organized and ready to use, put them in activity boxes.

When you put everything you need for one kind of activity into a box or dishpan, you have made an *activity box*. This helps you keep many different things ready for children to play with without taking up much room. Activity boxes help you set up new activities quickly because you won't have to run around at the last minute to find the toys you need. You can store activity boxes in a closet or on a shelf. The activity boxes hold things to add variety to the things you have out every day in the activity centers. Label each box so that you know what's inside. A picture on the box will help the children know what's inside.

As you and the children put things back into an activity box, make sure that all the pieces are there and that they are clean. If you are careful to do that, you can count on the materials being in good shape the next time you need them. On pages 22 and 24 there are ideas for indoor and outdoor activity boxes.

Activity box ideas

Playhouse activity boxes

Fancy tea party box has a pretty tea set, place mats, small vase, and dry flowers.

Cleaning box has small brooms, mops, dust pans, brushes, and a toy carpet sweeper. Make sure you have at least two of each and enough so that everyone who wants to can clean house together.

Restaurant box has paper cook's hats, menus, and paper plates.

Store box has empty food boxes, empty cans (make sure they are clean and have no sharp edges), a small play cash register and telephone, paper bags to put food in, and play money.

Grown-up play box has toy or real telephones of different kinds, cameras, radios, and walkie-talkies.

Dress-up activity boxes

Shoe box has things to play shoe store, including sandals, high heels, men's shoes, sneakers, and baby shoes. Make sure all the shoes are clean and sprayed inside with disinfectant.

Jewelry and sunglasses box has old strings of beads, clip-on earrings, rings, and sunglasses. Make sure the beads are secure on the strings.

Block center activity boxes

Airplane box has different types and sizes of airplanes.

Wild animals box has toys to use to build zoos.

Farm animals box has familiar animals, including pets, to use in playing farm.

Small cars and trucks box has toys to use when building garages and roads.

Street signs box has a stop-and-go sign and a railroad crossing sign.

People box has toy people of different kinds, including different races and ages.

Trains box has a small hook-together train set, with or without tracks.

Book center activity boxes

Flannel board boxes have a different story or set of pictures, each in its own small, labeled box. Include a box with a boy and girl and different clothes to put on them, a face with different eyes, noses, mouths, and ears to make funny faces, as well as some pieces for favorite stories.

Puppet boxes have finger puppets and hand puppets, each type in a different box.

Picture games boxes have lotto, sequence cards, matching cards, and other picture games.

Puzzle and small-muscle toy boxes

Easy puzzles are stored on a labeled puzzle rack or in a labeled box, to be taken out a few at a time and put in the center. Put the name of the puzzle on the back of each piece.

Harder puzzles are stored on a labeled puzzle rack or in a labeled box, to be taken out a few at a time as children are ready. Put the name of the puzzle on the back of each piece.

Beads and strings box has beads of different kinds and strings with a knot on the end and a firm tip for stringing.

Put-together toys are in their own labeled boxes. In order to cut down on fighting, have several boxes of the same toys and put them out in the center at the same time.

Art center boxes

Story-picture box has crayons or felt pens in several small containers and paper of different sizes and shapes to draw on.

Play dough mixing box has a recipe, containers of salt, flour and color, measuring cups, and bowls to use with the children to mix play dough.

Art activity boxes each have the materials needed to do some of the activities in the art section of this book, such as stringing things, stamping things, and texture cards.

Music activities boxes

Sound container box has different types of sound containers to match.

Instruments box has tambourines, wrist and ankle bells, and rhythm sticks.

Dance props box has scarves, pretty fabrics, dance skirts, and capes.

Outdoor play boxes

Sand toys box has dump trucks, shovels and scoops of different sizes, pots, pans, dishes, and cans.

Water toys box has unbreakable pitchers, cups, cans; baby dolls to bathe.

Painter box has pails or cans to carry water and medium-thick house-painter brushes.

Action hats box has washable hats for construction workers, firefighters, bus drivers, pilots, mail carriers, and police.

Ball box has balls of various sizes, and maybe a target with holes to toss balls into or an old wastepaper basket to use as a basketball hoop.

Outdoor Play

Be sure to set up an outdoor play space and use it every day when the weather permits. Check to see that the area is safe and free of any health problems. Have weeds cut, be sure none of the plants is poisonous, and get rid of harmful bugs. Check daily, before you take the children out, to see that there is no trash in the area.

A fence around the area makes it easier to keep the children safely inside. It will also keep dangers out. A rolling cart or wagon for carrying activity boxes with balls, wheel toys, sand toys, and other materials makes going outdoors easier. The children can help take things out. If you are doing a special activity or using large equipment, be sure to set up ahead of time. Once the outdoor area is set up, you will only need to get the children out and back inside again.

Outdoor space can also be organized as activity centers. Some of the centers you have outdoors will be fixed, but others can be moved in or out. When you make activity boxes, make some you can use outdoors, such as the ones listed on page 00.

Some outdoor activity centers Threes enjoy are the following.

- climbing center with safe, low climbers, a rocking boat, sturdy boxes to climb into or on top of

- sand box with play dishes, shovels, and pails (Be sure to cover the sand to keep animals out, and check to see that it's clean before letting the children play.)

- water play with a little pool in hot weather, and a water play table or buckets and tubs on warm days for washing baby dolls and doll clothes, playing with dishes and pans

- art center where the easel or painting table can be brought out and where messy activities like fingerpainting can be done

- active play space where children can use wheel toys such as trucks to ride on and doll carriages to push, play with balls of different sizes, or dance to music (Be sure active play spaces are away from the quieter spaces.)

Trips

Threes like to see new things, but any trip outside the play yard needs a lot of planning. Don't even think of taking a trip until every child feels secure about coming to the center. Ask parents and other helpers to come along on a trip so that you have enough adults to keep the children safe.

Walking trips are easier than bus or car trips. A car trip is a big job because each child needs a seat belt or safety seat to be really safe, and there should be a second adult with the driver. Anyway, most Threes like a short walk to a nearby place just as well as a longer trip. Even for a walking trip, you should have one adult for every three to four children. Have the adults and children hold hands as they walk because Threes can

run away and get into danger very quickly. Any walking trip should be short so that children don't get tired or bored. Before the trip, talk about things you might see. Point these things out on your walk.

Get written permission from parents for any trip that takes children away from the center. Tell the parents when you will be going, where you will be going, when you will be back, and if they need to do anything special for their children that day. Remind parents again the day before the trip.

You don't even have to take Threes away from the center to have some interesting trips. Try a trip to another part of your building, such as the office or kitchen. A trip in your own play yard can be fun if you take a small group out at a time when the other children are indoors. Do something different on a play yard trip, such as catching insects or collecting leaves.

Threes are still very young children and do not need to be taken on many trips. Later in the year, when they are almost four, plan some walking trips to add something special to your program. A picnic or longer trip at the end of the year is a special treat and can be fun for the child's whole family.

Planning Activities Around Topics

Many caregivers find that it helps planning when they pick a topic and look for activities to do on that topic. You remember that in the first years of school, teachers plan units on subjects such as community helpers and the family. You can do this, too. However, you need to remember that three-year-olds have a short attention span and like to change toys and activities often. So you can't use the same activities that work with kindergarteners. The activities you use in a unit for Threes should be very simple.

Units can last less than a day or go on several weeks. For example, you may have a new goldfish for your room. You want your Threes to learn about that fish and other kinds of fish, too, so you could do a unit on fish.

As part of the unit, you could put easy picture books about fish into the book corner and put pictures of fish up where the children can see them. Talk about fish with the children to see what they can tell you and then give them more information. You might put plastic fish in the water table, have the children pretend to be fish as they move to some watery music, and have fish-shaped paper for the children to paint or color in their own way. You might add a trip to the pet store to buy fish food, too.

Once you pick a topic, you can find related activities in the sections of this book, including stories, songs, and fingerplays. Pages 28 and 29 list some topics that you could build a unit around. You can add your own ideas, too.

Myself:	body parts
	what I like
	my toys
	my clothes
Families:	parents
	grandparents
	brothers and sisters
Mothers and babies:	animal babies
	human babies
	when I was a baby
	baby brothers and sisters
The weather:	cold, warm, rainy, sunny
	the clothes we wear
	where we play in different weather
	seasons
Animals:	pets
	zoo animals
	farm animals
	animal families
The Senses:	smells
	colors
	sounds
	textures
Big, middle-sized, and little:	houses
	animals
	shapes
	people
Nature:	water
	rocks
	pine cones
	leaves
Going places:	cars
	trucks
	buses
	bicycles
	trains
	airplanes
	boats

Health and safety: foods
brushing teeth
fire safety
traffic safety

Our neighborhood: grocery store
library
fire station
pet store
shopping center

Sample Unit

As an example of how you might choose related activities on a topic for a month, let's think through how a unit on families might work. This example is for a long unit with many topics. Some of your units may be much shorter and last only a few days or a week.

Monthly Unit Topic: Families

WEEK 1	***Everybody has a family***	*Materials and Activities*
	Who is in your family?	Magazine pictures of families of different races
	Talk about the children's families.	
	Talk about parents, brothers and sisters, grandparents, aunts and uncles, cousins.	Pictures of the children's families
	What do all families need?	Books on families to read at storytime
	Talk about food, a place to live, someone to take care of them	Play people in the block area
		Dollhouse with family and furniture
		Something new to add interest in the playhouse
		Songs about family members
		Activities in this book on family members.

WEEK 2	**Families have fun together**	*Materials and Activities*
	Where does your family go together?	Places to build in the block corner
	Talk about trips to the zoo and to the beach.	Books on family fun
	What games do you play at home?	Songs about fun times
	What are your favorite times at home?	Pictures of their families on vacation brought in by children
	Talk about bath time, story before bed.	Activities in this book on family fun.
	What pets do you have?	

WEEK 3	**Families work together**	*Materials and Activities*
	What jobs does each family member do at home?	Pictures of people of all ages and races doing home jobs
	Talk about what mother, father, children do.	Make place mats
	Show how to set the table, wipe up spills.	Work pictures and books during storytime
	Show jobs children can do to help.	Songs about work
	Talk about different jobs children do at the center. (clean up, set table)	Work activities in this book.

WEEK 4	**Families have holidays together**	*Materials and Activities*
	What holidays does your family celebrate?	Pictures of families celebrating together
	Talk about birthdays, Thanksgiving, Christmas, Chanukah.	Holiday songs
	Talk about visiting grandparents.	Holiday books
	Talk about special foods eaten at celebrations.	Activities in this book on family holidays.

Weekly Planning

The unit activities you do take a very short time during the day, so don't plan *only* for the unit. When you plan for the week, remember that you will need to plan many self-directed and teacher-directed activities for the children every day in addition to the unit activities. Also, not all the activities planned for that week must be related to the unit. The unit can help you bring many different ideas and facts to the children's attention. The repetition in a unit also helps three-year-olds learn some basic ideas and words better. But you will need to plan many more activities.

When you get down to practical planning for children, you need to think of what you will do day by day. Making a daily plan can help you think of teacher-directed activities that you can add to the children's self-directed play. The daily plan can help you think of new toys to bring out that day, and ways to change activity centers by using some different activity boxes. In your daily plan, try to pick out at least two activities for younger Threes and two for older Threes. Over a week's time, include activities from all four sections of this book.

There is a sample form for a weekly plan on pages 34 and 35. You could put your completed plan up on the wall as a reminder. Also use the plan as a guide when you get your materials ready for the next day.

Planning for Individual Children

Every three-year-old is an individual with his own pattern of what he can and can't do. No two children of the same age will be able to do exactly the same things. By using the "Threes Can" lists on pages 40 and 41, you can find some of the things each one of the children can do. Using the "Threes Can" lists, take a few minutes to watch each one of your Threes and write down what he or she can do.

The "Threes Can" lists were not meant to be used in screening for problems. They cannot tell you how fast or slow a child is in his development. These lists can only help you notice more of what the children can do. Without the help of a list, you usually see only the big advances a child makes. A list can help you become a better observer so you see more of the little advances a child is working on every day.

When you know some of the things a child in your group can do, then you will know which activities in this book best suit him or her. For each of the activities in this book, a "Threes Can" is listed that tells what skill the activity will let the child practice. If you think a child can do that skill or is trying to learn to do it, then try the activity with her.

When you plan, try to think of several children who would enjoy the activity you chose. Jot down their names on a written planning form so that you will remember to try the activity with them. Sometimes there will be one or two children that you plan a special activity for. During a slow time of day, try that special activity with one or two children. You might try it when some children are napping and others are up, or when some children have left for the day. The important thing is to plan some activities that are right for each child in your group every day.

Writing an Activity Plan

It is easy to do a written activity plan using the activities in this book. Each activity has a number and a name. Just put the number and name of the activity you want to use with each child in the right place on the planning form. You will probably be able to use the same activity for a small group of children who are able to do the same things. Jot down the names of the children near the activity to remind you.

On pages 34 and 35, there is a weekly planning form. Post your weekly plan where you can see it. Having the children's names on the written plan helps you to make sure that you are keeping each child in mind. If anyone else has to take over for you, things will go more smoothly with a written plan.

Your written plan should list the *new* activities you want to try. You will also want to repeat old familiar activities that went well last week because Threes enjoy repeating activities. The reason for planning is to be ready with a lot of activities and materials. It is better to plan too much than too little. Always have some extra things ready in case you need them. This way the children will be happy and learn new things all day, during routines and at play times.

When you have written your activity plan, look it over and ask yourself:

Have I used routines such as meals and snacks to do activities whenever possible?

Have I planned for both the morning and afternoon playtimes?

Are there outdoor play activities daily, weather permitting?

Are self-directed activities and toys available all through the day?

Remember in carrying out your written plan, to prepare for activities by getting the materials together and going over the instructions; think of questions to ask the children and things to talk about for different activities; and use a warm touch and soft voice.

On the next three pages you will find a sample Activity Plan Form. The first one is filled in to show you how to use it. Copy the blank form if you wish, and change it to fit your needs. If you are already using a written plan form and you are happy with it, by all means stay with it. Remember, this is only a sample to help you come up with the written planning form for Threes that suits you best.

Activity Plan

Center or Home _____   Week of _____

Age Group _____   Caregiver _____

Fill in activity name and number and children's names in each box.

AM

	Monday	Tuesday
Listening and Talking (Books and Pictures, Conversation)	2 Read and Ask Rosa, Nicky, Rebecca, Anna, Juan, David 9:30	40 Hide the Picture Emma, Jimmy, Jesse 9:00
Physical Activities (Large Muscles, Small Muscles)	101 Stairs Rosa 10:30 on her way outside	Repeat 101 Stairs Rosa 10:30 on her way outside
Creative Activities (Art, Blocks, Dramatic Play, Music)	233 Baby's Bath Time Anna, Juan, David 11:00 outdoor time	208 Big Boxes as Outdoor Blocks Emma, Juan, Jimmy 11:00 outdoor time
Learning from the World (Nature; Numbers; Five Senses; Shape, Size, and Color)		351 Number Sort Game Noah, Yoshiko, La Shawna 10:00

PM

	Monday	Tuesday
Listening and Talking (Books and Pictures, Conversation)		Repeat 2 Read and Ask Rosa, Nicky, Rebecca Anna, Juan, David 3:00
Physical Activities (Large Muscles, Small Muscles)	132 Stringing Beads David, La Shawna 2:00	121 Follow the Leader Emma, Jesse 2:00 after nap
Creative Activities (Art, Blocks, Dramatic Play, Music)	162 Tempera Painting Rosa, Nicky, Rebecca 2:00	253 Tape Children's Singing Rebecca, Anna 4:00
Learning from the World (Nature; Numbers; Five Senses; Shape, Size, and Color)	297 Wet Sand / Dry Sand Yoshiko, David 3:00	

Activity Plan

Center or Home _____ Week of _____

Age Group _____ Caregiver _____

Fill in activity name and number and children's names in each box.

AM

	Monday	**Tuesday**
Listening and Talking (Books and Pictures, Conversation)		
Physical Activities (Large Muscles, Small Muscles)		
Creative Activities (Art, Blocks, Dramatic Play, Music)		
Learning from the World (Nature; Numbers; Five Senses; Shape, Size, and Color)		

PM

	Monday	**Tuesday**
Listening and Talking (Books and Pictures, Conversation)		
Physical Activities (Large Muscles, Small Muscles)		
Creative Activities (Art, Blocks, Dramatic Play, Music)		
Learning from the World (Nature; Numbers; Five Senses; Shape, Size, and Color)		

AM

Wednesday	Thursday	Friday

PM

Wednesday	Thursday	Friday

Finding the Right Activities

The activities for Threes have been broken into two age groups. Each group is shown by a picture.

stands for what a child 36 to 42 months can do

stands for what a child 42 to 48 months can do

Every activity has one of these two pictures to make it easy to pick out the right activities for each child in your care. You can use these activities for a three-year-old who is developing normally, more slowly, or faster than usual for his age. Just choose an activity based on what each child *can do*. Each activity in this book tells what the three-year-old should be able to do in order to take part in the activity. Remember, what the child can do is more important than the child's age in choosing the right activity.

The first activities in each section are easier ones than those that come later. For example, in the first color activities, children are asked to match colors. The later color activities ask the children to sort colors and point to a few colors when they are named.

On pages 40 and 41 you will find a list of many things Threes can do in each of the two age groups. Take time to look at these pages. It may surprise you to see what you can or can't expect from Threes.

When You Start to Use the Activities

Before you start

- Look at the "Threes Can" lists. Watch and think about each child. What can each one do?

- Pick out the best "Threes Can" picture for each of your children. This will help you plan for each one of them.

- Which children seem to be on a similar level in large- and small-muscle skills, in listening and talking, and in play interests? Plan some activities for those small groups.

- Look at all four activity sections and ask yourself the following questions:

    Which activities do I have the materials for?

    Which activities do I think each child will be able to enjoy?

Which activities do I have time to do?

Which activities would I like to start with?

Can I relate any of these activities to a topic and add it to a simple unit?

First week

■ Plan one activity for each of your children to do alone or in a small group.

■ Try to use each of the four activity sections.

■ Use the activities you choose with different children throughout the day.

■ Go back over the plan at the end of the week, and ask yourself these questions about how things went.

Which activities went best?

Do I need to make any changes in the interest centers?

Do I need to make any changes in the daily schedule?

Do I need to make any new activity boxes?

Second week

■ Plan one new activity for each child or small group of children.

■ Repeat the old activities that children enjoyed.

■ Try each new activity at least once during the week and favorites more than once.

■ Go back over the plan at the end of the week and ask yourself the questions about how things went.

Third week

■ Plan at least two new activities for every child or small group of children.

■ Fill in the activities on the written plan.

■ Go back over the plan at the end of the week and ask yourself the questions about how things went.

Fourth week

■ Try to think of a unit topic that would take only one week to complete.

■ Choose some activities from each section for each group around this topic.

■ Fill in the written plan.

■ Go back over the plan at the end of the week and ask yourself the questions about how things went.

Writing Your Own Activities

Any number of the activities you will find in this book may be familiar to you. That's because many of the activities are ones that parents and caregivers have always used to encourage children to grow and learn. There will also be some activities you've never used before because no one can think of every activity or even remember all the ones that have been done in the past. That's why activity books keep you on your toes with lots of new ideas. And there may be some activities that you have enjoyed doing with Threes that are not in this book. As you remember them, write them down in the blank activity boxes at the end of each section. This will make it easier to remember and use the activities as you write your activity plans.

When you work with three-year-olds, you will find that you have to think up some of your own activities to meet their needs, suit your interests, and make the best use of the toys you have on hand. Here's how to write your own activities.

■ First, think about what one child can do. Use the "Threes Can" lists to help focus on a skill the child would like to practice.

■ Next, think about what you need to do to help the child practice the skill: Ask yourself the following questions:

Will the activity be teacher- or child-directed?

What toys, equipment, or other materials will I need, if any?

Where will the activity work well?

How long will the activity take?

How many children can take part in the activity?

Will I have to get things ready ahead of time?

Exactly what must I do to make the activity happen?

What kinds of things can I say to help with the child's learning?

■ Write out your activity in a blank activity box. Try it out to see how it works. Make changes if you need to.

Activity Checklists

At the beginning of each activity section in this book, you will find a checklist. The checklist is to help you see how well the setting you create for children meets their needs for learning in that area. It's a good idea to try out these checklists to see what the strengths and weaknesses of your child care setting are for each type of activity in the book. Then you can see where improvements are needed and use the checklists as a guide for making changes.

You can do all the checklists at one time if you wish, or pick one or two to work on at first and then do the others when you are ready. As you carefully read each statement on the checklists, look around your child care setting and think about the things you do with the children.

Carefully follow these directions as you do the checklists.

1. On each checklist you will find that the statements are followed by blanks under two age ranges. Note the ages of the children in your setting and rate the statements for those ages.

2. If you find much evidence that a statement is *true* for an age group, put a check in the blank.

3. If you find clear evidence that a statement is *not true,* put an X in the blank.

4. Make notes next to a statement if you are not sure about whether it should get a check or an X.

If people other than you want to use the checklists, they will need to spend enough time observing in the room to really find out what they need to know. It takes about two hours in a morning to get most of the information needed to complete all the checklists. If the other observers do not see or hear everything needed to complete the checklists, then they will have to set aside time to ask you some questions about the child care setting. However, they should be sure to observe first.

Observers may see things differently from the way you see things. If there is a chance to talk about the differences, both of you will probably end up with some good new ideas.

"Threes Can" Lists

The following pages give you more information on what Threes can do. It is important to remember that these lists are only general guidelines and cannot be used to find out whether a child is or is not developing normally. These lists are not a screening test. If you are worried about a child in your care, you should advise the parents to find a professional who can do some special tests. The parents could talk to their family doctor for suggestions. Or they could find out about special services by asking the child care professionals who come to your center, such as the day care specialist or social worker.

The "Threes Can" lists are meant to help you become more aware of some of the things most three-year-olds can do. The lists are actually made up of many of the Threes Can indicators from the activities. Without a list to follow, it is hard to be aware of the new little things each child is learning to do. But it is these new little things that we need to encourage in order to help children grow. We want to help each child practice these small advances as he plays with toys, listens to stories, answers our questions, and takes part in all the play activities. Then the big things will come more easily in their own time.

Threes Can List

From 36 to 42 months, some things Threes can do are

36 MONTHS

- begin to take turns and try to share
- play with another child
- sing simple songs; do fingerplays
- talk in short sentences
- run around corners and things in their path
- count two or three things
- use simple art materials
- stack up to nine blocks or inch cubes
- tell a little about what they are doing
- play very easy circle games
- do easy picture matching
- kick a ball; throw a ball 10 feet
- balance on one foot for a second
- show or tell use of something
- put blocks in a row; make a three-block bridge
- put on and take off most clothes
- do simple matching: colors, shapes, real things to outlines
- know when to wear familiar clothes
- match one to one
- help tell a story
- walk up stairs, alternating feet
- use fingers to show age
- put together two halves to make a whole
- balance and walk on a 5″-wide board
- use some words that tell "where," (*up, down, in,* or *out*)
- try to copy simple shapes
- do an easy five-to-ten-piece puzzle
- tell a little about things they make
- talk about things they have just done
- begin to pedal a tricycle
- catch a big ball bounced from three feet away

42 MONTHS
- talk about their scribbles or drawings when asked

Threes Can List

From 42 to 48 months, some things Threes can do are

42 MONTHS
- take part in a short group time
- tell about something they have done
- talk to friends while playing
- do a five-to-ten-piece puzzle
- point to a color or shape you name
- talk about some things they will do
- copy counting to 10
- screw a lid onto a jar
- try to trace over simple designs and around simple objects
- recognize some opposites
- hop on one foot
- do simple block building
- do simple comparing
- count three or more things
- play simple guessing games
- balance on one foot for five seconds
- begin to do a forward somersault
- walk heel to toe
- give simple reasons
- tell how to do some things
- understand *same/different*
- know names of familiar rooms and furniture
- close a space with four blocks
- match simple bead or block patterns
- trace a cross and diamond
- begin to pump on a swing
- do easy sorting, by one characteristic, with adult help
- name two or three colors or shapes
48 MONTHS
- put three things in order, such as hard to soft, full to empty

Activity Guide

Look at this page carefully. It gives you an idea of how the activities in this book are written. By using underlining, italics, and pictures as short cuts, the activities tell you a lot in a few words. Each activity has a name and number.

There are also activity tips and notes that you should be sure to read in this book. Some of the notes have safety tips and important practical ideas.

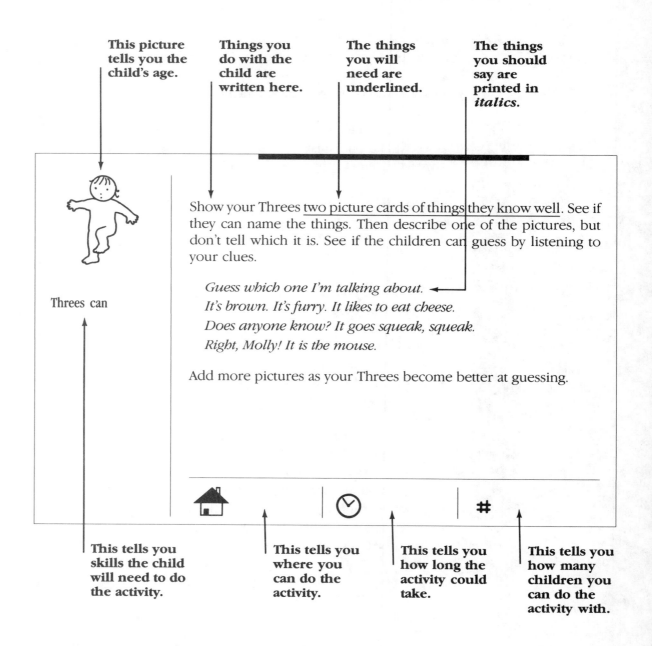

This picture tells you the child's age.

Things you do with the child are written here.

The things you will need are underlined.

The things you should say are printed in *italics*.

Threes can

Show your Threes <u>two picture cards of things</u> they know well. See if they can name the things. Then describe one of the pictures, but don't tell which it is. See if the children can guess by listening to your clues.

Guess which one I'm talking about.
It's brown. It's furry. It likes to eat cheese.
Does anyone know? It goes squeak, squeak.
Right, Molly! It is the mouse.

Add more pictures as your Threes become better at guessing.

This tells you skills the child will need to do the activity.

This tells you where you can do the activity.

This tells you how long the activity could take.

This tells you how many children you can do the activity with.

When You Want to Know More

Here is a list of some good materials to use when you wish to add to the ideas in this book. These are just a few of the many resources that are available to people who work with three-year-olds. Ask at your public library for help in finding the books that are listed, as well as other titles.

Ferguson-Florissant School District. *Games to Grow On for Three-Year-Olds.*

This small book is packed with ideas that help three-year-olds learn and have fun at the same time. Topics include cooking, "rhyme time," water, nuts and bolts, and holiday activities. A list of ages and stages of development for Threes is given. Florissant, Missouri: Ferguson-Florissant School District, Early Education, 1976. (The school district address is 655 January Avenue, Florissant, MO 63135.)

Gordon, Ira and Barry Guinagh and R. Emile Jester. *Child Learning Through Child Play: Learning Activities for Two- and Three-Year Olds.*

There are many ideas for games to play with three-year-olds in the seven sections of this book. The sections include sorting and matching games, building an understanding of patterns, recognition games, word play, developing physical coordination, and imaginative play and creative activities. New York: St. Martin's Press, Inc., 1972.

Leach, Penelope. *Your Baby and Child: From Birth to Age Five.*

This book covers most areas of child care for three-year-olds. A long chapter on children from two and a half to five tells about routine care, such as feeding or toilet training, as well as playing, thinking, and learning how to behave. New York: Alfred A. Knopf, Inc., 1978.

Redleaf, Rhoda. *Open the Door. Let's Explore: Neighborhood Field Trips for Young Children.*

This book gives ideas for over twenty easy-to-take walks or fieldtrips. Many include activities to do before, during, and after the walk: songs and fingerplays, cooking, nature, art, stories, and pretend play. There are also sections on planning trips, safety, hints for happier trips, and sample forms to use. St. Paul, Minn.: Toys 'N Things Press, a division of Resources for Child Caring, Inc., 1983.

Sparling, Joseph and Isabelle Lewis. *Learningames for Threes and Fours: A Guide to Adult-Child Play.*

This book has one hundred activities for adults to do with three- and four-year-olds. The games are matched with typical new behaviors that are listed for children, aged 36–42, 42–48, 48–54, and 54–60 months. The "how" and "why," plus photographs, are given for each game. New York: Walker & Co., division of Walker Publishing Co., Inc., 1984.

Materials Index

The Materials Index lists the activities in this book by the toys, equipment, or other supplies needed for each activity. The index can be used in several ways. You can look for different activities to do with the toys you have. Or you can use the index as a guide as you make up a shopping list for your program.

A

Acorns: 313, 350, 357
Airplanes, toy: 191, 213
Airport, toy: 191
Animals, stuffed: 199, 288, 316, 327
Animals, toy: 191, 205, 213, 316, 338, 364
Aprons, waterproof: 136, 160, 227, 296

B

Bags, cloth and pillow cases: 107, 250, 434
Bags, paper: 237, 350, 362, 401
Balls: 48, 89, 91, 97, 102, 117, 125, 126, 244, 357
Band aids: 241
Barns, toy: 191
Baskets: 102
Bead pattern cards: 427
Beads, $\frac{1}{2}$": 132, 427
Beanbags: 109, 431
Beans, dry: 154, 323
Bells: 248, 385
Birdfeeder and birdfood: 304
Blankets: 106, 210, 223, 231, 339, 369, 389
Blocks, fit together: 146, 207
Blocks, large: 108, 111, 116, 119, 191, 192, 194, 196, 200, 202, 204, 210, 217, 220, 240
Blocks, table: 129, 145, 194, 207, 213, 216, 364, 396, 423, 429, 433
Blocks, unit: 191, 194, 201, 206, 209, 213, 214, 215, 218, 232, 277
Board: 108, 116, 131, 138, 139, 144, 217, 228
Board, metal: 363
Books: 1, 2, 7, 26, 27, 106, 123, 197, 198, 200, 214, 223, 229, 231, 236, 238, 239, 240, 241, 244, 245, 248, 249, 269, 334, 371, 381, 415
Books to make: 9, 12, 18, 22, 358, 371
Bottles, plastic: 178, 226, 232, 244
Bowls: 127, 131, 146, 151, 154, 156, 166, 168, 172, 323, 359
Boxes: 10, 11, 16, 17, 88, 96, 102, 107, 109, 116, 117, 119, 126, 132, 138, 154, 170, 180, 185, 190, 203, 208, 232, 235, 243, 244, 245, 246, 247, 248, 250, 340, 351, 356, 386, 387, 389, 399, 404, 405, 407, 411, 431
Bowling pins, plastic: 125
Brooms: 230
Broomstick horse: 114
Brushes: 247
Bubbles: 104
Buckets: 136, 227, 230, 247
Bugs: 311, 315
Buttons: 349, 356

C

Camera: 13, 31
Cardboard: 12, 22, 122, 133, 137, 174, 214, 248, 270, 320, 375, 380, 399, 400, 406, 409, 411, 432
Cars, trucks, toy: 191, 197, 201, 209

Cart: 202
Cash register, toy: 20, 237
Catalogs: 3, 12, 22, 42, 137
Cellophane paper: 375
Chalk: 168
Cheerleading pom-pons: 266
Clay: 399
Clock, toy: 368
Cloth, material: 182, 214, 226, 356, 370, 386, 399, 400, 404, 409, 411, 432
Clothes, childrens: 55, 302, 408
Clothesline: 156, 163
Clothespins: 156, 163, 227
Contact paper, clear: 4, 11, 12, 22, 31, 42, 122, 133, 137, 169, 270, 294, 320, 354, 403, 405
Contact paper, colorful: 138, 170, 274, 431
Containers, empty food: 20, 203, 237, 362
Containers (plastic margarine tubs, juice cans, film cans, etc.): 14, 61, 128, 159, 175, 184, 190, 203, 274, 275, 295, 303, 313, 337, 349, 355, 357, 363, 370, 373, 374, 376, 414, 426, 435
Containers, see-through: 309, 315, 384
Cookie cutters: 297
Cook's hat and apron: 225
Cot: 231
Cotton balls: 370, 396
Crayons: 61, 88, 143, 148, 157, 159, 189, 319, 380, 416
Cubes, 1": 129, 145, 355, 357, 410
Cup hooks: 131
Cups, paint: 162, 173, 183
Cups, paper: 153, 324, 342, 359, 388
Cups, plastic: 88, 136, 154, 156, 295, 296, 297, 306, 377

D

Dishes, unbreakable: 210, 221, 228, 234, 297
Dishpan: 20, 109, 127, 129, 146, 147, 148, 151, 154, 155, 156, 160, 169, 182, 197, 207, 216, 231, 233, 234, 262, 295, 296, 297, 300, 303, 310, 321, 326, 332, 355, 384, 400, 409, 410, 433
Dishsoap: 234
Doctor things: 241
Dolls: 77, 199, 221, 223, 226, 231, 233, 242, 257, 296, 339
Doll bed: 223
Doll clothes: 227, 242
Dress-up clothes: 149, 152, 222
Dustpan and brush: 295

E

Easel: 162
Envelopes (used): 250
Extract (peppermint, vanilla): 370

F

Feather: 313, 378
Feelie Bag: 14, 313, 357, 426, 435
Felt: 11, 21, 326, 341
Filmstrip projector: 140
Fingerpaint: 160, 171, 188
Fishnet: 163
Fit-together toys: 146, 151
Flannelboard: 11, 17, 25, 37, 326, 341

Flannelboard people: 17, 21
Flannelboard pictures: 25, 37
Flashlight: 140, 241, 389
Flour: 166
Flowers: 298, 314
Foil, aluminum: 248
Folders: 158
Food: 141, 309, 318, 333, 345, 359, 373, 377, 382, 388, 392, 398, 402
Food color: 166
Food, play: 20, 237, 362
Forks: 225, 351
Freezer: 310
Furniture, doll house: 219
Funnel: 295, 296

G

Garage, toy: 191
Gardening tools: 236
Geoboards: 128
Glass: 399
Gloves and mittens: 235
Glue: 3, 4, 12, 31, 41, 133, 137, 147, 178, 185, 375, 386, 400, 409, 411, 432
Grasshopper and cricket: 315
Gravel: 303

H

Hairbrush: 88
Hammer: 88, 144, 239, 248
Hats: 238, 244, 247, 248
Hoops: 119
Hose: 238, 248, 295
Housekeeping furniture: 77, 221
Houses, toy: 191

I

Icecube trays: 310
Interlocking toys: 146, 151, 207

J

Jars, plastic: 155, 274, 275

K

Knife, X-acto or razor blade: 375, 421
Knives, plastic: 141, 225

L

Ladder: 105, 116
Lawn mower, toy: 236
Leaves: 189, 313, 319, 320, 350
Lemon: 377
Locks: 139

M

Magazines: 3, 22, 110, 137
Magnet: 246, 300
Magnet board: 363
Magnet numbers: 363

Magnifying glass: 305, 307, 323
Mail, junk: 250
Markers: 143, 157, 164, 177, 179, 212, 416, 436
Mat: 295, 296
Masks: 179, 243
Matching game: 322
Mattress: 231
Measuring cups: 166, 225, 344
Measuring spoons: 344
Metal: 399
Mirror: 179, 243, 245, 283
Money, play: 20
Mop: 296
Music box: 264
Musical instruments: 255, 256, 262, 267, 278, 279, 290, 292

N

Nails, large head: 144, 239
Name labels: 23
Nesting blocks: 429
Newspaper: 168, 178, 189, 393, 413

O

Oil: 166, 383

P

Paint, powder: 185
Paint roller and pan: 247
Paintbrushes: 88, 162, 173, 184
Paints: 162, 173, 176, 183, 184, 413, 430, 431
Paper: 3, 41, 140, 143, 147, 148, 157, 159, 162, 164, 167, 169, 170, 173, 175, 177, 178, 182,
     184, 185, 187, 188, 189, 190, 246, 319, 325, 348, 354, 358, 412, 413, 416, 421, 430, 436
Paper clips: 189, 246, 349
Paper, construction: 167, 168, 169, 412
Paper, giftwrap: 167
Paper plates: 179
Paper punch: 133
Paper roll: 171, 183, 420
Paper, textured: 182
Paper towels: 160, 176, 184, 342
Paste: 167, 169, 182, 348, 412
Pebbles: 190, 303, 349, 374
Pegboard and pegs: 127, 332, 414
Pencils: 157, 175
People, toy: 191
Pets: 308, 316, 318
Photos at home: 8
Photos at school: 8
Photos of children: 23, 31
Photos of families: 34
Photo albums: 13, 34
Picture labels: 191, 221
Pictures and picture cards: 3, 4, 5, 10, 14, 16, 20, 29, 30, 33, 35, 179, 234, 240, 293, 294, 298,
     299, 304, 325, 329, 351, 360, 391, 394, 428
Pictures of animals: 107, 110, 205, 308, 322, 328, 330
Pictures of familiar things: 6, 9, 15, 40, 133, 197, 198, 235, 245, 270
Pictures, matching, counting, opposites, sets: 4, 18, 24, 39, 322, 340, 348, 360, 361

Pictures of people: 41, 137, 223, 226, 231, 246, 247, 249, 252, 308, 328
Pie plate: 176
Pillows, cushions: 231, 369
Pitchers: 136, 154, 306, 377, 388
Plants: 306, 314, 390
Plaster of Paris: 190
Plastic: 399
Poker chips: 138
Popcorn: 383
Poster board: 4, 31, 403, 405
Potato masher: 225
Potatoes: 430
Pots and pans: 221, 228, 383
Puppets: 19, 38, 288
Purses: 240
Puzzles: 134, 419

R

Rags: 227, 230
Record player: 26
Records or tapes: 26, 48, 100, 255, 263, 265, 266, 267, 280, 283, 286, 397
Ribbon: 178, 179
Rice, dry: 154
Riding toys with pedals: 99, 238
Rocks: 350
Rope: 227
Rubber: 399
Rubber bands: 128
Rubber pants: 226
Rug: 105, 108, 110, 111

S

Salt: 166
Sand: 180, 185, 190, 297, 344, 374, 384
Sand table: 135, 213, 295, 303
Sandpaper: 11, 411
Scarves: 266
Scissors: 88, 169
Seeds: 324
Shape sorting boxes: 418
Shape stencils: 421
Sheet: 140, 212
Shells: 190, 313
Shelves, low: 134, 191, 207, 237
Shoelaces: 132, 172
Shoes: 150
Shopping cart: 237, 362
Shower caps: 232
Shower curtain: 136, 212, 296
Sink and float toys: 296, 321
Slide: 103, 119
Snails or slugs: 309
Soap: 88, 160, 227, 233
Sock: 313
Soft toys: 106, 369
Soil: 303, 324
Sorting board: 24, 299, 361, 425, 428

Spices: 370
Sponges: 230, 234, 396, 430
Spoons, scoops: 88, 154, 225, 228, 295, 296, 303, 342, 351
Stamps and seals: 250
Staples: 179, 358, 386
Steering wheel: 240
Stethoscope: 241
Stick: 246
Stickers: 170, 325, 358, 412
Stones: 303
Stool: 116
Streamers: 266
String, yarn: 12, 22, 133, 174, 178, 179, 190, 246, 370
Stump: 144
Styrofoam: 239
Sugar: 377
Sunglasses: 244
Swings: 118

T

Tape: 122, 132, 133, 174, 186, 189, 274, 275, 281, 319, 374, 393
Tape, masking: 95, 119, 193, 208, 212, 226, 424
Tape recorder: 26, 29, 220, 253, 391
Telephones, toy: 83, 224
Tents: 106, 119
Timer: 368
Tissue paper: 147, 281
Tools, plastic: 238, 239, 255, 303
Towels: 136, 232, 234, 244, 295, 296
Train track: 201
Trains, toy: 198, 201
Trays: 160, 171, 172, 180, 188
Tricycles: 99
Tub: 296
Tubes, cardboard: 281
Tunnel: 119
Twigs: 213

V

Vinyl picture stick-ons (color forms): 130

W

Wagons: 202, 235, 237, 248
Waiting list: 57
Wallpaper: 167
Washcloths: 233
Washers, different sized: 131
Water: 136, 160, 166, 184, 227, 230, 233, 234, 296, 297, 306, 310, 323, 324, 344, 377
Water table: 136, 296, 321
Watering can: 236
Wheelbarrow, toy: 236
Whisk: 225
Wood: 399

Active Learning
for Threes

Planning for Threes

Here's Why

Words are important to three-year-olds as a way of telling you what they want. Words also help a child think and remember. Three-year-olds are able to do more with words every day. Most can talk in short, simple sentences, say familiar nursery rhymes, talk about what they see in pictures, ask many questions, and answer some questions, too. But Threes still have lots to learn before they can talk clearly. In fact, children are usually about six years old before they can be easily understood. You can help Threes continue to practice talking by asking questions, listening with interest, and adding to what Threes say. That's what this book is all about.

In the Books and Pictures section you will find ideas for using pictures to help your Threes practice some new thinking skills, such as naming, matching, guessing, or comparing. You will also find activities in which Threes get the warm, personal experiences with books that make learning to read more fun later on.

The Conversation activities give you ideas on helping Threes use talking to get along with others, share feelings and ideas, work on new self-help skills, follow directions, and show what they know and remember. Some of the activities in this section are just meant to be fun as you and the Threes play with words together. Listening and talking should be a big part of everything you do with Threes. The activities in this book can get you started helping Threes improve their new skills with words.

Materials and Notes
Books and Pictures

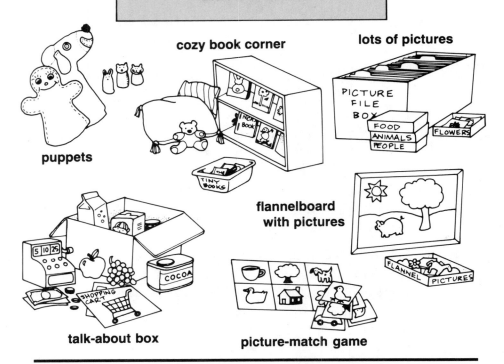

puppets

cozy book corner

lots of pictures

flannelboard with pictures

talk-about box

picture-match game

- Keep the book corner area small, for two to four children at a time. Make it comfortable and well-lighted. Add pillows, carpet, cuddly toys, and a small chair or two near a little table.

- Have books with pictures of things you are talking about with your Threes. Be sure that the books show people of many ages, races, and cultures in a positive way. Change books often.

- Keep the book corner organized and neat and keep books in good shape. Talk with your Threes about caring for books. Place most books so the child can see their front covers.

- Include new story books and old favorites. Add books that help children learn about new ideas.

- Add some other book corner materials. Try finger puppets in a little box, a flannelboard with shapes and pictures, or some sets of picture cards. Don't have too many of these added materials in the book corner at one time so that pieces won't get mixed up or lost.

- See Tips for Story Times and Ideas on Pictures for Threes, pages 75–78.

Activity Checklist

Books and Pictures

Book and picture activities for Threes include the use of colorful pictures and designs placed where children can see and touch them, sturdy picture books, and simple picture games. Threes enjoy being read to and looking at books on their own. They are able to talk about the pictures they see, help you tell a favorite story, and play easy picture-matching games on their own, once they've been shown how. Threes are developing a memory for their favorite stories and enjoy trying to retell them.

Check for each age group	*36–42 mo*	*42–48 mo*
1. Many pictures are placed where children can easily see and touch them.	—	—
2. A cozy book area with a variety of books is available to child most of the day.	—	—
3. Pictures and picture books are colorful and have clear illustrations of people and things that interest Threes.	—	—
4. Pictures of people are not sexist and show different races and ages in positive ways.	—	—
5. Books children use are sturdy, in good condition, and displayed with front covers showing.	—	—
6. New pictures and books are added often.	—	—
7. Adult and children often talk about pictures.	—	—
8. Adult asks questions about pictures to encourage children's ideas.	—	—
9. Adult reads with children every day, either individually or in small groups.	—	—
10. Adult shows children how to play simple age-appropriate picture games. Games are available for regular independent use.	—	—
11. Other story-telling materials, such as a flannelboard with sets of pictures, hand puppets or finger puppets, are set out for children to use.	—	—

1

Get to Know the Book Corner

Set up a <u>book corner</u> for your Threes. Take a few children at a time on a "tour" around this area. Talk about all the things in the book corner. Ask questions to see if your Threes know how to choose, look at, and put away books. You can act out what to do with the children. Give words to what you do. Use the word *library* to talk about the book corner.

Stacy, you know how to use the books here, don't you?
Can you show us? We'll watch.
First you look at the books.
Then you find one you want to look at.
Good, I see you chose your favorite book.

Threes can

- look at books on their own
- help clean up

 indoors | 3–5 min | 1–4 Threes

2

Read and Ask

Read a <u>very simple story</u> to a small group of Threes. (See Tips for Story Time, page 75.) As you finish reading a page, see if the children can answer some easy questions about what's happening. Hold the book so that they can see the pictures. Then use questions that ask what, who, where, when, or how.

What's happened to the hungry caterpillar?
That's right. He got big and fat.
Do you remember what he ate?
Let's look at the pictures. What did he eat?

Be ready for lots of children to answer at once, or for no one to talk. Encourage children to listen as another child talks. Ask easier questions if children do not answer.

Threes can

- listen to short story
- answer easy questions

 in or out | 3–7 min | 1–9 Threes

3

Threes can

- paste or glue
- talk about pictures

Poster Making

Have your Threes help you make picture posters to go with the ideas you talk about. For example, if you are talking about toys, make posters that show different kinds of toys or people using them. Cut out <u>lots of the pictures</u> you need from <u>magazines and catalogs</u>. Then your Threes can look at them and help you <u>glue</u> the ones they like onto a <u>large sheet of sturdy paper</u>.

Talk about the pictures as you work. Ask questions to help the children talk, too.

Hang up the posters when they are done. Look at and talk about them often. Take the posters down after a week or two, but save them to show and talk about again.

 indoors | 10–20 min | # 1–6 Threes

4

Threes can

- do easy picture matching

Big Lotto Game

Cut out <u>eight or ten pairs of matching pictures</u>. <u>Glue</u> one picture from each pair onto a <u>large piece of posterboard</u>. Cover with <u>clear contact paper</u>. Make <u>picture cards</u> with the other half of the pictures. Show your Threes how to place each picture card onto its matching picture. Help them look at the picture card and each picture on the board until they find the one that matches. Talk about the pictures as you work together.

What's this picture, Jerry?
A dog, that's right. It's a big brown dog.
Can you find the same dog here?
Look at it carefully.

 in or out | 3–10 min | # 1–4 Threes

5

Threes can

■ talk about pictures

Peek-a-Boo Picture Board

Make a <u>peek-a-boo picture board</u> for your three-year-olds. (You will find directions for making one on page 79.) Put <u>new pictures</u> on the board each day. When children look to see what the pictures are, help them talk about what they see.

What do you see under there, Fay?
Yes, kittens. Do you see anything else?
Yes, the mommy. That must be the mother cat.
She has four kittens. See, one, two, three, four.
What are the kittens doing?

 indoors   2–4 min   # 1–3 Threes

6

Threes can

■ guess easy riddles

Riddle Guessing

Show your Threes <u>two picture cards of things they know well</u>. See if they can name the things. Then describe one of the pictures, but don't tell which it is. See if the children can guess by listening to your clues.

Guess which one I'm talking about.
It's brown. It's furry. It likes to eat cheese.
Does anyone know? It goes squeak, squeak.
Right, Molly! It is the mouse.

Add more pictures as your Threes become better at guessing.

 in or out   3–10 min   # 1–15 Threes

7

Threes can

- understand many words
- answer easy questions

Look for Details

Look at a book with your Threes. Use a <u>book that has lots of small, interesting things in its pictures</u>. Go through the pages slowly. Help the children find, name, and talk about as many things in the pictures as possible. See if they can find things you name.

Charles, can you find the girl who is sawing the wood?
That's right. And what is this boy doing?

 in or out 3–10 min 1–3 Threes

8

Threes can

- tell actions in pictures

Sequence Card Story

Buy or make a <u>set of easy, three-step sequence cards</u>. (You will find some examples to copy on page 81.) Try making sequence cards from photos taken at school or at home. Put the cards out in order, from left to right. Point to the pictures as you tell the Threes what is happening. Then see if the children can tell you about the story. Ask questions to see if the children can point to a card you are describing.

Which card shows the girl brushing her teeth?
And now what is she doing?

Put the cards in the book corner for the children to use. Many Threes will want to put the cards in a different order. Enjoy the special way young children see things.

 in or out 3–10 min 1–3 Threes

9

Threes can

■ show or tell use of something

Pictures of Things we Use

Make picture cards, a book, or a poster of "Things We Use." Include pictures such as a cup, a bar of soap, a car, cot, chair, and others. Look at the pictures with the children. Ask questions to help them tell how we use the things in the pictures. See if they answer with words or actions. Do some pretend actions along with the words.

What's this, Ginger? Right, a cot.
What is the cot for? Right, naptime.
We sleep on cots, don't we?
Let's pretend to be asleep.

 in or out | 3–10 min | **#** 1–15 Threes

10

Threes can

■ do very easy sorting

First Sorting

Make sets of picture cards that show foods and toys. (See Ideas on Pictures for Threes on page 76.) Have four or five cards in each set.

Put out two boxes the cards will fit into. Tell your Threes you are going to sort the cards. Show them which box will hold the toy pictures and which will hold the food pictures.

Then hold up a picture for all to see. Ask if it is a toy or a food. As the children answer, put the card into the correct box. Help with the answer if you need to. Continue until all cards are sorted.

Leave the cards and boxes on a low shelf where one or two children can use them on their own. Try other sets of cards, such as clothes, animals, or flowers.

 in or out | 3–7 min | **#** 1–15 Threes

11

Flannelboard Grocery Store

Turn a <u>flannelboard</u> into a grocery store game. (See directions for making a flannelboard on page 279.) Cut out lots of <u>pictures</u> from food ads and labels from food containers. Put <u>clear contact paper</u> on the front. <u>Glue felt or sandpaper</u> to the back. Keep the pictures in a <u>box</u> near the flannelboard in the book corner.

Talk about all the foods with the children. See which ones they can name, which ones they like, and which ones they have tasted. See if the children will pretend to "buy" the foods from one another or just have fun moving them around the board.

Threes can

- name food pictures
- do simple pretend play

 indoors 3–10 min 1–2 Threes

12

What Are They Doing?

Have children help you make a picture book with <u>pictures you find in school supply catalogs</u>. Cut out pictures that show children using the things your Threes use, such as blocks, puzzles, tables and chairs, cots, and others. Then let the children help <u>glue</u> these onto <u>sturdy cardboard pages</u>. Let the pages dry, and cover with <u>clear contact paper</u> if you wish. Tie the pages together with <u>yarn or string</u>.

Ask questions to help your Threes talk about the pictures while you are making the book. Put the book in the book corner for the children to use every day.

Threes can

- say what people are doing
- answer easy questions

 indoors 7–20 min 1–5 Threes

13

Threes can

- talk about pictures
- answer easy questions

Kids' Photo Album

Take photos of the children once in a while. Take pictures on special days, such as birthdays or holidays. Be sure to have many pictures of the children doing everyday things, too. Put the photos into a sturdy photo album with plastic pages that will protect them. Put the album in the book corner for your Threes to use. Talk about the pictures with the children. Help them remember as they look.

Who is this? Do you remember?
That's Fran. She moved away. Who is this standing next to Fran? Yes, that's you!
What are you and Fran doing?

Add new pictures to the album. Make more than one album if there are problems with sharing.

 in or out | 6–15 min | 1–5 Threes

14

Threes can

- recognize some familiar things by touch

Feelie Box Picture Game

Put a plastic margarine tub into a large, stretchy sock to make a feelie box. Have some familiar things that will fit into the box, such as a crayon, key, block, paint brush, or spoon. Make picture cards that show these things. Put one of the things into the feelie box while the child looks away. Then show the child two cards, one of which is a picture of the thing in the box. Let the child reach into the box and feel. See if he can choose the picture of the thing he feels. See if he can name what the thing is and say a little about it. Ask easy questions to help with this.

Yes, it's a crayon. What do you do with a crayon?

 in or out | 2–10 min | 1–3 Threes

15

Threes can

■ say what people are doing in pictures

Picture Directions

Find or draw <u>pictures of things you often ask your Threes to do</u>. Include pictures of washing hands, picking up toys, sitting at the table or in a circle, or going outside. Look at the pictures with the children. See if they can tell you what is happening. On the same day, hold up and show the pictures instead of using words for your directions. Have the children tell you what they are to do.

Look here to see what I want you to do now.
See the picture? What does it tell you to do?
Right, wash hands. Let's wash up for snack.

 indoors　｜　 2–5 min　｜　 1–15 Threes

16

Threes can

■ name pictures and talk about them

"Things We Talk About" Picture Box

Make <u>picture cards</u> that go with the things you are talking about with your Threes. Put them into a special <u>box</u> that you keep in the book corner. Look at the pictures with the children. See what they can say about each one. You can add more to what they say.

That's right, Jenny. That is a fireman.
Do you remember Jake, the firefighter, who showed us around the fire station?
What was he wearing?

See if two of the children will look at the cards together. Show them how one can take out the card while the other can name what's in the picture.

 indoors　｜　 3–15 min　｜　 1–5 Threes

Activities for Listening and Talking

17

Threes can

- say when to wear some clothes

Flannelboard People with Clothes

Buy or make flannelboard people with different clothes. (See directions for making a flannelboard on page 279.) Include a bathing suit, a raincoat, boots, a coat, and others. Put these in a box next to the flannelboard in the book corner. Show the children how they can dress the people. Help them name the clothes and say when they would wear them.

What clothes did you dress the boy in, Charles?

Leave these in the book corner for the children to use on their own.

 indoors 3–15 min # 1–2 Threes

18

Threes can

- say some opposites

Opposite Pictures

Look with your Threes at a book or some pictures that show opposites. (Ask your public librarian for ideas on books.) Point to a picture and say a sentence about it.

This boy is up. He's up in the tree.

Ask a question to help the children say the opposite.

Where's the other boy? That's right. He's down.
He's down on the grass.

After some practice, see if anyone can tell you the opposite before you even ask the question. Don't be surprised if some Threes tell you everything about the pictures before you can say a word.

 in or out 3–6 min # 1–15 Threes

19

Threes can

- help tell a story

Story with Puppets

Have a few Threes use <u>hand puppets</u> to help you tell a very familiar story, such as "The Three Bears." Give each child a puppet to hold. Tell each who his puppet will be in the story. Have the children listen carefully so that they will know when to make their puppet talk. Begin telling the story. When the time comes for a child's puppet to say something, give help if needed.

The Mama Bear looked at her bowl.
And what did she say, Latoya?

If you don't have hand puppets, try this activity with toy animals or homemade stick puppets. (See directions for making stick puppets on page 83.)

 in or out 5–10 min 1–4 Threes

20

Threes can

- talk about familiar pictures and things

Picture-Toy Box

Make a picture-toy box to use with your Threes. For example, try a supermarket picture-toy box. Make <u>a few supermarket picture cards</u>. Add these to a <u>toy cash register</u>, some <u>empty food containers</u>, <u>play money</u>, and some <u>plastic fruits</u>. Put all into a <u>box or dishpan</u>.

Have the children take out one picture or thing at a time. Ask questions to see what the children can tell you. Add more information to what they say.

Leave the picture-toy box on a low shelf for your Threes to play with. Try other picture-toy boxes that the children will enjoy.

 in or out 5–15 min 1–3 Threes

21

Threes can

- use some words that tell "where"

"Where is the Man?" Flannelboard

Cut out a felt house-shape and a little felt man to use on the flannelboard. (Directions for making a flannelboard are on page 279.) Then play this game with your Threes.

Let them watch as you put the house on the board. Have them hide their eyes as you place the man next to, on top of, or under the house. As you do this, say, "Where is the man going to be?" Some children may peek, but that's fine. When the man is in place, have your Threes look and use words to tell you where he is.

Play again. Add other felt pieces to the game. Leave the game in a container in the book corner for a few children to use on their own.

 indoors 3–5 min **#** 1–15 Threes

22

Threes can

- name pictures

Book Making

Have children help as you make new books for the book corner. Tell them what the book will be about. Then all of you can look through old magazines or catalogs to find pictures you need. You can cut out the pictures and help the children paste them onto cardboard book pages. Write down the words the children say about the pictures. Cover pages with clear contact paper if you wish. Tie the pages together with yarn or string. Write the book's title on the front page.

Look at the books with the children. Talk about the pictures. See what the children can remember about how they made the books.

 indoors 5–20 min 1–5 Threes

23

Threes can

- recognize their whole name

Name Labels

Label things each child uses with his name printed in big, clear letters. Put children's name labels on their cubbies, cots, artwork, places in a circle, and coat hooks. Put a photo of each child on his cubby too.

  Point out the names often, but don't try to make children read them. Instead, talk about how a name lets you know what things belong to each child. Help children enjoy their names and the things that are just for them.

 indoors | 1–2 min | # 1 child at a time

24

Threes can

- do very easy sorting

Sorting Board Fun

Make some sorting boards for your Threes who enjoy picture sorting games. (You'll find directions for making sorting boards on page 348.) Put out a sorting board with two sets of cards. Show the child how to sort the cards into the right places. Talk about the pictures. Help the child say why each card goes where it does.

What's this picture, Cara?
Right, it's a boy.
Does it go here with the girls, or here with the boys?

 in or out | 5–15 min | # 1–2 Threes

25

Threes can

■ help tell a story

Flannelboard Stories

Buy or make <u>flannelboard pictures</u> to use as you tell a favorite story with a small group of your Threes. (See directions for making a flannelboard on page 279.) Give one or more pictures to each child. Let the child be "in charge" of placing those pictures on the <u>flannelboard</u> and moving them when needed. Have your Threes take part in the telling as much as you can. Use questions to help them say what is going on.

If your Threes are able to work well as a large group, try making up a story that has enough felt pictures for the whole group to use.

Leave the pictures in the book corner for the children to use on their own.

 indoors   5–10 min   1–5 Threes

26

Threes can

■ enjoy stories
■ turn pages
■ follow directions

Books with Records or Tapes

Play a <u>record or tape that goes with a picture book</u>. Show the children how to listen to the story and turn the pages at the right times. The record or tape should have a special sound, such as a bell ringing, to tell when to turn the page. Help your Threes listen for this. You will probably have to work the <u>record or tape player</u>. Your Threes will enjoy taking turns holding the books and turning the pages.

Try making your own tapes of favorite books. Read slowly, ring a bell as you turn the page, and wait ten seconds before starting the next page. Ask some fathers and mothers if they would read and record a story.

 indoors   4–10 min   1–3 Threes

27

Threes can

■ enjoy being read to

Poems

Read to your Threes from a <u>book of poems</u>. (Your public librarian can help you find poetry for young children.) Try to pick poems that talk about things the children enjoy. Find poems with different rhythms, some that show different feelings, some that tell stories, and some that are just fun. Read slowly and show that you enjoy the poems. Talk about things the Threes might imagine as you read.

Here's a poem about swinging on a swing.
We go on swings outside, don't we?
Close your eyes while I read.
Pretend you're on a swing.

 in or out   3–7 min   1–15 Threes

28

Threes can

■ tell about something they have done

Sunshine Notes

When you and a child are happy about something she has done, write a <u>short Sunshine Note</u> for the child to give to her parents. (Sample Sunshine Notes for you to copy are on page 84.) Have the child help tell you what to write.

I liked the way you tasted the broccoli, Kimiko.
You found out that you like broccoli.
I'm so proud of you! Let's write a Sunshine Note to your mom
to tell her about it.
What should I write?

Read the notes you've written back to the children, and encourage parents to read them aloud too. Keep plenty of blank notes handy.

 in or out   2–5 min   1 child at a time

29

Threes can

- enjoy fingerplays and stories

Going on a Bear Hunt

Practice the Bear Hunt with your Threes. (You'll find the words on page 85.) Show them how to do all the movements. Then make a tape recording of the words and sounds to the Bear Hunt. Play the recording so that a few children can do the Bear Hunt on their own.

Add simple pictures that show the Bear Hunt steps. Put them where the children can easily see as they listen. Make sure the first step is on the left and the last is on the right so that the Threes can "read" the pictures in the right order.

 indoors | 5–10 min | 1–15 Threes

30

Threes can

- do easy puzzles

Picture Puzzles

Make three or four picture cards of big, bright, colorful, familiar things. Cut each in half with a wavy or zig-zag line. Show a child half of a picture. Ask her what she thinks the picture will be. Then hand her the other half and let her put it together. Talk about the whole picture.

That is a dog. You were right, Crystal.
What's the dog doing?

If this is easy for a child, let her work with more than one picture at a time, or cut each picture into three or four pieces.

 indoors | 3–7 min | 1–2 Threes

31

Threes can

- tell about a picture

Photograph Posters

Take photos of the children, or have parents bring some in for you to use. Glue the photos to a big piece of posterboard. Have each child tell you something he wants you to write under his picture. If he can't think of something to say, ask a question to help.

Here's your picture, Todd. What should I write under it?
Tell me what you're doing in the picture.

Cover the posterboard with clear contact paper. Hang the poster down low where Threes can see and touch it. Look at the poster often with your Threes. Read aloud what they had you write.

 indoors | 2–3 min | 1–2 Threes

32

Threes can

- help tell a familiar story

What Will Happen?

Begin to tell a familiar story to your Threes. Do this without a book so that the children listen without looking at pictures. Once you are into the story, choose places where the children might be able to help you tell what happens. Be ready to hear lots of different ideas besides the ones you expect. Show the children how happy you are with whatever they say.

Peter Rabbit hid under the flower pot.
And then what happened?

Try to make up a story with your Threes. See if they can help you make up what happens as the story grows. This can get pretty silly, so be ready to laugh.

 in or out | 3–7 min | 1–5 Threes

33

Threes can

- give simple reasons

Pictures About Feelings

Make a set of <u>flannelboard felt pieces shaped and colored like different fruits</u>. (See directions for making a flannelboard on page 279.) with the Threes. See if they can name the feelings in the pictures. You can add other words about feelings. Help the children talk about why each person might be feeling the way he or she does.

I think the boy is sad too, Caitlin.
Why is he sad? What happened to his ice cream cone?
Right. It fell down. Would that make you sad?

 in or out   4–8 min   1–12 Threes

34

Threes can

- talk about familiar things

Family Photo Album

Ask children's parents to bring in <u>family photos</u> for you to put into a Family Photo Album. Put the photos in an album that has <u>clear plastic covers</u> for the pages, or cover pictures with clear contact paper.

   Have each child talk about his family as you place the pictures on the album pages. Bring in a picture of you and your family too.

There's your mom and your grandma, Tyrone.
But who's this here with you?
He's your dog? What's his name?

 in or out   5–20 min   1–6 Threes

35

Threes can

- talk about pictures

Special Picture Place

Set up a "Special Picture Place" on a wall, the back of a bookcase, or a bulletin board. Put up <u>pictures</u> of the things you and the children are talking about at the time. As topics change, be sure to change the pictures. Point out the pictures in your talks. Ask questions to help the children talk about them.

That's right, Andrea. Cars have wheels.
There are lots of other things with wheels.
Let's look at our special picture place.
What else do you see with wheels?

 indoors 2–4 min 1–15 Threes

36

Threes can

- enjoy books
- follow some directions

Library or Bookmobile Visit

Take your Threes on a visit to the library. First, plan your visit with the librarian. Then get the children ready. Talk about the library before you go. Explain library rules, and talk about how to handle the books there. Make sure you have one adult along for every four children. Then go on your visit.

Let the children look at books for a while. If there's time, have a short story or other fun library activity. If possible, let each child choose a book that you can check out. Keep these in a special place so that they don't get mixed up with other books.

If you cannot make library visits often, see if a Bookmobile will visit.

 in or out 45–90 min 1–4 per adult

37

Threes can

- do simple sorting

Flannelboard Sorting Game

Make a set of <u>flannelboard felt pieces shaped and colored like different fruits</u>. (See directions for making a flannelboard on page 279.) Include six red apples, six oranges, six yellow bananas, six purple plums, and six green pears. Show the child how to play fruit store with these. Let him pretend to be the fruit seller. Have him sort and arrange all the fruits so the same ones are together. Make sure to tell the child the names of all the fruits and give him a chance to say them too.

The child may want to play with the felt fruits in other ways, too. Store the fruits in a box. Leave them with the <u>flannelboard</u> in the book corner.

 indoors | 7–15 min | 1–2 Threes

38

Threes can

- enjoy puppets

Finger Puppet Play

Make or buy <u>finger puppets</u> for your Threes. You can even draw eyes, a nose, and mouth on each child's "pointer" finger to make puppets. Help the children pretend different actions with their puppets. See if they can make their puppets run, fly, sleep, or jump. Help the three-year-olds make their puppets talk to another child's puppets. You may want to use a puppet to get the talking started. Give children two puppets each, and see if they will make the puppets talk to each other.

Who's your puppet, Larry?
And who is this on your finger, Holly?
Can they talk? My puppet can talk to yours.

 in or out | 4–10 min | 1–15 Threes

39

Threes can

■ tell what a familiar thing is used for

Missing Words Fill-In

Make a <u>set of picture cards</u> that include pairs that go together, such as soap and a bathtub, a chair and a table, a spoon and a cup, and an umbrella and a rainhat. Tell the children you are going to play a word-guessing game. Look at one pair of pictures with your Threes. As you look, say what one of the things is for. Then start saying what the other thing is for, but do not finish. Let the child guess the words.

Soap is for washing and a bathtub is for _____.

If your Threes don't say what you expect, just enjoy what they say in their own three-year-old way and have fun talking about the pictures.

 in or out | 2–7 min | 1–15 Threes

40

Threes can

■ remember many things

Hide the Picture

Show your Threes a clear <u>picture of a familiar thing</u>. Tell them to "look hard," because you are going to hide the picture and see if they remember what it was. Have them name the picture. After they have looked, have them close their eyes. Then hide the picture under a piece of paper. Have them open their eyes and try to tell you what it was.

If this is too easy, use two or three pictures and hide one while the children's eyes are closed. Don't worry if a few children peek. Just laugh and have fun with the guessing game anyway.

 in or out | 3–10 min | 1–15 Threes

41

Threes can

- talk about pictures

Making Baby Posters

Have your Threes find lots of <u>baby pictures</u> in <u>magazines and cata-</u><u>logs</u>. Be sure the children can find babies of all races. Cut out the pictures and help the children <u>glue</u> them to <u>large sheets of paper</u>. Look at the pictures, and talk with the Threes about what babies can and cannot do. Write their words near the pictures. Hang the posters where your Threes can see and touch them. Look at the posters with the children, and read the things they told you.

Which baby do you like, Debby? Oh, that one.
Do you remember what we wrote about that baby?
It says, "The baby drinks milk."

 indoors 10–20 min 1–5 Threes

42

Threes can

- recognize many pictures
- help clean up

Picture-Word Labels

Make picture labels to show your Threes where things go. Cut <u>pic-</u><u>tures</u> out of school supply <u>catalogs</u>, trace outlines of familiar things, or draw the pictures you will need. Have the Threes tell you what each thing is, and write what they say on the labels. Then use <u>clear</u> <u>contact paper</u> to stick these on shelves, dishpans, and other places where toys and supplies are kept. Talk about the labels with the children as they help you put them up.

What is this picture, Beth? Yes, it is a little toy car.
The picture and word "cars" tells us that the cars go in this dishpan.
Let's stick the label here and put the cars in.

 indoors 2–5 min 1–5 Threes

Tips for Story Times

Time

■ Plan at least one special time in your schedule for stories with your Threes. If the time works well, have a story or other talking activity at that time every day. Stories work well at the table after snack is cleared away or before lunch. A story as children wake up from nap also is good.

■ Be patient. Begin with a very short story time (about seven minutes). As children learn to listen with interest, have a longer story time, but stop as soon as interest is gone.

■ Use a fingerplay, song, or puppet to catch children's attention. Then read a short book. Also use pictures and flannelboard stories at this time. Remember that it's a time for children to listen, think, and talk.

Place

■ Plan a place for your story time. Choose a large enough space so that no one will be crowded. A rug helps tell children where they should be.

■ Choose an out-of-the way place where you won't be disturbed.

■ Find a place where children will pay attention, for example, away from toys on open shelves.

■ Give each child his own special space to sit. You can put chairs with names on them in a circle, or names on labels around a table. You can try putting names on a masking tape circle that you have put down on a rug. Or try giving each child his own carpet square or pillow to sit on.

■ Make sure every child can see and hear.

■ Keep the story place the same every day unless it does not work well. Changing children's places, making story time shorter, or having stories with fewer children might help.

Group size

■ Begin with a small group. Encourage children to take part, but don't force them.

■ If there are two adults, have two groups if you can. Or have one person read while the other sits with the children and helps them listen.

■ Plan other quiet activities for children who are not ready to listen to stories in a group.

■ Read to children alone or in a very small group during the day, whenever you can. Be sure you read to the children who cannot listen to stories in a larger group.

Reading

- Choose the book you will read ahead of time.

- Use books with big, clear, colorful pictures and not too many words. If there are too many words, tell the story in your own words, instead of reading it.

- Hold the book up facing the children so that all of them can see the pictures.

- Point out things on the pages that interest the children. Help them talk about what they see.

- Give the children a chance to help tell the story with you. For example, if the story is a familiar one, see if they can say what is coming next. If the story is a new one, have them guess what will happen.

- Show interest with your face and voice. Change your voice to match the story.

- Use a quiet voice when you want children to listen. Children pay more attention to a quiet voice than to a loud one.

- Look into each child's eyes often as you read or talk.

- Pick books that go with the ideas you are talking about at the time. For example, if it's fall, and children bring in pretty leaves from outside, read a book about fall leaves.

- Put books you read in the book corner for children to look at by themselves. If the book has thin pages, show the children how to turn the pages carefully.

- Read favorite books often.

Other Ideas

- Use puppets, a flannelboard, pictures, or real objects as you tell a story.

- Add to your book collection by using your public library. Ask if a Bookmobile will visit you and your Threes.

- Help children act out a very short, simple story that they know well.

Ideas on Pictures for Threes

Choosing Pictures

- Choose clear, colorful pictures that show things Threes know about—food, furniture, clothes, people.

- Choose clear pictures of new things you will be talking about and teaching your Threes—holidays, community helpers, people doing things.

- Make picture collections of different subjects: toys, colors (red things, blue things), animals, birds.

- Have big pictures and small ones.

- Have pictures that show one thing at a time and pictures that show many things.
- Choose pictures that show people of all ages and races doing many things alone or together.
- Choose non-sexist pictures that show men doing traditional women's jobs, such as giving baby a bath, and women doing traditional men's jobs, such as fighting fires.

Storing Pictures

- Make picture cards with the pictures you want children to use a lot. Glue the pictures onto sturdy cardboard. Cover with clear contact paper. Keep cards sets together.
- Put picture cards into separate, labeled boxes, or use a picture file box.
- Make a file box for your pictures. Use a large, sturdy cardboard box with folders labeled by topic. It helps to have plastic pages or contact paper over the pictures to protect them.

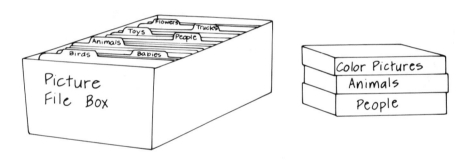

Finding Pictures

- Department store catalogs
- School supply catalogs
- Colorful newspaper ads
- Junk mail
- Photographs, postcards
- Old calendars, magazines, picture books, coloring books
- Pictures that parents and friends provide. Tell parents why you need pictures so that they can use some of your ideas at home.
- Free photos you can send for from groups such as the Dairy Association or dental groups.
- Free posters used as ads in stores, car sales places, and supermarkets. Ask managers if you can have these when they are no longer needed.

Displaying Pictures

- Hang pictures where Threes can see, reach, and touch them. Hang them on furniture, on walls or doors, or on bulletin boards.

- Use tape or clear contact paper to hang pictures. If you use bulletin boards, use thumbtacks or staples, but these should be out of Threes' reach.

- Tape pictures face-down to a large sheet of clear, thick vinyl. Turn the vinyl over so you can see the pictures. Hang it where Threes can see and touch it. Or put it on the floor for Threes to explore.

- Change pictures often.

- Put pictures into large, page-sized, soft vinyl photograph holders. You can usually get these in stores where cameras are sold. Hang these around the room where children can see and touch them.

- Use three-ring binders with clear vinyl pages to make a book of pictures. Change the pictures in the pages often.

- Put sturdy picture cards you have made into a box or on a tray. Put these on a shelf in the Book Corner for Threes.

Making your own picture books

1. Glue pictures onto same-size sturdy cardboard.
2. Add your own words or the children's if you wish.
3. Cover with clear contact paper.
4. Punch two or three holes on the left side or top of each page.
5. Tie pages together with strong string or narrow ribbon. Do not tie too tightly. Leave pages a bit loose so that they can be easily turned.

How to Make a Peek-a-Boo Board

1. Cut out six or more 8-inch squares of pretty cloth.
2. Sew the top edge of each square onto a yard of cloth, so that the squares become flaps that hang down. (Hem all rough sides if you wish.)

3. Nail or staple the cloth to a wall, the back of a bookcase, a board you can move around, or a closet door. Cover tacks or staples with strong tape so that children will not pull them out.
4. Use masking tape to hang picture cards behind each of the cloth flaps. Or pin them from the back of the cloth with a safety pin. Draw your own pictures, or cut them out from magazines, old children's books, catalogs, or coloring books.
5. Show children how to lift a flap to see the picture.
6. Change pictures often.

Sequence Cards

What They Are

- Sequence cards are picture cards that show the steps in a story. They show what happens first, second, and so on.
- There is often no one right answer when using the cards with young children. Use the cards only to help children talk about what they see and think.

How to Use Them

- Use only very easy sequence cards with your three-year-olds. Begin with cards that show three clear, familiar steps in what is happening.
- Threes probably won't put the cards in the same order you do. They should see the cards in their own creative ways. Listen to how they tell the story and enjoy it together.
- You can put the cards in order and tell the children how you see the story. Use the words *first, second,* and *last* as you talk.

How to Make Them

1. Find or draw pictures of the steps in the story you want to show.
2. Cut out the pictures.
3. Glue them to sturdy cardboard squares.
4. Cover them with clear contact paper.
5. Store the cards in a box or container. Keep each set separate with a rubber band or in its own little sandwich bag.

Topics for Cards

Getting up in the morning or going to bed

- Child sleeping in bed
- Child getting dressed
- Child all dressed and walking away from bed

Cooking and eating

- Stirring food on stove
- Serving food onto plate
- Eating food

Getting dressed or undressed

- Child with shirt and underclothes on, putting on pants
- Child putting on shoes
- Child dressed

Taking a bath or getting washed and dressed

- Clothes on
- In bath
- Drying off with towel

Sweeping the floor

- Dirty floor
- Person with broom, floor partly swept
- Person with broom, floor clean

Eating apple

- Person with whole apple
- Person with apple that has one bite out of it
- Person with apple core

Grocery shopping

- Person with empty shopping cart
- Person with full cart
- Person with bags of groceries

Sequence Cards to Use with Threes

- Cut these out. Color them if you wish.
- Glue the cards to cardboard squares.
- Cover them with clear contact paper.
- Have children put them in the order they see, or you can arrange the
- Talk about the pictures.

How to Make Stick Puppets

1. Find or draw a picture of what you want to use as the puppet. Try faces, animals, or anything else you or a child wants to make talk.

2. Cut out the picture, glue it to a larger piece of cardboard, and cover it with clear contact paper, or simply draw the picture onto the cardboard.

3. Make a holder for the picture. Try these ideas:

    Glue smaller pictures to popsicle sticks. Make them more secure with tape.

    Use one-inch brass brads or paper fasteners to hold the picture onto an empty paper towel or toilet paper roll. Poke two brads through the picture and into the roll. Then open the brads so they stay in place.

    Glue pictures to tongue depressors. Make more secure with tape.

    Cut out a cardboard holder as part of the cardboard you use to mount the picture. Make it sturdier by attaching a stick or some extra cardboard where it might bend.

Sunshine Note

Sunshine Note

Words to "The Bear Hunt"

We're going on a bear hunt.	*(slap hands on thighs to make walking*
Here we go!	*sounds)*
Let's go look for a bear.	
Here's a hill—	*(make hill with hands)*
We can't go under it.	*(make hand go down)*
We can't go around it.	*(make hands go around)*
We'll have to climb it.	
Let's climb!	*(climb with arms)*
Climb, climb, climb, climb.	
Wow! That was hard work.	*(wipe brow)*
Let's walk on.	*(slap thighs to make walking sounds)*
We're going on a bear hunt.	

Continue with:

Here's a lake . . . row	*(do movement for all of these, making*
Here's a swamp . . . squish	*walking sounds between each)*
Here's a jungle with vines . . . swing	
Here's a field of very tall grass . . . swish	
Here's a pond . . . swim	
Oh, here's a cave.	*(point to cave)*
Let's go inside.	
Ooooh! It's dark in here!	*(close eyes)*
And the walls are cold and slippery!	*(stretch out hands to feel)*
Aah! Here's something warm, and big, and fuzzy.	*(pretend to feel)*
EEK! It's a bear!!	
Run, Run, Run!	*(slap thighs fast)*

Do all verses and actions quickly in reverse.

After pretending to run down the hill, say,

Look! There's our house!
Quick, run inside! Lock the door!

Whew! We're safe!
Let's go on a bear hunt again sometime.

Materials and Notes

Conversation

someone to talk with

things children make

things children bring in

talker's hat

- Threes enjoy talking—to you and to each other. Try to keep the happy, busy sound of talking going on most of the day.

- Show children how much you enjoy their talk. Look at children as you listen to things they tell you. Ask many questions to get them to say more. (See page 6 for ideas about different kinds of questions.)

- Include parents in the talks you have with three-year-olds. Ask them about things the child does at home. Ask questions to help the child add to what they say.

Activity Checklist

Conversation

Conversation activities with Threes make use of the informal talking times that happen throughout the day. Many Threes can talk quite well, using many words and short sentences. They enjoy talking to adults and other children who will listen to them. They ask plenty of questions and answer easy questions you ask. The conversation activities you do with Threes don't have to be planned. They will happen when children find out that their talking and listening are important to you.

Check for each age group	*36–42 mo*	*42–48 mo*
1. There is much talking with every child about things that interest the child.	—	—
2. Adult speaks clearly and uses appropriate tone of voice.	—	—
3. Adult shows interest when children begin conversations or ask questions.	—	—
4. Adult asks simple questions to encourage children to talk, and listens to children's answers.	—	—
5. Adult makes eye contact when talking with child.	—	—
6. Adult talks with children about the routines and play they experience.	—	—
7. Adult has informal conversations with each child daily.	—	—
8. Adult adds more information to what children say.	—	—
9. Adult encourages children to talk and listen to each other in very small groups.	—	—
10. Adult encourages children to use talking to solve problems with each other and supplies words when needed.	—	—

43

Threes can

- tell a little about things they have done

Early Morning Talks

Show children how happy you are to see them each morning. Plan time to greet each one with a happy good morning hug and a little chat. Make time to do this even when you are busy or when everyone seems rushed.

Include parents in the little talks. See if they will help their children remember some nice things they did the night before, or what they plan to do over a weekend. Make sure you, the parents, and the children all take turns talking and listening to each other at this time.

 in or out 1–3 min 1–2 Threes

44

Threes can

- greet people

Hello and Goodbye

Help your Threes remember to say "hello" and "goodbye" at the right times. Add these words to pretend play in the house or block areas.

Daddy is going to the grocery store.
Say goodbye to daddy.

Or use these words as people come and go.

Here comes the mail truck.
Let's go say hello to Mr. Rudy.
He's bringing our mail.

 in or out 1–3 min 1–15 Threes

45

Threes can

- talk in short sentences

New Information for Threes

Think of a special idea you want your Threes to know more about. (A list of some special ideas for units that you might like to work on with your Threes is in the Planning section, page 28.) Choose an idea that you and the children will find fun and interesting. An example might be "things with wheels." Then write down many ways to talk about the idea. Use real things, books, pictures, fieldtrips, and anything else you can think of to help the children learn about the idea. Ask easy questions to help Threes talk and think about what they know.

Let's look for things in your play yard with wheels.
That's right, Juan. The tricycles have wheels.
Yes, Patrick. The lawn mower has wheels.
I didn't remember that!

 in or out   3–10 min   1–15 Threes

46

Threes can

- ask many questions

They Ask, You Answer

Try to listen to and answer the many questions your Threes may ask. Show them how pleased you are with the asking they do. If you don't know an answer, don't worry. Just say that you don't know but will try to find an answer with the child as soon as you can.

Keep the talk going by asking the child a question.

I don't know why our goldfish died, Kevin.
I think he got a fish disease. Then he died.
Should we get a new one? Where can we get it?

 in or out   1–5 min   1–15 Threes

47

Threes can

■ tell a little about what they are doing

Doll House Talk

When children are playing in the house area, ask questions so they will tell about what they are doing. Choose the right time to ask questions so you don't bother the play. Add your own ideas to the children's answers to help play go better.

Is that your baby, Sandra?
What are you doing with her?
Maybe you and Aretha can take your babies for a walk after their nap.

Ask about children's play in other areas, too.

 in or out | 1–3 min | 1–3 Threes

48

Threes can

■ play very easy circle games

■ recognize and say people's names

Name Game

Play this name game with your Threes. Have children sit in a circle. Play <u>music</u> as the children pass a <u>ball</u> around the circle. Stop the music. Have the others name the child who is holding the ball. Play again. Make sure everyone is named.

A game like this helps your Threes know and use people's names. They will learn the names as you use them in different ways every day. Tell everyone the name of new children or adults. Help children use names to get people's attention.

Sara, you don't need to pull Tamara when you want her to listen. Say her name. Then she will look at you.

 in or out | 5–15 min | 1–15 Threes

49

Threes can

■ use many words

Real Words for Things

Help children use exact words for things. When they point to something or use words like "it," "them," or "those," see if you can get them to use the real words for what they mean. Many times you will have to say the words they need.

What do you want, Shamon?
Oh, that's a funnel. Carrie is using it now.
There's another funnel in the sand box.
Would you like to go and get the funnel?

 in or out   1–2 min   1–2 Threes

50

Threes can

■ talk in short sentences

Look and Talk

Look to see what attracts children's attention. As the Threes watch, touch, try out, or play with something, see if they will talk about it. Use questions to help them talk and think.

What are you looking at, Maria?
Oh yes. I see the airplane too.
It's going so fast! I think it's a jet.
Where do you think it's going?

 in or out   1–2 min   1–15 Threes

51

Threes can

- answer some questions

Questions, Questions

Think about the questions you ask the children. Plan questions that need more than just a "yes" or "no" answer. Use your questions to help the children tell what, where, or who. Add easy questions that ask why, when, or how. Be ready to give answers to the harder questions when the children don't know what to say.

Try writing down a few questions you will be able to use each day. Ask them at the right time. See what answers you get.

What's new in our play yard?
Yes, there's new sand in the sandbox.
Where do you think it came from?
How did they get it into the yard?

 in or out   1–5 min   # 1–15 Threes

52

Threes can

- use short sentences

Meal and Snack Talk

Make meals and snacks happy talking times. Help children talk about what they are eating, the play they have just done, or things that are still to come. Try to sit with the children as they eat. Show them how pleased you are when they talk to you or each other.

Eating times may take a little longer with all this talk. If a child is finished and does not want to wait for others, have a quiet activity ready for the child to go to.

Things to talk about include:

shapes, color, and temperature of the food served

things the children did at play that day

new things that happened at home

new things that happened at school

 indoors   10–30 min   # 1–15 Threes

53

Threes can

- say what they are doing

Wash-up Talk

Help children talk about the steps they take as they do familiar things, such as washing hands.

You need to wash the paint off your hands, Betty.
Let's see what you do first.
Yes, you turn on the water. Then what?

When the children are done, help them remember the steps to what they did. Later, make up a story about washing hands. See if the children can help tell the story.

Little Bear's hands were very dirty. So he went to wash them.
How did he wash his hands?
What do you think he did first?

 in or out | 2–5 min | 1–2 Threes

54

Threes can

- help clean up

Let's Clean Up

Help children with clean-up by talking about each thing they need to do. Ask questions to help the Threes think through their work.

The blocks need to be put away, Tanya.
Now what goes in this dishpan? That's right, the little people.
Do you know where these little cars go, Sidney?
Yes. Please find the rest and put them in the box.
Now what do we need to put away?

 in or out | 5–15 min | 1–15 Threes

55

Dressing Words

Help Threes talk about what they do as they put on <u>clothes</u>. Add more to what they say. See if they know the words for different parts of the clothes they wear.

Threes can

■ put on most clothes

Are you having trouble with your jacket, Nicole?
What is the problem? The sleeve?
Oh yes, I see. The left sleeve is inside out.
Bring your jacket here and I'll show you what to do.

 in or out   1–2 min   1–2 Threes

56

Talk About Treasures

Pay attention to any "treasures" your Threes <u>find or bring in</u>. A treasure may be anything: a new pair of shoes, a favorite toy, or a pretty rock.

Notice these things. Ask questions to help the children talk about their treasures.

Threes can

■ answer some questions

What is that, Ginny? Yes, a box.
Is there anything in the box? I see.
That's some cotton. It's soft and white.
That looks like a little jewelry box.
Where did you get the box?
Was there anything else in the box?

 in or out   1–3 min   1–2 Threes

57

Threes can

■ begin to take turns

Taking Turns

Talk about taking turns as your Threes learn to do this. Make a "waiting list" for the most popular activities to be sure each child will get a chance.

Show the child her name on the list. Tell her that her name keeps her place in line for her. Help children see other fun things to do while they wait.

I know you want to work with the play dough, Isabella.
Let's put your name on the waiting list.
I'll be sure to call you as soon as the first child is done here.
Let's look for something else for you to do till I call you.

 in or out | 1–2 min | 1–15 Threes

58

Threes can

■ understand many common dangers

Why Be Careful?

Remind your Threes to be careful about things that may be dangerous. Do this often. Help the children talk about why care must be taken.

Sammy brought balloons for his birthday today.
Balloons are fun, but we have to be careful with them.
Do you remember our rule about balloons?
Don't put balloons in your _____.
That's right, Andy. Don't put balloons in your mouth.
Why don't you put balloons in your mouth?

 in or out | 2–5 min | 1–15 Threes

59

Threes can

- talk in short sentences

Special Talking Time

Plan to have a special talking time with each child every day. Make this a warm time when you listen to and talk with just the one child. Fit these times in whenever you can. Keep a checklist, if you need to, to be sure you talk to everyone.

You've been working so hard, Robert.
Tell me about your work in the sandbox.

 in or out | 1–3 min | 1 child at a time

60

Threes can

- say many words
- guess easy words

What Are We Going to Do?

Give children clues about what activity they are going to do. Show them some <u>things they will use</u>, and see if they can guess what the activity is.

What's this I'm holding? Yes, it's string.
And what's this? That's right, some beads.
Guess what you can do at this table today.

 indoors | 2–5 min | 1–15 Threes

61

Threes can

■ begin trying to share

Talk About Sharing

Give your Threes chances to share. For example, put one <u>container of crayons</u> between two friends. Talk about sharing, taking turns, and cooperating. Show the children how proud you are when they share.

I like the way you two are sharing the crayons.
It's hard when you both want to use the red crayon.
It's nice that Sherry gave you the red as soon as she was done.

Help children see how sharing helps everyone.

Jonathan brought in this big watermelon from his garden.
He wants to share it with all of us!

 in or out │   1–2 min │   1–15 Threes

62

Threes can

■ talk in short sentences

Talk—Don't Hit

Help Threes learn words to solve problems they have with others. Tell them to use words to say what they do not like. You will often have to help Threes find the words they need and make them feel safe as they work things out.

What's the matter, Andrew?
Benjamin is taking the blocks you are using?
Tell him you need these. Tell him to get his own.
Show him the blocks he can use on the shelf.

 in or out │   2–5 min │   1–3 Threes

63

Threes can

- say a little about things they make

What Did You Make?

Ask questions to help your Threes tell you about the <u>things they make</u>. Help them talk about art work, sand play, block building, and more. See if they can remember what they used and some of what they did.

What did you make, Luz? A cake? What kind of cake?
Yes, it's a play dough cake.
How did you make these holes in it? . . .
Who will eat the cake?

 in or out | 1–2 min | 1–2 Threes

64

Threes can

- talk about things they have just done

Remember

Ask questions to help the children remember things they did at play time. Make notes, if you need to, about who did what so that you can ask the right questions.

What did you play with in the house corner this morning, Terry? I saw you with the baby stroller.
Who was in the stroller? Yes, the bear.
Where were you going with the bear?

Help children remember other things that happened in the day, such as what snack they ate or what story you read.

 in or out | 1–2 min | 1–3 Threes

65

Threes can

■ enjoy word play

Silly-Nilly Words

Have fun enjoying silly word play with your Threes. Use your imagination to add funny rhymes or sounds to words all of you use every day.

We're having carrot sticks for lunch today.
This is a munchie crunchie lunchie!

Let's zip up your zipper.
Here it goes. Zipper zapper zip!

 in or out 1–2 min 1–15 Threes

66

Threes can

■ name actions

Guess What I'm Doing

Act out some very familiar, easy-to-guess things your Threes do often. Act out getting dressed, drinking, eating, going to sleep, or taking a bath. Do the actions without words. See if the children can say what you're doing.

If they have trouble guessing, then add words to your actions.

First I put on my underwear. Then my shirt.
Then my pants and socks and shoes.
Can you guess what I am doing?

 in or out 3–7 min 1–15 Threes

67

Threes can

- talk in short sentences

Rhyming Words

Point out and repeat words the children say or hear that rhyme. Be excited about these words and show that they can be fun.

Listen, Paul. You made a rhyme! You said, "My coat is new, it's blue."
New. Blue. They rhyme. That was a little poem you made up!

Don't expect Threes to do rhyming on purpose. This will come later and be easier if they have enjoyed rhymes with you.

 in or out   1–2 min   1–3 Threes

68

Threes can

- talk about some things they will do

What Are We Going to Do?

Talk about things your Threes will do soon. Later, ask questions to see what they remember.

Remember, I told you this morning what we will do later.
Do you remember? What did I say?
That's right, Ray. We're going to go swimming!
What did you bring to swim in?

 in or out   2–5 min   1–15 Threes

69

Threes can

■ use short sentences

Words for Changes

Help the three-year-olds talk about simple changes they see. Ask questions to help them out.

Our room looks different this morning.
What's changed in our room? That's right!
The chairs are on top of the tables.
Look at how shiny the floors are now!
What happened to the floors?

 in or out   1–3 min # 1–15 Threes

70

Threes can

■ tell how to do some things

Child as Teacher

Whenever possible, let children who know how to do something teach others who don't know how. Encourage the children to use words as they show what to do.

Lottie, please tell Debbie how to hang up her painting.
Show her and use words to tell her.

Children can be very helpful in teaching one another playground skills, such as pumping on the swing.

 in or out   1–5 min # 1–3 Threes

71

Listen to Them Talk

Take time to listen to your Threes as they talk to each other. Note who is talking, what they talk about, and who tends to not talk very much. Use what you find out in a gentle way to help the non-talkers say more.

You can ask the non-talkers what they were doing, what they were playing with, and with whom they were playing.

Anna, what were you and Tina doing in the book corner?

Threes can

- talk to friends while playing

 in or out | 4–10 min | 1–15 Threes

72

Same and Not the Same

Talk about <u>things that are the same or different</u>. Do this as a part of each day, not just as a special activity or game.

What are Marla and Carrie wearing that are the same?
That's right! Their shoes.
T.J. and Tommy both have on overalls.
Are they the same?

Threes can

- do simple comparing

 in or out | 1–2 min | 1–15 Threes

73

Threes can

■ whisper

Whisper Game

Play a fun whisper game with two children. Whisper something into the first child's ear. Have that child whisper it to the next child. See if that child can tell you what you said.

Play over and over. Each of you can take a turn being first. Remind Threes not to talk loudly into other's ears because it hurts.

This game may tickle and words get mixed up, so be ready to laugh at a lot of nonsense.

 in or out   2–4 min   # 2–3 Threes

74

Threes can

■ use short sentences

Talk-About Table

Set aside a <u>little table</u> where you and your Threes can put <u>new things to talk about</u> every day. You can put something that goes with the special things you and the children are talking about. For example, if you're doing a unit on fruits, put a new fruit on the table to taste and talk about each day.

The children can add whatever interests them. Make sure that things on the Talk-About Table are safe to touch and hold.

As the Threes stop by the table, talk about the names of each thing, who it belongs to, what you do with it, and how it looks or feels. Be sure the children know that the things on the table need to stay on the table. Change the things every day.

 indoors   3–5 min   # 1–6 Threes

75

Threes can

■ remember some things

Who Are Your Parents? Where Do You Live?

Help all your Threes learn their parents' first and last names and addresses. Have parents help with this. Teach the children this information and help them repeat it often. Try to get each child to say it slowly and clearly.

What's your daddy's name, Emma?
Jim? That's his first name. Do you know the rest?
That's right. And where do you live?

 in or out 1–3 min 1 child at a time

76

Threes can

■ follow easy directions
■ understand *no* and *not*

Simon Says

Give your Threes practice in following directions. Play an easy "Simon Says" game. Stand in front of the children and slowly do the actions as you tell them what Simon says to do. When you don't want the children to do an action, say "Simon says do not do it."

Simon says touch your toes.
Simon says stand up straight.
Simon says do not *jump.*
Simon says reach up high.

Don't worry if your Threes aren't great at the game yet. Just enjoy the exercise and fun.

 in or out 4–7 min 1–15 Threes

77

Threes can

■ say what to do when thirsty, hungry

Baby's Hungry. What Should I Do?

Sit in the <u>playhouse corner</u> as children play there. Hold a <u>baby doll</u>. Tell a child that your baby is hungry. Ask what you should do. See if the child can help you by telling and showing you how to feed the baby.

See if a child can tell you what to do when the baby doll is:

tired

wet

thirsty

dirty

cold

crying.

 indoors | 2–10 min | 1–3 Threes

78

Threes can

■ take part in a short group time

Gathering-Time Talk

Gather most of your Threes together for a very short talking and sharing time. You may want to do this as part of a story time.

Have one child at a time tell things to the group. Ask questions to help the children think of things to say. Have the children talk about what they did at play time, something they made or brought in, or things that go with what you and the children are working on.

To call attention to the talker, have the talker wear a <u>"talker's hat"</u> or hold something special which is passed from talker to talker. Help the others look at and listen to the one who is speaking.

 in or out | 3–7 min | 5–15 Threes

79

Threes can

■ follow two-step directions

Hunt and Find

Hide a <u>familiar thing</u> somewhere in the room. Tell the children what you have hidden. Give them two-step directions to follow until they find the thing.

I have hidden our little brown teddy bear.
Do what I say and you will find it.
Go to the block shelf and look near the dishpan of cars.

 in or out   2–3 min   # 1–2 Threes

80

Threes can

■ say please and thank you

Please and Thank You

Use "please," "thank you," "excuse me," "I'm sorry," and other polite words in everything you do with the children. In a gentle way, help them remember to use these words.

Don't force the words if a child doesn't mean them. Show how happy you are when they use these words on their own.

Jona, I like the way you said "I'm sorry," when you bumped B.J.'s blocks. Lauren, you need to say "Excuse me, Rodney," if you want to get past.

 in or out   1–2 min   1–15 Threes

81

Threes can

- use short sentences
- say what people are doing

Watch and Talk

When you see a child watching others play, see if you can help the child talk about what the others are doing. Ask questions to help.

You're waiting to paint, aren't you, Seth?
Let's watch Patty together.
What is Patty doing with her brush now?
Yes, dipping it in the paint.
She's dipping it in the red paint.
And now what is she doing?

 in or out | 2–3 min | 1–2 Threes

82

Threes can

- guess easy words

Guess the Word

Play a word-guessing game with your Threes. Give them easy clues until they guess the familiar thing you are talking about.

Guess what animal I'm thinking about.
It has four legs.
No, it's not a dog. Listen to all the clues.
It has long ears. It goes hop hop hop.
We saw one yesterday. It lives in a hutch.

 in or out | 2–7 min | 1–15 Threes

83

Threes can

- answer the telephone

Telephone Words

Practice talking on the telephone with a three-year-old. Use <u>two toy telephones</u>. Have questions ready to ask the child before you play so the talk will go better. You may have to guide the child in what to say and do.

Ring, ring. Your telephone is ringing, Sonya.
Pick up the telephone and say hello.
Good! Hello, Sonya. This is Judy.
Who was playing with you outside?

Remind children not to nod "yes" or "no" on the phone. They need to use words people can hear.

 indoors   2–3 min   1 child at a time

84

Threes can

- talk about things that will happen

Goodbye Talk

As children get ready to go home, talk with each child about what she has done that day. Look at and talk about things children are taking home. Have parents help tell about what the children will do when they go home. Say something about the plans for the next day.

What are you going to do at home, Dorothy? Play with your puppy?
Is there anything else Dorothy will do, Mrs. Gale?
Wow, Dorothy! I bet you like helping your mom feed the chickens! I'll see you tomorrow, Dorothy.
Do you remember what we will do tomorrow?

 in or out   2–5 min   1–2 Threes

85

Threes can

- follow two-step directions

Follow the Leader

Play a follow-the-leader game with your Threes. Instead of having them follow you, have them follow directions you give.

Run to the fence and hop up and down.
Now run to the climber and go down the slide.

Try to give two directions in one sentence.

 in or out 3–8 min # 1–15 Threes

86

Threes can

- play simple guessing games

Places We Know and Go

Tell your Threes all about a very familiar place. Don't name the place. See if they can guess what the place is. Try this with a supermarket, library, park or playground, zoo, shopping center, or farm. Also try telling about different rooms.

Guess what place I'm talking about.
When you go in, you take a shopping cart.
Then you look at all kinds of foods.
There are fruits, vegetables, foods in cans, frozen foods, milk, and bread.
You put these into your cart to buy.
Do you know what place it is?

 in or out 2–7 min # 1–15 Threes

87

Threes can

- tell what to do

What Do We Do?

Tell your Threes a little story that ends with someone who is cold, hungry, thirsty, tired, muddy, or too hot. Ask the children what the person in the story should do.

Once there was a little boy named Winston. He woke up and saw that it was a snowy day. So he got dressed and ran out to play in the snow. After a while he said, "Brrrr! I'm cold!" What do you think Winston should do?

Enjoy the many creative answers your Threes might give.

 in or out 2–10 min # 1–15 Threes

88

Threes can

- understand what things are used for
- do simple pretend play

What Are They Used For?

Collect these things in a <u>box</u>: <u>spoon</u>, <u>cup</u>, <u>paint brush</u>, <u>hair brush</u>, <u>soap</u>, <u>safe scissors</u>, <u>plastic hammer</u>, and <u>crayon</u>. Look at these with your Threes. Have them name each and say how it is used.

Then play this guessing game. Do actions to pretend you are using one of the things. Have the children guess and point to what they think it is. Let the children take turns pretending, too. Then you can help with the guessing.

 in or out 3–7 min # 2–4 Threes

Your Own Activities: Listening and Talking

Write your own activities in these blank boxes. You will find more information on writing your own activities in the Planning section, page 38.

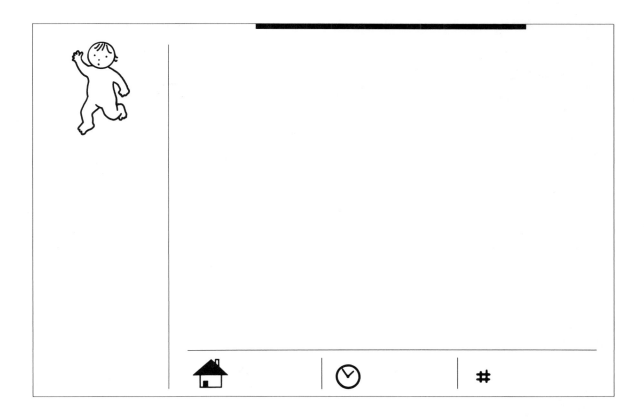

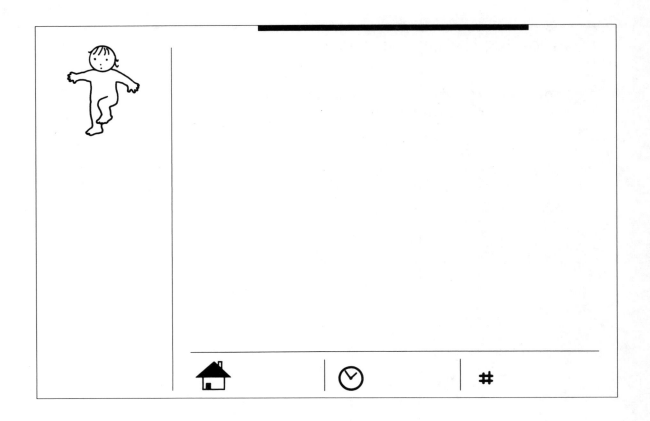

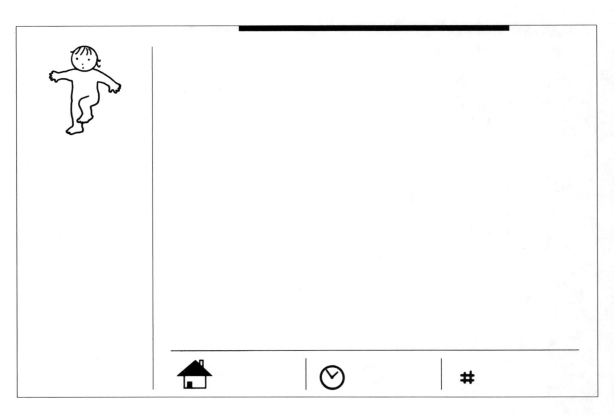

Activities for
Listening and Talking

Index
of Activities for Listening and Talking

Baby's Hungry—What Should I
    Do?   77
Big Lotto Game   4
Book Making   22
Books with Records or Tapes   26
Child as Teacher   70
Doll House Talk   47
Dressing Words   55
Early Morning Talks   43
Family Photo Album   34
Feelie Box Picture Game   14
Finger Puppet Play   38
First Sorting   10
Flannelboard Sorting Game   37
Flannelboard Stories   25
Flannelboard People with
    Clothes   17
Flannelboard Grocery Store   12
Follow the Leader   85
Gathering Time Talk   78
Get to Know the Book Corner   1
Going on a Bear Hunt   29
Good Bye Talk   84
Guess the Word   82
Guess What I'm Doing   66
Hello and Good-Bye   44
Hide the Picture   40
Hunt and Find   79
Kid's Photo Album   13
Let's Clean Up   54
Library or Bookmobile Visit   36
Listen to Them Talk   71
Look and Talk   50
Look for Details   7
Making Baby Posters   41
Meal and Snack Talk   52
Missing Words Fill-In   39
Name Game   48
Name Labels   23
New Information for Threes   45
Opposite Pictures   18
Peek-A-Boo Picture Board   5
Photograph Posters   31
Picture Directions   15
Picture Puzzles   30
Picture-Toy Box   20

Picture-Word Labels   42
Pictures About Feelings   33
Pictures of Things We Use   9
Places We Know and Go   86
Please and Thank-You   80
Poems   27
Poster Making   3
Questions, Questions   51
Read and Ask   2
Real Words for Things   49
Remember   64
Rhyming Words   67
Riddle Guessing   6
Same and Not the Same   72
Sequence Card Study   8
Silly-Nilly Words   65
Simon Says   76
Sorting Board Fun   24
Special Picture Place   35
Special Talking Time   59
Story with Puppets   19
Sunshine Notes   28
Taking Turns   57
Talk—Don't Hit   62
Talk About Table   74
Talk About Sharing   61
Talk About Treasures   56
Telephone Words   83
They Ask, You Answer   46
Things We Talk About Picture
    Box   16
Wash-Up Talk   53
Watch and Talk   81
What Are They Used For?   88
What Are They Doing?   12
What Are We Going To Do?   68
What Did You Make?   63
What Do We Do?   87
What Will Happen?   32
What's That Sound?   11
Where Is the Man? Flannelboard   21
Whisper Game   73
Who Are Your Parents? Where Do
    You Live?   75
Why Be Careful?   58
Words for Changes   69

Here's Why

*T*hrees enjoy physical activity. When they are actively moving around, they seem happy and involved. Often a sad time can be turned into a happy one by taking a break and going outdoors. Daily active play both indoors and outdoors in a safe space is important for a group of Threes.

While they are using their muscles, Threes can learn more than physical skills. They can learn about how things relate in space—in or out, up or down, near or far. They are open to learning the words they need to think and talk about what they are doing. The ideas in this section give children many safe and enjoyable large-muscle activities.

Three-year-olds also need lots of practice in using their fingers and hands. Activities with materials that use these small muscles, such as puzzles, pegboards, and beads, give Threes chances to solve simple problems and use their eyes and hands together.

Each activity in the sections for large- and small-muscle development includes some ideas for the caregiver to help children learn words and other thinking skills as they enjoy physical activity. Physical activities are learning activities, and you have to plan for them as carefully as you do for other learning. Every new thing Threes learn to do with their large and small muscles builds their feelings of confidence and pride in what they can do by themselves.

Materials and Notes
Large Muscles

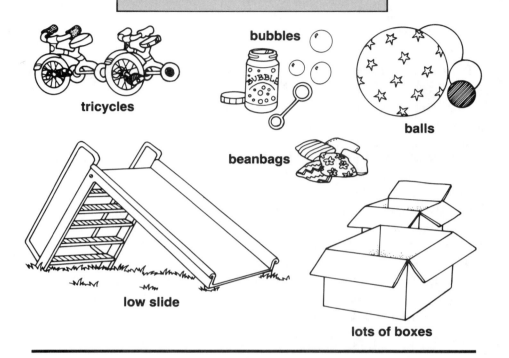

tricycles

bubbles

balls

beanbags

low slide

lots of boxes

- Set up large-muscle play spaces for your Threes both indoors and out. Be sure the floor or ground under climbers, slides, swings, and other equipment is softly covered with a thick mat, wood chips, sand, or grass.

- Threes will practice running, climbing, and jumping on their own. Give them lots of time and space to do this in their own special way.

- All climbing and riding toys must be safe and in good condition. Check equipment for rough splinters, sharp edges, loose nuts or bolts, or hidden nails. Use low, wide slides for Threes.

- Give parents ideas for safe large-muscle activities for children at home. Talk about how things in the home, such as grocery store boxes, blankets, and balls can be used in many fun ways.

- See ideas for making tents and broomstick horses on page 135.

Activity Checklist
Large Muscles

Large-muscle activities with Threes include experiences in which the arm, leg, and body muscles are used and strengthened. Large-muscle activities for three-year-olds include climbing, running, throwing, balancing, pedaling wheel toys, swinging, and many others. Equipment should be the right size for Threes.

Check for each age group	*36–42 mo*	*42–48 mo*
1. Adult carefully supervises large-muscle activities both indoors and outdoors.	—	—
2. Safe, fenced, open space is provided for large-muscle play outdoors.	—	—
3. Safe open space is provided indoors for large-muscle play with some suitable equipment, especially during bad weather.	—	—
4. Safe, sturdy, age-appropriate large-muscle equipment (riding toys, wagons, slides, balls, a jungle gym, swings) is available for children's daily use outdoors.	—	—
5. Duplicates of popular large-muscle toys are available.	—	—
6. Equipment encourages a variety of skills, such as climbing, balancing, walking, running, swinging, and pedaling.	—	—
7. Surfaces in large-muscle play areas are suitable for different types of play (smooth areas for running and wheel toys, cushioned surfaces under climbing equipment).	—	—
8. A safe area for riding pedal toys is available, separated from swings and other equipment.	—	—
9. Adult talks to children about the large-muscle activities they do.	—	—
10. Adult encourages independence and new skills, such as pumping on the swings, when children seem ready.	—	—

89

Threes can

- catch large ball with arms straight out

Catching Balls

Stand about three or four feet from your three-year-old. Tell him you are going to throw him the <u>ball</u>, and ask him to stretch his arms way out. Gently toss him a <u>lightweight ball</u> that is about six to eight inches across. After he has caught the ball, ask him to throw it back to you. Enjoy this back-and-forth game of catch and be ready for other Threes to join in your fun.

Here it comes, Tony. Ready?
Good catching!
Now can you throw it back to me?

 in or out | 2–7 min | 1–5 Threes

90

Threes can

- move their bodies without moving their feet

Trees in the Wind

Pretend to be trees with a group of your Threes. Have them stretch their arms out wide and move as if they were blowing in the wind. Talk about different kinds of weather and act out how the trees would move in each.
    Try some of these ideas:

a big thunderstorm

a heavy snowstorm

an autumn day when leaves are falling

a still, quiet summer day

 in or out | 3–7 min | 1–15 Threes

91

Threes can

- run well
- kick a ball

Kick and Run

Take your Threes outside to a big open space on a nice day, and give them each a <u>ball</u> to kick and chase. Have them kick the balls as hard as they can and then run to kick them again. Let the children enjoy darting in between each other, as well as around the playground equipment and then back to you.

Run and get it, Melika. Go fast. Good kicking!
You kicked the ball all the way to the swings.

 outdoors | 5–10 min | **#** 1–15 Threes

92

Threes can

- hop forward six feet

Hop Like a Frog

Pretend to be frogs with your three-year-olds. Hop around the room or the play yard as you chase a bug, hide behind a tree, or jump into the sand box. Ask your Threes to talk about what they are doing.

What does a frog say, Jimmy?
That's right! Ribbet, ribbet, ribbet.

 in or out | 2–7 min | **#** 1–15 Threes

93

Threes can

■ jump forward

Jump Over the Cracks

Play a jumping game with your Threes. Jump over the cracks in a sidewalk, driveway, or tile floor. Have them practice jumping with both feet together so they have to do more than just step over each crack.

Jump up high, Vicky. There, you did it!
Can you find another crack to jump over?

 in or out | 1–10 min | **#** 1–15 Threes

94

Threes can

■ walk on tiptoes

Tiptoe Time

Have tiptoe times with your Threes. Try walking on tiptoes as you move from one activity to another or go to get your coats. When you go outside, run to the fence or swings on your tiptoes. Try tiptoeing with shoes on and with shoes off. Think up new ways in your own room to enjoy a little tiptoe time.
    Try one of these other ideas:

    a hopping time
    a crawling time
    a backwards-walking time
    a flap-like-a-bird time
    a waddle-like-a-duck time

 in or out | 2–3 min | **#** 1–15 Threes

95

Threes can

- walk a few steps on a line

Walking on a Line

Use wide masking tape to make a long path on the floor for your Threes to follow. Put in corners, curves, or even short loops. Have the path end up some place special, such as the art area, the sand table, or even the bathroom. Your children will probably step off the line now and then. It will be hard for them to keep their balance for the whole time they are on the line.

Slow down, Aaron. Then you will stay on the line better. Try holding out your arms to balance, like this.

 indoors 1–3 min 1–4 Threes

96

Threes can

- climb over things
- tumble

Box Play

Bring in a few large appliance boxes from a local store. Put these boxes outside on a dry, soft area for the three-year-olds' free play. Let them have fun using them in their own way for climbing, rolling, tumbling, pushing, or hiding. Ask them to tell you about what they are doing.

Where are you hiding, Jay? Are you under that box? Tell me what you and your friends are doing in there.

Be sure to have enough boxes so that children won't be crowded when they play.

 outdoors 3–20 min 1–4 Threes

97

Threes can

- catch a ball bounced from three feet away

Catch a Bounced Ball

Stand about three feet from your three-year-old. Gently bounce a <u>big ball</u> to her so she can catch it with two hands. Try to make it bounce up at about her waist or chest level. This will be the easiest place for her to catch. Ask her to bounce it back to you. Enjoy a playful game of bouncing the ball, and be ready for others to join in your fun.

You got it, Terry! That was good catching!
Can you bounce it to me?

 in or out   2–10 min   1–3 Threes

98

Threes can

- run, jump, and hop
- follow easy directions

Red Rover

Have your Threes stand on one side of the room or play yard. Call to them from the other side and say:

Red Rover, Red Rover, everybody run over!

Have them all follow your direction and run across the play area. Laugh and have fun with the children as you change the direction each time.

Try some of these ideas:

jump over

crawl over

roll over

twirl over

all the boys walk over

all the girls march over

 in or out   3–10 min   1–15 Threes

99

Tricycles

Set up a big, clear area outside in your play yard for <u>tricycles</u>. Put out <u>other riding toys that have pedals</u>, too. Make sure these wheel toys won't be in the way of other play. Help your Threes learn to push the pedals with their feet as they steer the tricycles. Have them talk with you about what they are doing.

Push hard, Donald. You need strong legs to get up the hill.

Be sure to have enough tricycles out so you don't have a problem with sharing. If you don't have enough, use a timer so that everyone gets a turn.

Put the children's names on a waiting list down where they can see. Check them off as they get their turns.

Threes can

- begin to pedal a tricycle

 outdoors | 3–15 min | 1–15 Threes

100

March and Stop

Put on a <u>lively record</u> for your Threes to march to. After they have marched around the room once, turn the record off and tell the children to stop where they are. Tell them they can march whenever they hear the music, but when it stops, they need to stop, too. It will take a little time for the children to learn how to stop and start with the music, so make a game of it and laugh with them as they practice.

You can stop and start some of these actions to music, too.

clapping

patting the floor

patting your head

jumping

stamping

shaking your hands

Threes can

- march
- follow easy directions

 in or out | 3–7 min | 1–15 Threes

101

Threes can

- walk upstairs,
  alternating feet

Stairs

Give the three-year-old chances to practice walking up and down stairs. Help her learn to hold onto the rail as she climbs the steps. Be sure to take enough time with this activity so that you don't rush the child. Allow the child to go at her own pace. See if she can alternate feet as she walks up the stairs.

Where are we walking, Donna?
That's right, we're walking up the stairs.
Do you have stairs like this in your home?

 in or out | 2–3 min | 1–2 Threes

102

Threes can

- throw a ball
- follow easy directions

Basketball Time

Put a big basket or box in the middle of your room. Give your Threes a few small, soft balls to toss into the box. Have fun throwing the balls in different ways or from different directions. Try some of these ideas to add something special to your "basketball" game:

raise the box on a table or chair

throw the ball between your knees as you bend over

dress up like basketball players in sneakers, shorts, and T-shirts

nail a sturdy basket or box low on a tree outside (be sure to cut the bottom out first)

bounce the ball before it goes in the basket

 in or out | 2–10 min | 1–8 Threes

103

Threes can

- use a small slide on their own

Slides

Set up a <u>slide</u> for your three-year-olds. Watch them carefully as they climb up the steps and slide down. Talk to them about how to use the slide safely. Encourage children to take turns, and see that the slide is clear before they slide down.

What are you doing, Anthony?
That's right, you are sliding.
Now hop up so that Keia can have her turn.
Thank you!
Good, Keia! You waited till the slide was clear.

 in or out | 1–10 min | # 1–5 Threes

104

Threes can

- run and jump
- follow easy directions

Bubbles to Chase and Pop

Blow <u>bubbles</u> for the three-year-olds to chase and pop. Blow some up high so that they have to stretch, reach, and jump. Blow others down low so that your Threes have to bend and stoop. Laugh and have fun with your children as they enjoy a playful bubble chase.

Run, Vicky, run! Catch that bubble.
Oops! What happened to it?
Where did it go?

If some of your Threes want to, see if they can blow a few bubbles for their friends to chase. Make sure the bubble pipes or straws are clean for each child.

 outdoors | 3–15 min | # 1–15 Threes

105

Threes can

- balance on one foot

Walk Through a Ladder

Lay a <u>ladder</u> down flat on a <u>rug</u> or other soft area. Let your Threes walk through the ladder, stepping over each rung carefully. You may want to hold the child's hand at first because stepping like this may throw him off balance.

Lift up your feet, Marshall.
Great! Do you want to do it again?

 in or out   2–3 min # 1–2 Threes

106

Threes can

- crawl
- follow easy directions

Tents

Make <u>tents</u> for your Threes to crawl in and play under. (You'll find tent ideas on page 135.) Put a few <u>books, soft toys, and blankets</u> under each tent to add to their play. Help your Threes use their tents in many creative ways.

I can't find Randi! Does anyone know where she is?
Oh thank you, Huang, she's under the blue blanket, isn't she?

Put up several tents so that children won't be crowded as they play.

 in or out   3–20 min # 1–3 Threes

107

Threes can

- follow easy directions
- recognize and tell about some animals

Move Like the Animals

Put pictures of several familiar animals into a feelie bag or box. Tell the child to close his eyes, reach in, and pick one out. Ask him to tell you about the animal he chooses. Talk about its name, how it looks, and how it moves.

Then all of you can move the way the animal would. Wave your arms, take big giant steps, crawl on the floor, or hop around the room just like the animal in the picture. After you have moved the way one animal does, put the picture back in the box and have a child choose another.

 in or out | 2–10 min | 1–7 Threes

108

Threes can

- balance and walk along a 5″ wide board

Balance on the Board

Lay a long, flat, 5–6″ wide board on two or three sturdy wooden blocks. This will raise the board off the ground an inch or two. Be sure the board is over a rug or other soft area. Walk along the board as the Threes watch.

Come look at me. I hold my arms out to balance.
Would you like to try?

As each child comes for a first turn, hold his hand and help him across slowly. Show him how to put one foot in front of the other so he won't fall. Leave the board out in the open area for the Threes to walk across and use in their own special way. Encourage children to take turns helping each other balance.

 in or out | 2–3 min | 1–4 Threes

109

Threes can

■ throw a ball

Beanbag Toss

Cut out a <u>10-inch circle</u> from the side of a <u>big cardboard box</u>. Draw an animal's face on that side of the box so the hole becomes its mouth. Set out a <u>basket or dishpan</u> of <u>beanbags</u> for the children to toss into the animal's mouth. Stand a few feet away from the box and throw a beanbag as you tell your Threes what you are doing. Then let them have fun on their own tossing the beanbags and "feeding" the animal.

Look, John Paul. The lion ate your beanbag.
Do you think he is still hungry?

 in or out | 2–10 min | 1–5 Threes

110

Threes can

■ balance on one foot

Storks and Cranes

Look in a few <u>old nature magazines</u> for <u>pictures of storks, cranes, flamingos, or other long-legged birds</u>. Show your Threes the pictures, and talk about how the birds look on their long, skinny legs. Point out that many of the birds sleep while standing on one foot with the other leg tucked up under their bodies. Then take your Threes to a <u>soft rug or grassy area</u> and pretend to be these birds. Practice standing on one foot, flapping your wings, catching fish with your long neck and beak, or any other things the birds are doing in the pictures.

You look just like the tall flamingo we saw in the picture.
What do you think he eats for dinner?

 in or out | 3–5 min | 1–15 Threes

111

Threes can

- jump off a step

Jump Off the Block

Put out several <u>large, sturdy wooden blocks</u> in an open area with a <u>soft rug or grass</u>. Play a follow-the-leader game with a few of your Threes. March or walk around some of the blocks and jump off the tops of others. Leave the blocks out after you've finished so that the children can go back and use them on their own.

Leslie, you're up so high!
What are you standing on?
A block, that's right.
Can you jump down?

 in or out   3–10 min   1–7 Threes

112

Threes can

- begin to do a forward somersault

Tumbling Time

Take your three-year-olds to an <u>open, soft area</u>. As you help one child do a forward somersault, help her remember to keep her neck and knees tucked into her chest. Help the child push up with her arms to keep weight off her neck. Don't worry if she rolls sideways or can't quite get all the way over on her own. Just laugh together as she tumbles and rolls in whatever safe way she can. Always stay near and watch tumbling carefully.

Yea! You went all the way over, Temika. Wasn't that fun?
What did the trees look like when you were upside down?

 in or out   2–5 min   1 child at a time

113

Big Step/Little Step Walk

Take a big step/little step walk with your Threes. Have the children copy the kinds of steps you take as you go on your walk. Take big giant steps so that the children have to reach and stretch, then take tiny baby steps so that they need to balance as they walk heel-toe. Have the children talk to you about the size of the steps.

What kind of step was that, Germaine?
A big step or a little step? That's right!
We took lots of big giant steps.

Make sure to have enough adults along if you go outside the yard.

Threes can

■ walk heel to toe
■ follow easy directions

 in or out 2–15 min 1–6 Threes

114

Broomstick Horses

Put out a <u>broomstick horse</u> for each of your three-year-olds who want to play. (You'll find directions for making broomstick horses on page 135.) Show them how to step over the stick and then "ride" the horse. Give them lots of room as they enjoy using the horses in their own creative way around the room or play yard.

Does your horse have a name, Annette?
It does? Can you tell me what it is?

Threes can

■ begin to gallop

 in or out 3–10 min 1–15 Threes

Activities for Physical Development

115

Threes can

- walk backwards a few steps

Backwards Walk

Walk backwards with your three-year-olds. Choose a place to go, such as the housekeeping area or the cubbies, and then try to walk there backwards. Go slowly at first, and make sure there is nothing in the child's way. At first you will need to be very careful. Later, the child will be able to walk around a table or chair.

You're walking backwards, Lee.
Now can you change direction and walk forward to me?

 in or out | 2–3 min | # 1–6 Threes

116

Threes can

- pick up and carry heavier things

Playground Things to Move

Put several pieces of movable equipment in the play yard for your Threes to move around themselves. Let the children set them up however they want. Help them be creative as you ask them to tell you what they are doing. Try some of these ideas:

a long, flat wooden board
cardboard boxes
sturdy blocks or bricks
a stool or a few chairs
a small ladder
wooden or metal triangles to make ramps

Watch carefully to make sure things are safe.

 outdoors | 3–15 min | # 1–6 Threes

117

Threes can

- throw a ball
- run

Throwing Far Away

Take your Threes to an open field or play yard. Bring along a big box of <u>many different-sized balls</u>. Let a child choose her own ball and then see how far she can throw it. After all the balls have been thrown, have fun running and laughing as you collect all the balls and bring them back to the box to throw again.

Wow, what a throw, Stacy! It went all the way to the fence. How did you get to be so strong?

 outdoors | 3–10 min | 1–15 Threes

118

Threes can

- begin to pump their legs

Swings

Take your three-year-old to a swing set with <u>low, safe swings</u>. Help him to get into the swing, and then give him a little push. Remind the child to hold on tightly. As he swings, help him learn to move his legs so he can pump to make the swing go by himself. This will take a little time to learn, so let him practice a little each day until the child can do it on his own. It will help if he watches a child who can pump.

You're swinging so high, Norman.
I think you might even touch the sky.
Can you move your legs to keep the swing moving?

 outdoors | 2–5 min | 1–3 Threes

Activities for Physical Development

119

Threes can

- run, kick, jump, and climb
- follow easy directions

Obstacle Course

Set up an obstacle course for your Threes. Make sure it is in a safe, open area where they have lots of room to play and practice using their large muscles.

Try some of these ideas in your obstacle course:

<u>blocks</u> to step on and over

<u>hoops</u> to jump in and out of

<u>small slides</u> to climb and slide down

<u>tape lines</u> to run, walk, or crawl on

<u>boxes</u> to climb in

<u>tunnels</u> or tents to crawl through

<u>places</u> to hop on one foot

 in or out | 3–15 min | 1–15 Threes

120

Threes can

- follow easy directions

Exercise Time

On a day when the weather is too bad to go out, have an exercise class with your Threes to use up some of their extra energy. Push the tables and chairs against a wall, and put away all the toys so you have a large, safe, open area. Try some of these exercises with children who are interested:

stretch high and low

twist back and forth

run, jump, hop, or crawl

swing your arms or legs

march with big, high steps

bicycle kick with the legs while lying down

Make sure the children are spread out so that they have enough space. Add music for more fun.

 indoors | 3–15 min | 1–15 Threes

121

Follow the Leader

Stand in front of a small group of Threes and ask them to copy what you do. As they copy you, ask them to name what they are doing. Try some of these actions:

shake your head, arms, or feet

pat your head, tummy, or nose

jump up, then touch the floor

wiggle your fingers or nose

turn in a circle

walk, run, or hop as you do some actions

sing a song while you move

start and stop an action so that they have to be completely still for a few seconds

Threes can

■ follow easy directions

 in or out 3–10 min 1–15 Threes

122

Follow the Footsteps

Cut out 25 or 30 large footprints from sturdy cardboard. Cover them with contact paper. Tape them down to the floor in a path for your Threes to follow. Make some footsteps close together and others far apart, so that the children have to change the size of their steps.

What are you stepping on, Mary?
That's right. Those are big blue footprints.
Where do you think they will go?

After the children feel comfortable with this, have them start at the end so that they can follow the footprints backwards.

Threes can

■ walk heel-toe
■ follow easy directions

 indoors 2–3 min 1–5 Threes

123

Threes can

- follow easy directions
- run, tumble, or climb
- balance on one foot

Circus Days

Read a <u>book about the circus</u> with your Threes. Talk with them about what they like best about the circus. Then set up a circus day for them with some of their favorite things to do. Let them dress up like animals or paint their faces like clowns as they have fun playing circus. Try some of these ideas, but feel free to add ideas of your own:

tightrope walker	lay a long rope or piece of masking tape on the floor to walk across
horses	set out broomstick horses to ride on
dancing animals	put out large stuffed animals to hold and carry, then turn on music to dance to
tumbling	put out a big, soft rug or mat to tumble and roll across

 in or out   30 min–1 hr   **#** 1–15 Threes

124

Threes can

- follow easy directions
- run, crawl, hop, and walk backward

Change Your Speed and Direction

Play movement games with your Threes in which they have to change their speed or direction. Give the children easy directions, and then ask them to tell you what they are doing. Try some of these ideas:

Change Direction	Change Speed
run to the tree and back	walk very slowly to the post, then walk back fast
walk around the table, then turn around	clap fast, then slow
walk one way, then the other	walk, then run, then walk
sway side to side	crawl fast, then slow
hop one way, then the other	hop fast, then slow
walk forward, then backward	roll slow, then fast

 in or out   2–10 min   **#** 1–15 Threes

Activities for Physical Development

125

Threes can

- roll a ball
- follow easy directions

Bowling

Set up five or six <u>big plastic bowling pins</u> at one end of the room. It helps to mark the place to stand with masking tape. Stand three or four feet away from the pins with your three-year-olds. As they watch, roll a <u>ball</u> at the pins to knock them down. Show the Threes how to set the pins back up, and let children take turns trying to knock down the pins all by themselves.

You did it, Karen. You knocked three pins over.

If you don't have any plastic pins, you can stand cardboard blocks up on one end and then knock them over. On another day, try plastic milk bottles or tall plastic jars.

 in or out | 2–5 min | 1–3 Threes

126

Threes can

- kick a ball
- run

Kick It in the Goal

Turn a <u>big box</u> on its side and put it at one end of the play yard. Set out a <u>few large rubber balls</u> at the other end of the play yard. Have your Threes try to run, chase, and kick the ball across the yard and then kick it into the box when they get to the other end.

Get the ball, Debby!
That's right, kick it hard.
Oops! What happened?
Where did your ball go?

 outdoors | 2–10 min | 1–4 Threes

Tent Ideas

- Put a blanket or sheet over a table.
- String a rope between two trees outside and throw a big blanket or sheet over it.
- Cut large openings in the ends of a large box and lay it on its side. Throw a blanket or sheet over it.
- Make a house shape with large snap-together plastic panels.
- Throw two or three old blankets over a small climber in the play yard.

How to Make Broomstick Horses

1. Draw eyes and a mouth on each side of a lunch bag.

2. Fill the bag half full with crumpled newspaper.
3. Tie the open end of the bag around the top of a child-sized broom or mop. Use a piece of string that is at least two feet long so that the ends can be tied together to make the horse's reins.

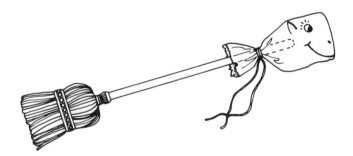

4. If you don't have any child-sized brooms, you can get one-inch-wide dowels from a hardware store. Cut these so they are about three feet long.

Materials and Notes

Small Muscles

pegs and pegboards

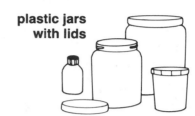

plastic jars with lids

geoboard with rubber bands

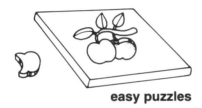

easy puzzles

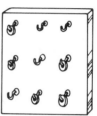

ring board with washers

- Store each toy with many pieces in its own sturdy box, dishpan, or plastic container. Put a picture label showing the toy on the box. Put only a few of these on a low shelf at a time so pieces don't get mixed up or lost.

- Check often for broken or lost pieces. Lost pieces frustrate children and keep them from finishing an activity with success.

- See if parents will make some of the homemade games talked about in the activities for your children to use.

- Give parents ideas about how they can use things in the home for their child to do small-muscle activities (stringing spools or large buttons; filling a plastic bowl with dried beans or rice; screwing large bolts onto fat nuts).

- See ideas for making activity boards, pages 156 and 348–350.

Activity Checklist

Small Muscles

Small-muscle activities with Threes include experiences in which children learn to control hand and finger movements. As eye-hand coordination improves, Threes enjoy dressing themselves, scribbling with crayons, cutting with safe scissors, and playing with toys that have many small pieces. Their ability to draw improves so that they can trace around shapes and draw simple designs.

Check for each age group	*36–42 mo*	*42–48 mo*
1. A variety of safe small-muscle toys for children to explore with fingers and hands is available for children to use by themselves daily.	—	—
2. Safe small-muscle toys are organized by type and stored on low, open shelves for children's free use.	—	—
3. Small-muscle toys are changed regularly.	—	—
4. Duplicates of popular toys are available.	—	—
5. Adult shows children how to use small-muscle toys as needed.	—	—
6. Toys are clean and in good condition.	—	—
7. Protected space is set aside for play with small-muscle toys.	—	—
8. Children are encouraged to serve and feed themselves.	—	—
9. Safe scissors are available for use, and children are helped to learn to cut.	—	—

127

Threes can

- put pegs in a pegboard

Pegs and Pegboards

Put two or three pegboards into a dishpan. Add a butter tub or plastic bowl of pegs that fit into the pegboards. Leave the dishpan out on an open shelf for your three-year-old's play. See if she can talk about the size and color of the pegs as she puts them into the holes. Be sure to have two or three dishpans so you can have different sized pegs and pegboards in each. Put these out at different times.

What are you making, Deirdre?
You have so many red pegs in your pegboard.
Are you going to fill all of the holes with little red pegs?

 in or out   2–10 min   1–4 Threes

128

Threes can

- handle small things with fingers

Geoboards

Make a few geoboards for your Threes. (Directions for making geoboards are on page 153.) Put them out with a butter tub full of colorful rubber bands. Stretch one of the rubber bands around a few nails to make a shape. Talk with the child about what it looks like and how you made it. Then give him the rubber bands and let him have fun making his own shapes and figures by stretching them around the nails.

Stretch it, Robin. There you go, it's on the nail now.
Look what you made! That's a blue triangle.

Note: Show the three-year-old how to hold the rubber bands down with two hands so that they don't fly off the nails.

 in or out   2–10 min   1–4 Threes

129

Building Tall Towers

Put a set of <u>inch cubes</u> into a <u>dishpan or box</u>. Set the box out on a low table or work space for your three-year-old. As the child begins to play with the blocks, ask her to make a tall tower. Have her see how high she can stack the blocks on her own. If the tower falls down, count the blocks that made up the tower. Then have fun building it up again, or let her play with the cubes in her own way.

Wow, Keisha! You had so many blocks in your tower.
Can you help me count them?

Threes can

- stack inch cubes

 in or out | 2–10 min | 1–4 Threes

130

Vinyl Picture Stick-ons

Give each three-year-old in a small group a set of <u>vinyl picture stick-ons</u>. Show him how to peel off the pictures and place them on the picture card. Let him have fun creating his own picture as he takes off and puts on new pieces. Ask him questions about the picture story he makes.

Those people in your picture have raincoats on, Darryl.
Is it going to rain on them?
It is? I'm glad you dressed them for the rain!

Note: Vinyl picture stick-ons are sometimes called "Color Forms" and can be found in book, toy, or school supply stores.

Threes can

- pick up thin things with thumb and pointer finger

 in or out | 2–10 min | 1–3 Threes

131

Threes can

- string small beads
- use small pegs and pegboard

Ring Board

Screw 15 or 20 round cup hooks into a plywood board. Set the board up in a safe place where it will not be knocked over. Put a handful of different-sized washers in a small plastic bowl. Give the bowl with these flat, round washers to the three-year-old, and show her how she can hang each one over a hook. Let her fit the rest of the washers over each hook in her own way. When she is finished, she can have more fun putting the rings back into the bowl.

What are you doing, Sandy?
Where are you putting the rings?
On the hooks, that's right!

 in or out   2–10 min   1 child at a time

132

Threes can

- string small beads

Stringing Beads

Tie a large knot in one end of a sturdy shoestring. Make sure the other end has a 1″ plastic tip on it. If it does not, wrap a short piece of tape around the end to make it more sturdy. Give the child this shoestring along with a small box of $\frac{1}{2}$″ beads. Show him how to push the string through one end of the bead and pull it out of the other. Help him move the bead down to the bottom of his string. Then let him string the rest of the beads on his own. When he is finished, tie the two ends of the string together so that he can wear the beads he has strung as a necklace.

One, two, three, four, five. Five red beads.
You have five little red beads on your necklace.

 in or out   3–10 min   1–6 Threes

133

Threes can

- weave yarn through holes in a card

Lacing Cards

Cut out <u>simple pictures of familiar things</u> from <u>catalogs, coloring books, or magazines</u>. <u>Glue</u> the pictures onto <u>sturdy cardboard</u> and cover with <u>clear contact paper</u>. Punch several holes around the outside of each picture with a <u>paper punch</u>. Tie a <u>shoestring or heavy piece of yarn</u> through one of the holes. Make sure the other end of the string has <u>tape</u> wrapped around it to make a firm tip. Give the picture card to the three-year-old and show her how the string can go in and out of the holes. Don't worry about which hole she puts the string into. Let her choose her own pattern.

Oh, Cecelia, your cat has a red string going right through his ear. Can you put the string through the hole in his tail, too?

 in or out 2–10 min # 1–4 Threes

134

Threes can

- do easy puzzles

Puzzle Place

Set up a place in your room for <u>puzzles</u>. (You'll find ideas for puzzles on page 154.) Put the puzzles on <u>low shelves</u> where the children can easily reach them. If possible, put easy puzzles on one shelf and harder ones on another. Keep only a few puzzles out at a time. Make sure you have a flat, open work area near the puzzle shelf. A low table or clear floor space works best. Talk to the children about one or two easy rules for this area so Threes can choose and play with puzzles on their own.

Where is Big Bird's head, Aaron? There it is! You found it. You'd better put it in or else he won't be able to eat his lunch.

 indoors 3–10 min # 1–7 Threes

Activities for Physical Development

135

Threes can

- copy simple designs

Copy Designs in the Sand

Sit near a three-year-old as she plays in the sand table or sand box. While she watches, make a line in the sand with your finger and ask her to make one just like it. After she can copy a simple line, try making a circle or a crossed line for her to copy. Give her a chance to make her own designs in the sand for you to copy. Have fun with your three-year-old as you spend this playful time in the sand together.

Can you make a circle like mine?
That's good, round and round.
Doesn't the sand feel cool on our fingers?

 in or out   3–15 min   1–4 Threes

136

Threes can

- pour into a cup with little spilling

Pitchers and Cups

Put out a few plastic cups and pitchers in a water table or bucket of water. Let a few of your Threes have fun playing freely in the water, filling and dumping the pitchers and cups. Have them practice pouring from the big pitcher into the smaller cups as if they were pouring juice for snack. If you are doing this activity inside, you may want to put down an old shower curtain or some towels in case water splashes out, and have smocks ready to keep children dry.

You have a very full pitcher, Maurice.
Can you pour some water out into these cups?
Good job!

Watch carefully so that a child does not drink dirty water or use the same cup as another child.

 in or out   3–15 min   1–4 Threes

137

Threes can

- join two halves to make a whole

People Puzzles

Cut out large pictures of people from old magazines or catalogs. Glue them onto sturdy cardboard and cover with clear contact paper. Then cut each picture into two to four large pieces and give them to the child to put together. After he can put one person together easily, give him the pieces to two or three people at the same time. See if he can put each one together all by himself.

You have the legs and the arms, Dante.
Where do you think they go? That's right.
Who is that in your puzzle?

 indoors | 3–10 min | 1–6 Threes

138

Threes can

- use thumb and pointer finger together well

Poker Chip Drop-in Games

Cut a narrow slot in the lid of a shoe box, so that a poker chip will just fit through. You can cover the box with contact paper or decorate it if you wish. Put 20–30 poker chips in the box, and place it on a low shelf for the children. Show the children how to open the box, dump out the chips, put the lid back on the box, and drop the chips through the slot. Remind children to put all the chips back in the box before putting it away.

Use other safe containers with lids to make other drop-in games. If your Threes play without putting things in their mouths, try smaller things, such as pennies, to drop in.

 indoors | 2–10 min | 1–2 Threes

139

Threes can

- use thumb and pointer finger together well

Lock Board

Make a <u>wooden board with locks</u> for your Threes to use. (You'll find directions for making two kinds of lock boards on pages 155–156.) Show the children how to use the different types of locks. Keep the boards out on a low shelf so that children can use them on their own.

Can you open this lock with a key, Thomas?
Which key will you use?

 in or out 2–10 min 1 child at a time

140

Threes can

- wiggle a few fingers

Shadow Shapes

Set up a <u>filmstrip projector or bright flashlight</u> so that it shines on a <u>clean wall</u>, an <u>old sheet</u>, or a <u>large sheet of white paper</u>. Wave your hand in front of the light, and wiggle your fingers so that the child can watch them move in the light. Then give her a chance to wiggle her fingers and make her own shadow shapes in front of the light.

I see the shadow of your hand.
I can see your fingers wiggling like worms.

 indoors 2–5 min 1–4 Threes

141

Threes can

■ spread soft foods

Spreading Peanut Butter

At snack time give each three-year-old a piece of <u>toast</u> and a <u>dull plastic knife</u>. Put a little cup or jar of <u>peanut butter</u> in front of him, and let him scoop some out onto his piece of toast. Then ask him to spread it all around the toast with his knife. After he spreads it around, take away the knife and let him enjoy his peanut butter snack.

That looks like a yummy snack, Christopher.
What do you have on your toast?
Peanut butter, that's right!

 in or out   2–5 min   **#** 1–6 Threes

142

Threes can

■ draw very simple pictures

Follow-the-Path Game

Make some big follow-the-path cards for your Threes to try out. (You'll find directions for making these on page 154.) Put these cards out on a low shelf for the children to use.

Have a few easy and a few more difficult cards out. Show children how to use the cards, and then let them choose how to play with them on their own.

Where is your little man going, Katya?
He went all the way to his house.

 in or out   2–10 min   1–4 Threes

143

Threes can

■ trace over simple designs

Tracing

Draw a big circle or a few lines on a piece of <u>paper</u>. Give the paper to the three-year-old along with a <u>crayon or marker</u> and ask him to trace over the same line you just drew. Don't worry if he goes off the line or has a hard time with corners or curves. This will be hard for him at first, but as he grows older, it will become easier. After he traces over your line, let him finish the picture in his own creative way.

Good tracing, Jason.
You really tried to follow my line.
What shape did we make?
Now you make a picture!

 in or out 3–5 min 1–6 Threes

144

Threes can

■ hammer nails and pegs

Hammer and Nails

<u>Hammer</u> a few <u>nails</u> with large heads, such as roofing nails, partway into an <u>old stump or thick wooden board</u>. Give your three-year-old a hammer and let him hammer the nails the rest of the way into the wood. Be sure to watch carefully to see that he cannot get hurt or that the board does not move. Keep other children away from the child with the hammer so that he doesn't hit any one by mistake.

That nail went all the way into the tree stump!
Can you hammer another one just like that?
Let's count how many hits it takes.

 outdoors 3–5 min 1 child at a time

145

Threes can

■ copy a three-block bridge

Copy a Bridge of Blocks

Make a bridge with three <u>1″ cubes</u> for your three-year-old as she watches. Leave your cubes up for her to look at, and then give her three 1″ cubes to make into her own bridge. As she stacks, help her to see that there is a space between the two bottom cubes and that the top cube fits over that space.

One, two, three.
You have three blocks in your bridge, just like mine.
If we take them apart do you think you could do it again?

Give her more cubes and let her play in her own way.

 in or out 2–3 min 1–3 Threes

146

Threes can

■ take things apart and put them together

Fit Them Together

Put a set of <u>blocks or toys that fit together</u> in a <u>large plastic bowl or dishpan</u>. Set the bowl out in a clear work space or on a low table for the three-year-olds' free play. Toys that work best for Threes are those that pull apart and fit together easily, such as Lego Bricks, Bristle Blocks, or Tinkertoys.

What are you building, Leon?
An airplane, what a great idea!

Be sure each set of toys is kept in its own dishpan. Do not dump many kinds of toys into one pan.

 in or out 3–15 min 1–3 Threes

147

Threes can

- squeeze with hands and fingers

Crumple and Glue

Give your three-year-old a piece of <u>paper</u>, and let her squeeze a small bottle of <u>glue</u> to make a squiggly line all over her paper. Then put the glue out of reach and set out a <u>dishpan</u> full of small pieces of <u>colored tissue paper</u>. Tell the child to take one piece of paper from the dishpan, crumple it up, and stick it onto her glue. Let her do this until her paper is full of pretty tissue paper balls.

I see blue, red, and green balls on your paper, Rebecca.
You did a great job.
Can you show me all the red balls?

 indoors 3–10 min 1–7 Threes

148

Threes can

- trace around simple things

Tracing Around Things

Put a few <u>small, simple toys</u> (a wooden car, a block, and a doll's plate, for example) into a <u>dishpan</u> with some <u>crayons and paper</u>. Show the child how you can put a toy on top of your paper and trace around it. Let him choose the toy he wants to trace, hold it down, and then trace it on his own paper. The lines will not be perfect, but let him have fun picking out new things to trace and add to his picture.

You drew a red line all the way around the car.
You traced around the car.

 in or out 3–7 min 1–5 Threes

149

Threes can

■ button large buttons

Buttoning

Collect several <u>old adult vests or sweaters that have large buttons</u>. Put these out in your dress-up area for the Threes to wear as they play. When a child puts the vest on himself or on a doll, show him how to push the button through the button hole. Be sure to let him play with and wear the vest in his own way, even if it is buttoned a little crooked.

What are you wearing, Douglas?
A sweater, that's right!
Did you button that button all by yourself?

 in or out 3–15 min 1–3 Threes

150

Threes can

■ weave yarn randomly

Lacing Old Shoes

Bring in a few pair of <u>clean adult shoes that lace up</u>. Make sure they have sturdy laces with plastic tips on each end. Put these shoes in your dress-up area for the Threes to wear as they play. Show the children how to push the laces in and out of the holes to lace them up. Let them enjoy lacing and playing with the shoes in their own creative three-year-old way.

Can you push the laces through the holes so you won't trip?

Be sure to spray shoes children use with a disinfectant and have children wear socks with the shoes.

 in or out 3–10 min 1–3 Threes

151

Threes can

■ use put-together toys

Put Tiny Pieces Together

Find a few sets of <u>toys that have very small pieces</u> that fit together. Put each set in its own <u>dishpan or plastic bowl</u>, and put them out on a low shelf for the Threes' free play. Make sure only one set at a time is taken off the shelf and that the pieces are all kept in their own bowl. As the child plays, help him to pick up the tiny pieces and fit them together.

Try some of these ideas:

Cooties

tiny pegs and pegboards

Lite-Brite

little beads to string or stack

little people that stack

 in or out | 3–15 min | 1–3 Threes

152

Threes can

■ zip easy zippers

Zipping Zippers

Put a few <u>jackets or pants that have large, easy zippers</u> into your dress-up area. Let your children wear these clothes as they pretend. As a child puts on something that has a zipper, help him to get the bottom started, and then see if he can zip it up the rest of the way by himself. Do this same thing when he wears his own jacket so that he can begin to do more and more for himself.

Do you need a little help starting your zipper, Joey?
Oh boy! I guess you don't.
You did it all by yourself!

 in or out | 2–3 min | 1–3 Threes

153

Threes can

- pick up tiny things

Tiny Rock Hunt

Give each child a <u>paper cup</u>. Then take Threes outside for a tiny rock hunt. Ask them to find the littlest rocks that they can and then to put them in their cups. After you have finished your hunting time outside, bring the children in and dump all the rocks out into a pile. Have a short discussion with your Threes about the different sizes of rocks they found. Ask them lots of questions to get them to use words like *big, little,* and *bigger.*

How many rocks did you find, Cleo?
Wow! Your cup is almost full!
I bet you have at least 20 tiny rocks in your cup.

 in or out | 5–15 min | 1–15 Threes

154

Threes can

- enjoy sand play
- pour from a cup or pitcher

Rice Play/Bean Play

Fill a <u>long, flat box or dishpan</u> with <u>dried beans or rice</u>. If you have enough, you may want to use an empty sand or water table. Add things to fill and dump, such as <u>plastic bowls, cups, pitchers, spoons, or other small scoops</u>. Let your Threes have fun playing, filling, and dumping in their own creative way.

What do you have in your pitcher, Kenji? Beans, that's right!
How many cups can you fill with your pitcher of beans?

On another day, put only small things to fill and dump into the dishpan, such as doll-sized spoons and plastic bottles with small openings.

 in or out | 3–15 min | 1–4 Threes

Activities for Physical Development

155

Threes can

- screw a lid onto a jar

Jars and Lids

Put a few <u>plastic jars with screw lids</u> into a <u>dishpan</u>. Add some <u>small toys that will fit into the jars</u>. Give your three-year-old a jar and ask her to drop in one of the toys. Then ask her to find the lid that fits the jar and to screw it on. Let her play freely with the jars and their lids as she hides, dumps, opens, and shakes the toys in the jars.

Who is hiding in your jar, Maria? A red bear?
Do you think he likes being in there all by himself?

 in or out 2–10 min 1–4 Threes

156

Threes can

- pinch a clothespin

Clothespin Play

Put 15–20 <u>clothespins</u> in a <u>dishpan</u> with <u>several sturdy plastic cups or bowls</u>. Show the three-year-old how to pinch the clothespin open and place it onto one of the cups or bowls in the dishpan. Let the Threes play with the clothespins in their own way. Try some of these other clothespin ideas:

hang up doll clothes on a small <u>clothesline</u>

hang up art work on a small clothesline

clip paper to an easel with clothespins

count how many clothespins you can clip on a shoestring

 in or out 2–10 min 1–5 Threes

How to Make Geoboards

1. Cut a piece of 1-inch thick plywood into 7-inch squares. Sand all edges and corners until they are smooth.
2. Follow the pattern below and hammer 25 nails ½-inch deep into each plywood square. Use sturdy 2-inch nails with smooth, flat heads.

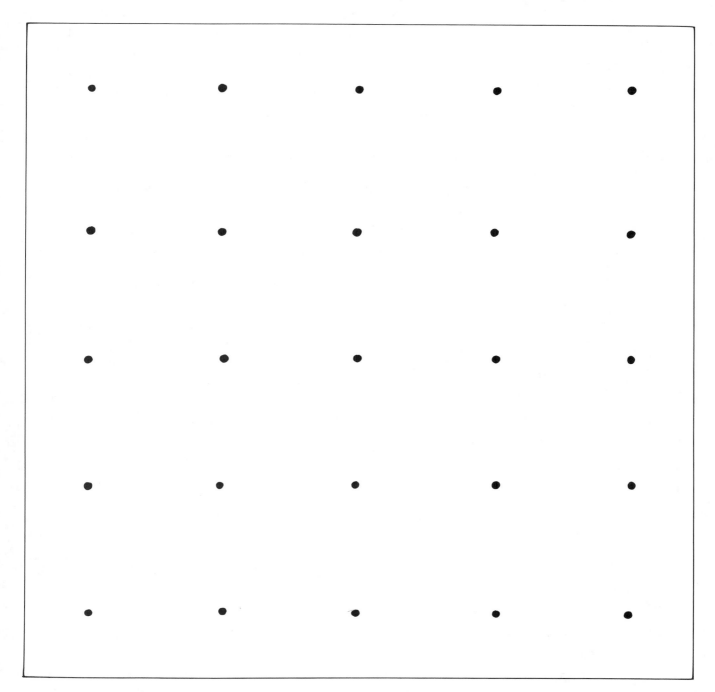

If you don't have any plywood, hammer a few nails into a stump or big log outside. Have fun making designs on it with rubber bands.

Puzzle Place Ideas

- Before you put puzzles out on the shelf, mark the back of each piece with the puzzle's name. This will help you tell which pieces go with each puzzle.

- Set puzzles out on a low, open shelf. Make sure the shelf is not cluttered with other toys and the puzzles are not piled on top of each other.

- Be sure to have a flat, open space near the shelf where the children can work on their puzzles. A low table or rug out of traffic works best.

- Have several different kinds of puzzles for the children to do. Choose ones that have different textures, numbers of pieces, colors, and sizes.

- Change the puzzles you have out for children. Don't keep all the puzzles out at the same time.

- If a child is already working on one puzzle, make sure he completes it before he takes out another. If the puzzle is too hard for him to work on his own, help him finish it so that he can choose another puzzle that will be more fun.

- Help children learn how to do a new puzzle one or two pieces at a time. Don't start by dumping out all the pieces at once. Take out one piece and let the child put it back. Then take out two and let him replace them. Continue this way until he can handle the whole puzzle on his own.

- Puzzle racks make it hard for children to see and choose puzzles. Use them for storing extra puzzles that you have not put out for the children's use. Separate easy from hard puzzles and label each rack.

- Puzzles for Threes should

    have five to nine pieces

    be colorful

    be of familiar things or people

    have some interlocking pieces

    be sturdy

    be of different textures (wood, rubber, plastic)

    be simple enough that the child can recognize each piece separately (for example, a hat, a face, a body, arms and legs would make a person; or wheels, a ladder, a firefighter and the truck would make a firefighter puzzle).

How to make follow-the-path cards

1. Use a large piece of sturdy cardboard or poster board for each card. Make each card about 12 inches square.
2. Draw a path for the child to follow on each card. Have some cards with very simple paths and others with more difficult paths. Make paths wide enough for a child's finger to follow easily, about one inch wide. Here are some examples. (Yours will be bigger.)

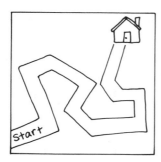  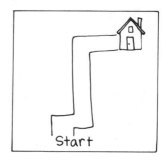

3. You can draw or glue pictures at the ends of the paths to make the paths more fun to use.

4. Cover the cards with clear contact paper.

To use:

- Let the child follow the path with her finger.

- Let the child draw along the path with a crayon or watercolor marker. Rub marks off with a paper towel so that the card can be used again.

- Let the child follow the path with little people, animals, or cars. Keep these things with the cards in a dishpan or box.

You can also use old game boards that have paths the children enjoy following.

Making Activity Boards

How to make a lock board
Sand the edges of an 18″ piece of plywood. Cover the edges with sturdy tape or contact paper if they are still a bit rough.

Easy Lock Board (for younger Threes)

- Tightly screw several different kinds of locks and bolts onto the board. Do not use locks with keys.

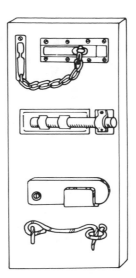

Lock Board with Keys (for older Threes)

1. Hammer two or three very large, sturdy staples into a board. You can get these at a hardware store. Or use hasps that open and close.
2. Put pictures under the flaps so that the children will see them if they get the lock open. A small unbreakable mirror under one flap is also fun.
3. Put different-sized padlocks on the staples or hasps.
4. Put the keys to the padlocks on a key ring. Attach the ring to a sturdy string and fasten it to the board so that the keys won't get lost.

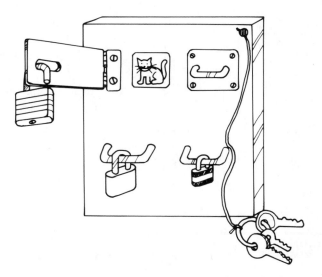

Put the Lock Board in a safe place where it can't tip over, or nail it to the end of a bookcase or cabinet where the children can easily reach and play with it.

Your Own Activities: Physical Development

Write your own activities in these blank boxes. You will find more information on writing your own activities in the Planning section, page 38.

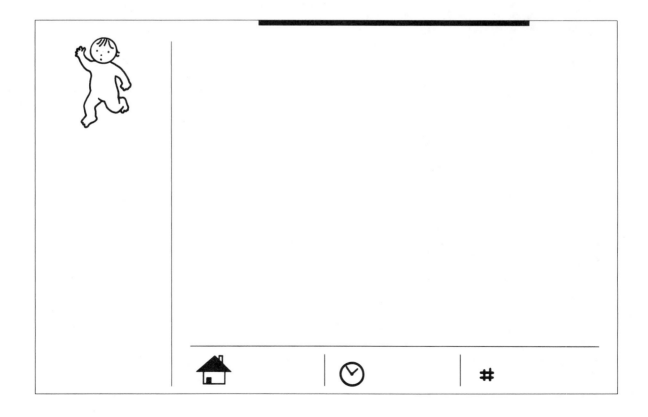

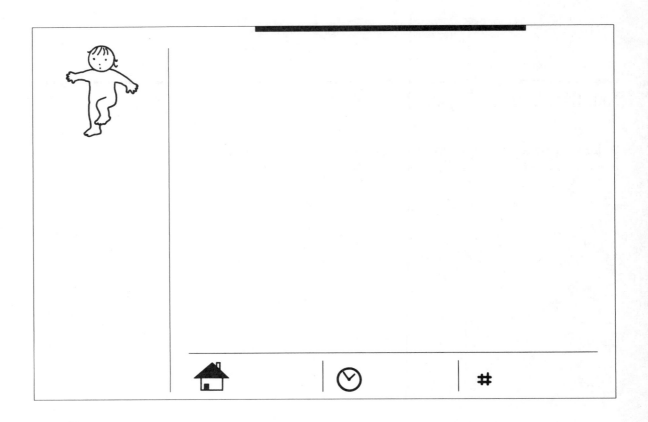

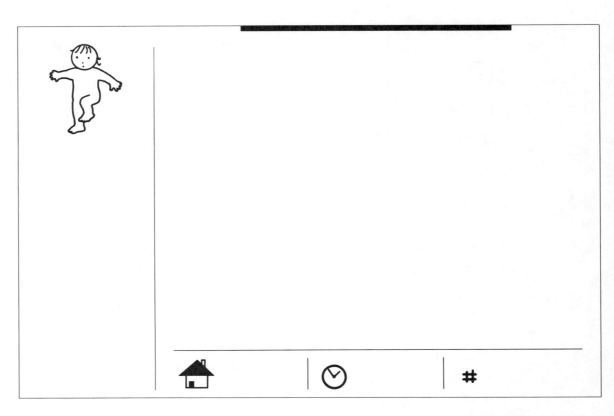

Activities for Physical Development

Index
of Activities for Physical Development

Backwards Walk   115
Balance on the Board   108
Basketball Time   102
Beanbag Toss   109
Big Step/Little Step   113
Bowling   125
Box Play   96
Broomstick Horses   114
Bubbles to Chase and Pop   104
Building Tall Towers   129
Buttoning   149
Catch a Bounced Ball   97
Catching Balls   89
Change Your Speed and
    Direction   124
Circus Days   123
Clothespin Play   156
Copy Designs in the Sand   135
Copy a Bridge of Blocks   145
Crumple and Glue   147
Exercise Time   120
Fit Them Together   146
Follow the Footsteps   122
Follow the Leader   121
Geoboards   128
Hammer and Nails   144
Hop Like a Frog   92
Jars and Lids   155
Jump Off the Block   111
Jump Over the Cracks   93
Kick and Run   91
Kick It in the Goal   126
Lacing Cards   133
Lacing Old Shoes   150

Lock Board   139
March and Step   100
Move Like the Animals   107
Obstacle Course   119
Pegs and Pegboards   127
People Puzzles   137
Pitchers and Cups   136
Playground Things to Move   116
Poker Chip Drop-in Games   138
Put Tiny Pieces Together   151
Puzzle Place   134
Red Rover   98
Rice Play/Bean Play   154
Ring Board   131
Shadow Shapes   140
Slides   103
Spreading Peanut Butter   141
Stairs   101
Storks and Cranes   110
Stringing Beads   132
Swings   118
Tents   106
Throwing Far Away   117
Tiny Rock Hunt   153
Tiptoe Time   94
Tracing   143
Tracing Around Things   148
Trees in the Wind   90
Tricycles   99
Tumbling Time   112
Vinyl Picture Stick-Ons   130
Walk Through a Ladder   105
Walking on a Line   95
Zipping Zippers   152

Here's Why

Art, blocks, dramatic play, and music give Threes chances to do interesting things by themselves that show clear results. Threes need to have many creative materials every day to use in their own ways.

Drawing and talking are two ways a young child has of developing understanding. Young Threes start out by scribbling, but many can draw recognizable things by the time they are three and a half. It takes a lot of practice in scribbling before a child learns to control his hands and focus his ideas well enough to draw a face we can all see. When children are allowed the time and practice to teach themselves to draw, they benefit most. Display the scribble drawings Threes make so they know how proud you are of what they can do by themselves.

The other creative activities are also important. Both music and dramatic play help to build memory for words and ideas. Threes love to sing along with familiar songs. They also enjoy pretending about the things they see happening around them.

When Threes play with blocks, they become aware of differences in shape, size, and weight. They also learn about balance as they build a big tower. Block play is a good way to learn how to share and how to play near others without bothering them.

Threes enjoy all the creative activities. They like the fact that they can do things themselves. They also enjoy the messy, active, noisy way the arts work. You can help them learn many other skills as they work with the activities in this section.

Materials and Notes

Art

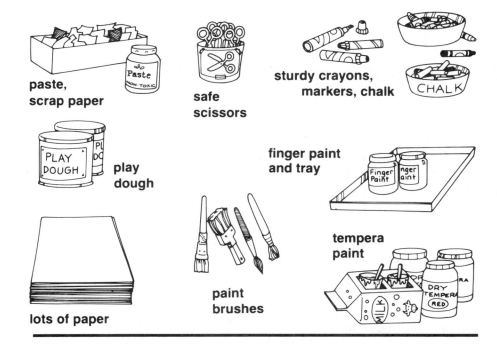

paste,
scrap paper

safe
scissors

sturdy crayons,
markers, chalk

CHALK

PLAY DOUGH

play
dough

finger paint
and tray

Finger Paint

lots of paper

paint
brushes

tempera
paint

DRY TEMPERA RED

- Make sure all the art materials you use are nontoxic.

- Have sturdy art equipment and supplies out for Threes to use every day.

- Put up lots of the children's art work to look at. Change the things you have up often.

- Encourage parents to hang up their children's work at home. Let them know that scribble drawings are an important step towards drawing things we can recognize. Scribbling also gets children ready for writing later on.

- Let the children use art materials in their own way. Do not have Threes copy things you have made.

- Do not ask Threes to color in coloring books. Coloring does not help them develop drawing skills.

- See Art Area Ideas and recipes for paint and play dough on pages 179–181.

Activity Checklist

Art

Art for Threes includes providing things for them to look at as well as art materials for them to use. Interest in handling art materials usually is well established by three. This is when the child starts to use drawing materials, fingerpaints, and play dough with greater control. Threes enjoy scribbling and drawing designs and may even start to draw faces and shapes towards the end of the year.

Check for each age group	*36–42 mo*	*42–48 mo*
1. Large, clear, brightly colored pictures of people and familiar things are placed where children can see them.	—	—
2. Children's drawings and other artwork are displayed where children can see them. Artwork is sent home with each child.	—	—
3. Adult talks to child about shape, color, and textures of things that the child experiences and about what the child is doing as he uses art materials.	—	—
4. Child is encouraged to feel, handle, and explore different textures (fabrics, papers, toys, play dough).	—	—
5. Adult offers some simple, nontoxic art materials for daily use, including paint, play dough, or pasting.	—	—
6. Child is offered art materials but is not forced to use them. Alternate activities are available.	—	—
7. Some drawing materials are available to child daily for independent use.	—	—
8. Several colors of paint with brushes are offered to the children to use on paper.	—	—
9. Fingerpainting with paint is provided.	—	—
10. A low, sturdy table or easel is used for art activities.	—	—
11. Children can help with easy clean-up.	—	—

157

Threes can

- use some art materials
- follow easy rules

Art Area Tour

Set up an <u>art area</u> for your Threes. (You will find Art Area Ideas on page 179.) Show the children the paper, crayons, watercolor markers, big thick pencils, and other art materials that are placed where they can reach to use freely. Talk about some art area rules such as the following.

Art Area Rules

Take one piece of paper at a time

Use art materials at the art table

Put art materials away when done

Throw away scraps

Put tops back on markers

Hang up pictures, put them out to dry, or put them into cubbies.

 indoors | 5–7 min | 1–6 Threes

158

Threes can

- scribble or draw simple forms

My Art Book

Save some of the <u>drawings made by each child</u> in <u>folders with their names</u>. Put the date on each drawing. When a child has ten drawings, staple the drawings into the folder for the child to give her parents. Go through each child's drawings with her and talk about them. Ask the parents to do the same. Talk about how the child's drawings have changed.

This is the first picture you made, Germaine.
See the colors you used?
And here's the next one.
You made long and short lines.

 in or out | 5–15 min | 1–2 Threes

159

Threes can

- scribble
- begin to share

Crayon Art

Put <u>several small containers of sturdy crayons</u> on a <u>low shelf</u>, along with lots of <u>paper</u> for your Threes to use freely. Have a small container for every one or two children. Add variety to crayon art by putting crayons out on a table with different colors or shapes of paper. Or put crayons and paper on the easel for a change of pace. Talk with the children about the colors they use as they draw.

I like all the blue lines you made, Charlene.
Where did you make a red line?

 in or out 2–15 min 1–6 Threes

160

Threes can

- fingerpaint

Fingerpaint on a Tray

Set some <u>large plastic trays</u> on a <u>low table</u>. Put <u>waterproof aprons</u> on the children who want to fingerpaint. Put a <u>dishpan with soapy water and paper towels</u> nearby for handwashing. Put <u>one or two tablespoons of fingerpaint</u> on each tray. (You'll find fingerpaint recipes on page 180.) Use a bright color like red or blue. Let the child fingerpaint in his own way. Talk about the different kinds of designs the children make.

You made big swirls here, Jimmy.
And you made squiggles and tiny dots, Jay.

 in or out 3–10 min 1–4 Threes

161

Threes can

■ do lots of artwork

Art Gallery

Make a special display space, an art gallery where Threes can put their favorite artwork. Use a wall, the backs of toy shelves, or doors. Let the children know that they can choose what they want to put there. Have enough space for everyone to use. It's good to have a shelf or windowsill for play dough or carpentry art, too.

Let children help hang up their work or choose where it should go. Help the children talk about what they have done so that they know you're interested.

Moira, do you want to hang this in our art gallery? Where would you like it to go?
Can you help with the tape?

Also hang children's work in other places in the room where they can easily see them.

 indoors │ 1–3 min │ **#** 1 child at a time

162

Threes can

■ use paints with a brush

Tempera Painting

Set up a <u>low easel</u> with <u>paper</u>, <u>two or three colors of thick paint</u> in <u>cups</u> that won't tip over, and <u>one sturdy, short handled brush for each color</u>. (You'll find paint recipes and directions for making a paint cup holder on pages 180–181.) Have a place ready to dry paintings.

Show the child how to wipe the brushes on the side of the cup to keep paint from dripping. Remind her to keep each brush in its own paint color, but have extra paint ready to replace mixed-up paints. Then let the child paint freely. Talk about the colors and designs in her artwork.

You used red and yellow, Kate.
See where red and yellow mixed to make orange?

Threes will enjoy painting with paper flat on a table, too.

 in or out │ 3–12 min │ 1–2 Threes

163

Threes can

- remember where things go
- squeeze with thumb and fingers

Hanging Pictures to Dry

Put up a <u>low clothesline or fishnet</u> where Threes can hang their art-work to dry. Have lots of <u>clothespins</u> ready. Show children how to bring wet pictures to the hanging place and get a clothespin. Then you can help them squeeze the clothespins to hold the pictures in place. Be sure that children's names are on their pictures and that there is plenty of room so pictures don't stick together. A wooden clothes drying rack can also be used.

 indoors 1–2 min 1–2 Threes

164

Threes can

- scribble
- begin to share

Watercolor Markers

Have <u>several containers of thick watercolor markers with sturdy tips</u> for Threes to use on their own. Let them try the markers on <u>paper of different sizes, shapes, and textures</u>. Show them how to take off and replace the marker caps. As Threes use the markers, talk about the bright colors and the designs they make.

You're using the green marker on bumpy wallpaper, David. Here's a design you did on smooth, slippery paper.

 in or out 2–10 min 1–5 Threes

165

Threes can

- talk about scribbles or drawings when asked

Picture Talks

When a three-year-old finishes a picture, talk about it with her. Ask easy questions to see how much she will say. Enjoy the different kinds of answers you will get from different children.

Tell me about your picture, Emma.
It's a monster?
How did you make your monster?
Yes, you painted it.
You used blue and green paint.

 in or out | 1–3 min | # 1 child at a time

166

Threes can

- follow easy directions
- enjoy play dough

Play Dough Fun

Have the children help you mix play dough. (A play dough recipe is on page 180.) Before children help, get all the things you will need—flour, salt, oil, color, water, measuring cups, and a big unbreakable bowl. Have the Threes help you measure, pour, and mix. Make one color at a time. When it is done, give each child some dough to use at a table in his own way. See how many things the Threes do with the play dough using just their hands. Help the children remember how they made the play dough.

What did you do to help make the play dough, Tony?
Yes, you stirred.
Now see what your hands are doing—patting, poking, and pinching the dough.

 in or out | 10–20 min | # 1–5 Threes

167

Paper Scraps Collage

Collect pretty paper scraps for your Threes to paste onto pieces of paper. Include scraps of construction paper, wallpaper, and gift wrapping. Give each child a little paste in a paper cup to use with a stick. Remind Threes to put paste on the correct side of each scrap and then to put the scrap on the bigger paper, paste-side down. Let them paste the scraps they like and make their own designs. Talk about the scraps they used when they are finished.

This is a scrap of birthday paper here, Maria.
Show me where you put the pink tissue paper.

Try collages made of pretty material scraps, too.

Threes can

- paste on right side
- point to a few colors you name

 indoors   3–15 min   1–6 Threes

168

Chalk Art

Cover a low table with newspaper. Put each child's name on the back of a piece of black construction paper. Wet the papers and put one in front of each child. Give each child a bowl with some large, brightly colored nontoxic chalks. Let the children draw on the wet paper. They may need to press hard to see their lines. When it dries, the chalk may rub off a little.

To keep chalk from rubbing off, use a brush to wet the paper with a mixture of half liquid starch and half water. Use a piece of sandpaper to clean chalks when done.

At other times, let your Threes use chalk on a chalkboard, or take chalk outside for drawing on the sidewalk.

Threes can

- scribble
- do simple comparing

 in or out   5–10 min   1–6 Threes

169

Threes can

- snip paper with scissors
- paste on right side

Cutting Paper Strips

Put a dishpan with colored paper strips about 1″ wide on a low table. Give each child small, safe scissors. Let each child pick a paper strip and cut it into pieces. Save the pieces so that the child can paste them on a piece of colored paper about 5″ × 8″. Talk about the colors he is pasting. Praise him for the good job he did of cutting with scissors.

On another day, have children place the pieces they cut onto the sticky side of clear contact paper. Turn the contact paper over to stick onto a larger piece of black paper and smooth it down.

 indoors | 3–10 min | 1–5 Threes

170

Threes can

- peel and stick stickers onto paper

Sticker Pictures

Collect free or inexpensive stickers for children to use. Have parents bring in the ones they get in "junk" mail. Also save scraps of contact paper to use as stickers. Keep all these in a box. Show your Threes how to peel the stickers away from the paper backing. Then they can put the stickers onto a piece of paper about 5 × 8 inches to make a design. When the children are done, talk about the colors and shapes of the stickers they used.

At another time, use free "junk" mail stamps the children can wet on a sponge and stick to half sheets of paper.

 indoors | 2–15 min | 1–6 Threes

171

Threes can

■ fingerpaint

Mural Fingerpainting

Cut a very large sheet of paper from a big paper roll. Hang this on the wall of a building, put it on a table, or on anything else that will make a solid back for the paper. Put out several trays that have fingerpaint on them. Show the children how to get fingerpaint on their hands and then make hand prints and other designs on the big paper.

Do this on a hot day, when the children can wear swim suits. Then you can rinse the paint off children with a hose before they cool off in a little wading pool.

 outdoors   2–10 min   1–7 Threes

172

Threes can

■ string beads

Stringing Things

Put out a tray with things to string that have big holes. (You'll find ideas for String Things on page 181.) Give each child a bowl in which to keep his stringing things and a string that has one tightly taped end and a knot on the other end. Let the children string the many kinds of string things in their own way. Let them keep their work. Talk with each child about the things he used.

Tell me what you put on your necklace, Nicholas.
Yes, those are pieces of straws.
Do you know what this is?

 in or out   3–15 min   1–6 Threes

173

Threes can

- paint with a brush
- use size words

Painting Little Pictures

Put onto a low table cups of <u>tempera paint</u> in a <u>paint cup holder</u>. Also put out some small paintbrushes and small pieces of <u>paper</u>. Let your Threes paint little pictures in their own way. Talk about the size of the brushes, paper, and the designs they make.

You're using the little brush in the purple paint, aren't you, Susie? Now what color will you use in your little painting?

If you wish, have an easel set up nearby and let children choose to paint big or small.

 in or out   5–15 min   1–6 Threes

174

Threes can

- weave yarn through holes in sewing cards

Sewing Designs

Punch holes in some <u>cardboard shapes</u>. Put these out with <u>pretty yarn</u>. Let the Threes each choose a shape and some yarn to work with. Tie one end of the yarn through one hole in the cardboard so it won't pull out. Wrap <u>tape</u> tightly around the loose end so the child will be able to push it through the holes. Let the child "sew" with the yarn in his own way to make a yarn design. If he wants to, let him use another color of yarn when he is done with the first. Talk with the child about his work.

Can you show me where the blue yarn goes over the yellow, Mark?

 in or out   3–15 min   1–4 Threes

175

Threes can

■ hold pencil with fingers

Pencil Pictures

Have in a <u>container</u> on the art shelf <u>soft lead pencils</u> that make dark marks for your Threes to use freely. Keep plenty of <u>paper</u> nearby for the children to use with the pencils.

Make pencil art a special activity by putting pencils out with special shapes of paper. For example, put out pencils to use with long, narrow paper, heart or star paper shapes, or with very tiny paper.

You made lots of tiny circles on this heart paper, Dinah.

 in or out | 2–10 min | 1–6 Threes

176

Threes can

■ follow directions

Gadget Prints

Make a stamp pad by putting many layers of <u>paper towels</u> in a <u>pie plate</u> and soaking them with <u>paint</u>. Have one stamp pad for every two or three children. Collect <u>things that will print</u>—an old potato masher, little cars with wheels, and spools. Show the Threes how to press these onto the stamp pad and then press them onto a piece of paper.

What made that print, Jaime?

At another time, cut crisp fruits and vegetables such as apples or squash in half to use with the stamp pad.

 in or out | 2–10 min | 1–6 Threes

177

Thin Markers

Bring out some <u>sturdy thin watercolor markers</u> for your Threes to try out with <u>small pieces of paper</u>. Look at the markers with the Threes before they use them. Talk about not pressing too hard and putting the tops back on when done. Also talk about the thin lines the markers will make. Let the children draw with the markers in their own way.

You made a face with the markers, Karen.
I see it has a blue nose.
What else does it have?

Threes can

- handle small things easily
- draw simple designs

 in or out 2–10 min 1–6 Threes

178

Yarn and Ribbon Pictures

Have <u>washable white glue in small squeeze bottles</u> for your Threes to use. Put the glue out on a table covered with <u>newspaper</u>. Add <u>yarn and ribbon scraps</u> for the children to glue to <u>pieces of paper</u>.
    Talk about how a little glue works well. Gently help the Threes use the right amount of glue to make things stick.

Good, Sarah. You are using a little dot of glue to make the yarn stick.

Threes can

- use glue in a squeeze bottle

 indoors 3–15 min 1–4 Threes

179

Threes can

- draw simple designs
- follow two-step directions

Paper Plate Masks

Look at some pictures of masks or some real masks with your Threes. Then cut eye holes in paper plates for your Threes to make into masks. Have the children use watercolor markers to color their masks in their own way. Let each child help you staple yarn or cloth strips to the plate so that it can be tied. Have a mirror nearby so children can see themselves in the masks they made. Talk about the different ways the Threes decorated their masks.

Matthew, you drew a nose and mouth on your mask.
You colored yours with lots of colors, Andre.

Try this before Halloween to help children get comfortable with masks. But do mask activities at other times, too.

 in or out　　 5–20 min　　 1–6 Threes

180

Threes can

- draw simple forms and figures

Sand Drawings

Put a thin layer (about ½ inch) of sand in a shallow box or tray for each child. Show the children how they can make designs in the sand with their fingers. The designs will show up better if the bottom of the box or tray is much darker or lighter than the sand color. Show children how to smooth sand over designs to make them disappear.

You made wavy lines with all your fingers together, Sherry.

 in or out　　 2–10 min　　 1–4 Threes

181

Threes can

- tell about their art
- be proud of things they make

Showing Artwork

Give Threes a chance to tell their friends about the <u>artwork</u> they have done. Have one child at a time show his work to a small group of Threes. Ask questions to help the child say a little about the art work.

What did you make, Tim?
What did you use to make this picture?
Did anyone else paint today?

Help the child put his work up in the art gallery.

 in or out 1–2 min 3–6 Threes

182

Threes can

- paste
- understand *rough* and *smooth*

Texture Collage

Put out on a <u>low table two dishpans with small pieces of textured paper and cloth.</u> Have smooth things such as shiny papers and silky cloth in one dishpan, and rough things like fine sandpaper in the other. Give each child some <u>paste</u> and a piece of <u>colored paper.</u>

Talk about the smooth things and the rough things as the children feel and paste them.

What are you going to paste on first, Evan?
A rough piece. Look at Jessie.
Her picture is made of smooth pieces.

 indoors 5–10 min 1–6 Threes

183

Threes can

- paint with a brush
- name a few colors
- do simple comparing

Great Big Pictures

Hang very big sheets of paper from a <u>roll of paper</u> on a wall out-doors. Have one sheet for each child. Put out <u>tempera paints</u> in a <u>paint cup holder</u> so that children can paint huge pictures. Use painters' brushes 1″ to 3″ wide. Let the children paint in their own way.

Talk about *big* and *small*. Help the children look at and compare their own designs with those of their friends.

You used mostly green paint, Latoya.
You made great big designs.
What did Jeremy do?

 outdoors | 3–10 min | **#** 1–5 Threes

184

Threes can

- follow two-step directions
- paint with a brush

Watercolor paintings

Put out <u>watercolor paints</u> with <u>small, sturdy brushes</u> for your Threes to use. Begin with two of the three primary paint colors (red, yellow, or blue). Have <u>margarine tubs filled with clean water</u> and <u>paper towels</u> ready. Wet a piece of white paper for each child.

Show them how to dip a brush into water, swirl it in a color, and paint on <u>paper</u>. Show them how to clean brushes in water as they change colors.

Talk about how the colors spread out on the paper, and what happens when colors mix together.

Look, Joel. You're getting orange.
How do you think you made orange?

Children can use paper towels to blot too-wet papers or brushes.
Rinse and blot paints dry when done to keep colors clean.

 in or out | 5–20 min | **#** 1–6 Threes

185

Sand and Glue Pictures

Show your Threes how to place a piece of <u>paper</u> into a <u>shallow box</u>. Let them squeeze <u>white glue</u> onto the paper in a design. Then have them sprinkle <u>sand</u> over the glue and carefully lift the paper so that the extra sand falls into the box.

Make this more fun by putting out colored sand in empty spice bottles that have covers with holes big enough for the fine sand to pass through. Color sand by mixing it with a little <u>dry tempera paint powder</u>.

You are letting the extra sand roll off the paper now.
What made the sand stick on the paper?

Threes can

- use glue in squeeze bottles
- make simple designs

 in or out 5–10 min 1–2 Threes

186

Using Tape

Give Threes chances to use <u>tape</u>. Help them use tape to hang up pictures they make, to seal papers they fold, or to attach small papers to a larger piece in a design. You will probably have to cut the pieces of tape for the Threes to use. Put lots of short pieces on the edge of a table for them to take.

Put the tape on the edge of the paper, James.
Now put the paper on the bigger piece.
Good! Now press it down.
It's sticking!

Threes can

- use tape with adult help

 indoors 1–5 min 1–5 Threes

187

Threes can

- tell about their artwork

Picture Stories

Give children <u>large pieces of paper</u> to draw on. Fold under the bottom part of the paper, about two or three inches from the bottom edge, so that they do not draw on that part. Let the children do a drawing on the part of the paper that is left.

When they are done, ask them to tell you about their drawings. Unfold the bottom of the paper and use that space to print what the child says. Read the child's words back to her.

Let me read what you said about your picture, Lashawna.
It says, "This is mommy and this is me."

 in or out 2–3 min 1–5 Threes

188

Threes can

- fingerpaint

Fingerpaint Prints

Have your Threes <u>fingerpaint</u> on a <u>tray</u>. Ask each child to tell you when he has made a design in the paint that he wants to keep as a print on paper. When the child is ready, have him wash and dry his hands. Then put his name on the back of a <u>piece of paper</u>. Help him gently smooth the front of the paper onto the paint and carefully lift it off. Talk about the print the child has made. Hang it up, or place it on a flat surface to dry.

We have to let someone else fingerpaint on the tray now.
You will be able to take this fingerpaint print home to show your mom, Charlotte.

 in or out 3–10 min 1–4 Threes

189

Crayon Rubbings

Put paper clips, leaves, or other flat objects on a table that is protected with newspaper. Cover them with a piece of paper and tape the paper down so that it won't move. Have the child color over the whole paper with the flat side of a crayon. Talk about the shapes that appear like magic.

Look, Ricky! What is this shape?
Color on it some more.
Then we'll see the whole thing.

Threes can

■ use crayons

 in or out   2–10 min   1–4 Threes

190

Sand Casting

Put one or two inches of sand in the bottom of a small, flat cardboard box. Have one box for each child. Wet the sand with a little water. Put out a tray of pebbles, shells, and other nature things that the children collected on walks outside. Let each child choose some of these and place them on the sand. For every box, mix plaster of Paris with water in a cottage cheese container until it is as thick as sour cream. Pour it over the sand. Press into the plaster a piece of paper with the child's name and a loop of string to use as a hanger. When the plaster is dry, lift it out and brush off the extra sand.

Let's look at all the things you put in the sand, Denise.
Can you tell me what they are?

Threes can

■ make a design

 in or out   5–20 min   1–4 Threes

Art Area Ideas

- Put easy-to-use art materials on a low shelf for Threes to use freely every day: sturdy crayons or watercolor markers, lots of paper, safe scissors.

- Put out other art materials as well for older Threes who can do more on their own.

- Let children use art materials in their own way. Don't show children something you have made and expect them to copy it. Let them use play dough to make their own original forms without cookie cutters. Then they will see the many shapes they can make with their own hands and imaginations.

- Show children where art materials are stored by putting picture labels on the shelf.

- Store art materials in many small containers instead of one big one. Giving one or two children a small container of art materials for themselves to use cuts down on fighting.

- Have art materials that need more help from you ready to bring out when you are free to watch them. Don't have all the children work at one time. Add these activities to the many other child-directed activities children can choose to do.

- Make sure that everyone who wants to gets a chance to do artwork. Keep the same special art activity out for more than one day if it is popular.

- Talk to children about their work. Show them you enjoy what they have made. Mention colors, shapes, and materials they used to make the work. Encourage children to talk about what they have made as they become able to do so.

- Protect the floor, tables, and walls in the art area. Accidents can easily happen with art materials.

- Have clean-up things, such as sponges, paper towels, and water, ready for children to use. Teach your Threes how to use these.

- Take the paper off crayons so they are easier to use.

- Cut the handles of paintbrushes to about 6″ so that they are easier for Threes to control. Smooth rough edges. Cut down legs on easels if easels are too high and can't be lowered.

- Use art materials outdoors as well as indoors, especially for messy activities such as fingerpainting.

- Put the children's artwork on display low on the wall or on the backs of bookshelves where the children can easily see their work. Change the display often.

Recipes

(Watch carefully to see that children don't try to eat any of the art materials.)

Brush Paint Recipe

This recipe will help keep down your painting costs because it uses very little dry tempera paint.

1. Mix 1 cup bentonite (an inexpensive clay product that you can get at a pottery supply company) with 2 quarts hot water.
2. Let the mixture stand in a large container with a lid for two or three days. Stir each day. It will be sticky and lumpy to begin with.
3. When the bentonite is smooth and thick, pour it into smaller jars.
4. Add 3 or more tablespoons of dry tempera paint to each jar. Stir.
5. Add more paint if the color is not bright enough. Add more water if the paint is too thick.
6. Pour paint into smaller unbreakable cups for children to use.
7. Keep jars covered.

Soap Fingerpaint

1. Mix 3 cups Ivory Snow Soap Flakes with one cup of water.
2. Beat with an eggbeater until it's thick.
3. Color with a few drops of food color. (You can also try shaving cream as fingerpaint.)

Easy Fingerpaint

1. Mix 2 cups of flour with $\frac{1}{4}$ cup of water. Add more water if needed and stir until the mixture is as thick as white glue.
2. Add a few drops of food color or a half teaspoon of tempera paint powder and mix. For a deeper color, add more food color or powder.
3. Let each child fingerpaint with 2 or 3 tablespoons of the mixture on large, sturdy paper, a plastic tray, a cookie sheet, or a table top.

Cooked Fingerpaint

1. Mix $\frac{1}{2}$ cup flour with 1 cup water. Stir until smooth.
2. Bring to a boil, still stirring. Cook until it is thick as pudding.
3. Cool.
4. Thin with dishwashing liquid until it is right for fingerpainting.
5. Add a few drops of food coloring.

Play Dough

1. Mix $1\frac{1}{2}$ cups of flour, $\frac{1}{2}$ cup salt, $\frac{1}{4}$ cup vegetable oil, about $\frac{1}{4}$ cup water, and a few drops of food coloring. (The color mixes most easily when added to the water.)
2. Knead until the dough is smooth and the color is well mixed.
3. Add more flour if the mixture is too wet. Add more water if the mixture is too dry.

4. Put in an airtight container. A coffee can works well. Don't use a plastic bag because it makes the dough too wet.
5. Store in the refrigerator.

Cup Holder

You can use a paper milk carton in a half pint, pint, or quart size. Rinse the carton out. Cut off one side of the carton. The open box that is left becomes a holder for two to three paint cups.

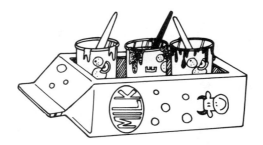

String Things

Collect anything that has a hole in it large enough for a coated wire or yarn with a taped end to pass through to use as things to string. Look for colored wires where telephone-repair workers have been at work, or ask your local telephone company for scraps. Cut plastic straws of different colors into 1″ lengths, punch holes in small shapes of colored paper, cut or punch holes in small foam or styrofoam shapes. Save large buttons, spools from thread, and large beads. Let parents know you are collecting things for children to string. Ask them to look out for things you could use.

Pencils

Most lead pencils are numbered to tell how soft the lead is. A number 2 pencil is usually a good dark writing pencil. Thick carpenter's pencils also work well. Most colored pencils do not make bright colors.

Materials and Notes

Blocks

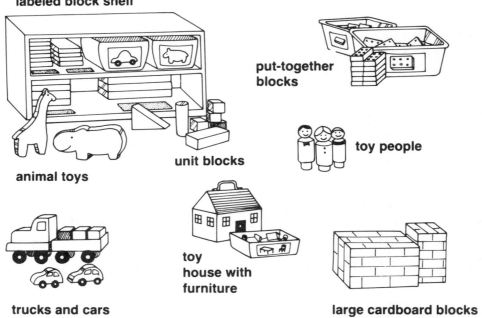

labeled block shelf

put-together blocks

animal toys

unit blocks

toy people

trucks and cars

toy house with furniture

large cardboard blocks

- Encourage both boys and girls to play in the block area.
- Show interest in what your Threes do with blocks. Try building with them and talking about what they build.
- Make sure children understand a few simple rules for using the blocks:

  don't knock the blocks down because someone can get hurt

  build in the block area, but not too close to the shelves

  get blocks from the shelves, not from other people's buildings

  walk around other people's buildings so they won't fall down

  put blocks and toys back on the labeled shelves.
- Make the block area interesting by changing the things on the shelves.
- Check blocks and block toys often for sharp edges, rust, or splinters.
- See Block Area Ideas on page 199.

Activity Checklist

Blocks

Block play for Threes includes use of any materials that can be stacked, such as colored cubes, wooden unit blocks, and foam, plastic, or cardboard blocks. Threes use blocks for loading and unloading games, to make tall stacks, as objects in pretend play, and later in the year, to build structures.

Check for each age group	*36–42 mo*	*42–48 mo*
1. Suitable indoor area is set up for block play (flat building surface, rug to cut down on noise, open storage shelf for blocks, enough blocks for several children to use at the same time).	—	—
2. Some outdoor block play is available with unit blocks, big hollow blocks and boards, or cardboard blocks.	—	—
3. Many kinds of blocks are used daily, such as plastic, wooden, colored, big, and small blocks.	—	—
4. Blocks used are safe for children (nontoxic coverings, no sharp edges, lightweight).	—	—
5. Adult talks with child about his block play (including how block looks, sounds, or feels; what he is doing with the blocks).	—	—
6. Blocks are sorted and stored in an organized way (separated by shape, size, and type).	—	—
7. Blocks are available on low, open shelves or in other open storage for independent use by children.	—	—
8. Shelves or other open storage areas are labeled with pictures to make clean-up easier for children.	—	—
9. Children can use blocks during play times, morning and afternoon.	—	—
10. Accessories for block play are added to blocks (boxes or wagons for loading play, little people or animals, little cars).	—	—

191

Threes can

- understand where things belong
- show how to use toys

Tour of the Block Area

Set up a block area with wooden or plastic unit blocks, a set of big cardboard blocks, and some block toys, such as small cars, airplanes, toy people, and animals. Add a toy house, barn, airport, or garage. To help children remember where things go, put picture labels and block outlines on the low, open shelves. Visit the block area with a few Threes at a time. Help children show their friends how they can:

    take blocks off a shelf to build
    take down a tower carefully
    put blocks away in the right place
    put toys away
    walk carefully around someone else's building

 indoors   5–7 min   2–4 Threes

192

Threes can

- stack blocks
- begin to take turns

Taking Turns with Blocks

Sit in the block area and begin to build a tower. Ask one or two children if they would like to help you. Take turns adding blocks to the tower. Ask two or three children to build a tower together. Help them take turns adding blocks.

Nicky put his block on. Now it's Susie's turn.
Nicky, you can get another block while Susie puts hers on the tower.

 indoors   4–10 min   1–4 Threes

193

Threes can

- begin to share

Spaces to Build

When you have several Threes who want to work in the <u>block area</u>, make sure no one builds too near the shelves. Help the Threes leave a clear path to the blocks for everyone. Give each child or small group its own space. Use <u>masking tape</u> on the floor to mark spaces, if you wish. Remind children to get blocks and toys from the shelves and to be careful of others' buildings.

I like the way you walked past Jinsy's blocks.
You went close, but you were so careful you didn't knock over her tower.

 indoors 2–6 min 2–4 Threes

194

Threes can

- use some size words

Talk About Block Shapes

As Threes play with <u>blocks</u>, talk about the shapes they are using. Tell the names of the shapes, use words for the block sizes, and say more about how the shapes look.

That's a rectangle you're holding, Terry.
See the corners of the rectangle?

Ask easy questions to see what the children can say about the blocks.

Is the rectangle big or small?
Can you find a smaller rectangle?

 in or out 1–2 min 1–2 Threes

195

Threes can

- match easy shapes
- help clean up

Sorting Game at Clean-up Time

Make cleaning up <u>blocks and block toys</u> into a sorting game. Show one block or toy to your Threes. Ask them to find all the others just like that one. Help them put the ones they find in the right place on the shelf. Then work on the next block shape or toy.

That's great! We found all the square blocks and put them away. Now which kind of block should we work on?

OK, let's find all the small rectangles.

 indoors   5–10 min   1–4 Threes

196

Threes can

- stack up to nine blocks
- use size words

Tall and Short Towers

Build lots of block towers with your Threes. Make some that are tall and some that are short. When everyone has finished building, walk around the towers. Point to each and ask whether it's tall or short. If the children are interested, count how many <u>blocks</u> are in each. Talk about how more blocks can make a taller tower when the towers are built of same-size blocks.

Yes, this is a very tall tower!

Do you see one that is taller?

Let's see how many blocks we used here.

 in or out   7–15 min   1–4 Threes

197

Threes can

- put four blocks in a row

Road Building

Look at a picture book about cars and roads with your Threes. Then put out a dishpan of little cars in the block area. Tell the Threes that you need a road for the cars to go on. Help them build a road made out of blocks. See if they will move the cars along the block road. Add a little toy house, garage, or airport. Talk about how the cars can go to each of these places on the road.

My car is going to the garage to get some gasoline.
Where's your car going, Cheryl?

Show the children how to add curves, corners, and side roads to one long main road.

 indoors 5–20 min 1–5 Threes

198

Threes can

- do simple pretend play

Toy Trains

Read a short picture book about trains to your Threes, or look at several train pictures with them. Put in the block area a sturdy little train set with cars that hook together easily. If there are tracks, show the children how the train can go on the tracks. Help them stack a few towers for train stations. Put out a container of inch cubes or little toy people to ride on the train.

Toot, toot. Here comes Gerald's train.
Gerald, stop at the station so Brian can load some blocks.

 indoors 5–20 min 1–2 Threes

199

Threes can

- say furniture names
- do simple pretend play

Dolls with Blocks

Bring several dolls and stuffed animals to the block area. Add some small cloth pieces for doll blankets and some doll dishes. Ask the children to help you make some houses for the babies.

What does baby need in her house?

Help children make houses for the dolls, with beds and any other things the children name. Ask questions to find out what else the house needs.

Where will baby eat? Where will she sleep?

 indoors | 5–20 min | 1–4 Threes

200

Threes can

- do simple pretend play
- put blocks in a row

Big Block Train, Bus, or Plane

Read a book about people on a train, bus, or airplane with your Threes. Talk about how all the people sit in rows behind a driver. Talk about what the driver is called and some of the things he or she might do or say. Talk about the passengers, too. Help your Threes use big cardboard blocks to make a train, bus, or plane. Then help them take turns being driver or passengers.

Annabel is the pilot, and she said "Coming in for a landing!" Let's sit down to be safe when the plane lands!

 in or out | 5–20 min | 1–8 Threes

201

Threes can

■ make a bridge of three blocks

Lots of Bridges

Build a <u>block road</u> or set up a <u>little train track</u>. Ask children to make lots of bridges for the <u>cars</u> or <u>train</u> to go under. Show them how to make a bridge that goes over the road or track. Then see if they can carefully push the cars or train through the bridge. Show the children that they can rebuild a bridge if it has fallen over.

I'm sorry your bridge fell over, Billy.
Do you want to build it again?
Let's see if this small car will go under the bridge.

 indoors 5–20 min 1–4 Threes

202

Threes can

■ talk about things they know
■ help clean up

Bringing Blocks Outdoors

On a nice day, tell your Threes that they can bring some <u>blocks</u> outside to build with. Ask the children to tell some ways they can bring blocks outside easily. For example, talk about having every child carry a few blocks or putting blocks in a <u>wagon or cart</u>. Then let children bring the blocks outside in the way they think will be easiest.

Once outside, have them use the blocks for building. When it's time to go in, help children collect all the blocks and return them to the shelves indoors. Make sure all the blocks are clean before you bring them indoors.

 outdoors 15–30 min 1–15 Threes

203

Threes can

- stack up to nine blocks
- talk about things they see

Stacking Things

Have <u>homemade things for your Threes to stack</u> in place of blocks. Try lots of margarine tubs with lids, coffee cans with lids, or empty cardboard food boxes. Keep these in a <u>big box</u> in the <u>block area</u>. As children make different kinds of towers, see if they can talk about the kinds of stacking toys they use.

What did you use to make your tower, Rebecca?
I see an oatmeal box. What else is there?

Make sure that all homemade toys are sturdy and safe and have no rough or sharp edges.

 in or out   5–15 min   1–4 Threes

204

Threes can

- do simple block building

Building a Big House

Work with your Threes to build a house that they can pretend to live in. Make an outline with <u>blocks</u> for the outside walls. Leave an opening for the door. Have the children build up the walls. Help them think of what they need inside the house.

Where is the door to your house?
Good, Peter. You made a bed for your baby in the bedroom.

At another time, try building an airport for airplanes or a parking lot for cars as a group project.

 in or out   10–20 min   1–4 Threes

205

Threes can

■ use four blocks to close in a space

Animal Cages

Look with your Threes at <u>pictures of animals in cages, pens or other fenced-in areas</u>. Talk about the pictures with the Threes. Hang the pictures in the <u>block area</u> where the children can see them. Put out some <u>toy farm and zoo animals</u> like the ones in the pictures. Ask the children to build homes to put the animals in.

You're building a house for the lion, David.
Do you know what a lion's home is called?

 indoors   3–15 min   # 1–5 Threes

206

Threes can

■ say how things are same and different

Same and Different Blocks

Show <u>two different blocks</u> to your Threes. For example, show a square and a rectangle. Ask them questions to help them tell how the blocks are the same or different from each other.

Are they the same color?
Are they the same size?
Are they the same shape?
Do they both have corners or curves?
Are they made of the same thing?

Help the Threes compare <u>several different kinds of blocks</u>: cylinder and square, big and little rectangles.

 in or out   4–8 min   # 1–15 Threes

207

Threes can

- use small building toys
- tell about a thing they make

Other Toys for Building

Have small building toys, such as table blocks, Lego Bricks, Tinkertoys, Lincoln Logs, or Bristle Blocks in labeled dishpans on a low, open shelf. Let your Threes use these to build in their own way. As they build, talk about the pieces they use. See if they can tell you something about their work.

What did you make, Sheila?
Oh yes, it is an airplane.
I see this long piece is the wings.

 in or out   3–20 min   1–2 Threes

208

Threes can

- lift big things
- stack blocks

Big Boxes as Outdoor Blocks

Bring in eight or ten big sturdy cartons or storage boxes for your Threes to use as blocks outdoors on a dry day. Tape the boxes closed with masking tape. Let the children stack them and build with them in many ways. Talk with them about the ways they use the boxes. They can also use these boxes as houses or boats.

You've stacked three boxes, Charles.
Are you going to put another on top?
Can you reach?

Throw away boxes when they become worn out.

 outdoors   3–20 min   1–4 Threes

209

Threes can

- understand some words that tell "where"

In, On, or Next to?

Build with your Threes a block garage for a toy car. See if they will place the car in, on, over, or next to the garage when you ask. Ask the child to move the car in a fun way to turn this into a game.

Your car is a flying car!
Make it fly over the garage.
Now it's landing.
Can you make it stop next to the garage?

 indoors | 2–7 min | 1–2 Threes

210

Threes can

- say furniture names
- do simple pretend play

Block Furniture

Ask the children to build furniture for themselves out of big cardboard blocks. Find out what they will do to make a bed, a chair, or a couch. Talk with them about what they have built.

I know what Dana has made.
She stacked two blocks on top of each other and is sitting on them.
What did Dana make, Robin?

Add a few housekeeping toys, such as blankets or tea sets to add more fun.

 in or out | 5–20 min | 1–4 Threes

211

Threes can

■ recognize some size and shape words

"Which Block? Game

Sit with a few Threes in the <u>block area</u> to play this "go and get it" game. Ask each child to bring a block from the shelf like the one you describe for him.

Danny, can you bring me a long block from the shelf?
Anna, can you bring me a curved block?

When the children bring their blocks, talk about each. Then see how they can put them together to make a block building.

Yes, Danny. This is a long block. It's a long rectangle.
Can it go on Sharika's cylinder?

 indoors   3–7 min   1–7 Threes

212

Threes can

■ do simple pretend play
■ stack blocks

Build a Little Town

Make a <u>masking tape road</u> on the floor in the <u>block area</u>, or draw a road with a <u>permanent marker</u> on part of an <u>old shower curtain or sheet</u> and spread this out on the block area floor. Encourage your Threes to make simple buildings along the road. Then let them add people and car toys. Talk about the town they have made.

Where's your car going, Antoine?
Is it going to the farm?

 indoors   5–20 min   1–4 Threes

213

Threes can

- do simple pretend play
- enjoy sand play

Blocks in Sand

Bring <u>unit blocks</u> or <u>smaller blocks</u> to use in the <u>sand table</u>. Let the Threes play freely with the blocks in sand. Talk about how the children hide blocks or stand them up at different angles. Add some <u>animal toys</u> and some <u>twigs</u> the children have collected. Then watch how your Threes play with these things. Clean the blocks before they are put back. Make sure the blocks do not get wet.

What did you build for the zebra, Fay? A fence?
I like the way you made trees out of these twigs.

 in or out   5–20 min   1–4 Threes

214

Threes can

- do simple block building
- pretend play

Blocks and Boats

Look at a <u>picture book about boats</u> with your Threes. Then make a <u>pretend blue lake or ocean</u> to use in the <u>block area</u>. For the water you can use a <u>sturdy blue piece of material</u> or <u>a piece of cardboard</u> that you and the Threes colored blue. Put your lake or ocean on the floor. Help the Threes remember some of the things they would see in water, such as boats or a dock. Help them use <u>blocks</u> to pretend about these things.

Toot, toot! My tugboat is coming to the dock!
Are you building a bigger dock, Donna?

 indoors   7–25 min   1–4 Threes

215

Threes can

■ do simple block
building

What Stacks, What Doesn't?

Build a tower with a few Threes, using <u>blocks of many shapes</u>. As you add each block, look at the tower and the block you are going to add. Try out and talk about the different ways the block could be added. Help the children guess when a block will balance and when it won't.

Do you think this square block will stay on top of this triangle or will it fall? Let's try and see.
Oh! What happened?

 in or out 3–7 min 1–3 Threes

216

Threes can

■ do simple sorting
■ stack blocks

Build with One Block Shape

Sort <u>table block shapes</u> into <u>several dishpans</u> with your Threes. Then let each child choose a shape to build with. Talk about the shape the child is using and what the child does with the blocks.

You're building with the square blocks, Kitty.
You've lined them up in a long line.

 in or out 3–7 min 1–3 Threes

217

Threes can

- do simple block building

Cardboard Blocks with Boards Outside

Bring <u>big cardboard blocks</u> outside on a nice dry day. Add some <u>three- to four-foot smooth, lightweight wooden boards</u> for your Threes to use with these blocks. Watch to see the ways they use these things together. See if the children build bridges, ramps, or see-saws.

Can you go under the bridge, Joshua?
I can see that it is safe.

Help children be careful as they move the boards so that no one is bumped. Be sure that blocks or boards won't fall if Threes climb on or go under them.

 outdoors   5–20 min   1–5 Threes

218

Threes can

- count three to ten blocks
- play with blocks

How Many Blocks?

Count the number of <u>blocks</u> your Threes use in their simple block buildings. Help each child point to one block at a time as she counts with you.

How many blocks did you use in this tower, Janet?
Let's count.
One, two, three, four, five, six.

 in or out   1–3 min   1–2 Threes

219

Threes can

- do simple block building
- recognize rooms in house

Build Your Own House

Put out <u>small, sturdy doll house furniture</u> in the <u>block area</u>. Ask children to build houses for the furniture. Tell them they can put furniture in the rooms. Watch to see the different ways your Threes build a house. Talk about what they do.

You made a square house with four long blocks, Anita.
Which room is this, with the bed?

 indoors | 3–15 min | 1–4 Threes

220

Threes can

- tell about things they make

Block Talk

When a child has built something with <u>blocks</u>, see if he will tell you a little about what he did. Ask questions to get him to say more.

What did you build, Jeremy?
Oh, a house for the daddy and the dog.
What do they like to do in the house?
The dog jumps out?
Show me how he does that.

Try tape recording the things a child says about his block building once in a while and play them back for the child to hear.

 in or out | 2–4 min | 1–2 Threes

Block Area Ideas for Threes

- Find a place for blocks that is out of traffic. A corner away from doorways works well.

- Make the block area big enough for at least three children to play in at the same time.

- Use open shelves no taller than the children to store blocks and the toys used with blocks.

- Label each place on the shelves with a picture of what goes there. Use outlines of blocks, or paste cut-outs of the blocks right on the shelf. Put the pictures near the front of the shelf and show the block with the long side to the front. The best way to get children to know where shapes belong is to start putting the block in the right place and have them copy you.

- Keep small toys to use with blocks in separate boxes, each labeled with a picture of the toys. Have small people, animals, little trucks, and airplanes to use with blocks. Have a separate box for each type of toy.

- Put the heavier blocks and toys on the lower shelves, so that they will be easier for the children to take out and put back by themselves.

- Put a flat rug that is good to build on in the block area to show the Threes where to play with the blocks. Remind them to build on the rug. If you do not have a flat rug, show the children how to build on a large, flat board so that their towers will have a steady base.

- Have different kinds of blocks: large cardboard or large wooden hollow blocks, wooden unit blocks, foam blocks, and different kinds of table blocks, such as Lego Bricks, inch cubes, and Lincoln Logs. Keep all of these organized in their own spaces. You do not need to have all of these kinds of blocks out at one time. Put some away and take out others to keep children interested.

- Put up pictures of bridges and buildings to add interest in building with blocks. Take pictures of the buildings children have made. Hang them where the children can see and talk about the pictures. Make these into a book if you wish.

- Have wooden or plastic houses, airports, barns, and filling stations near the blocks for the children to use with little toy people and cars. Keep these heavy play buildings on the bottom shelves or on the floor.

- Show children how to take the blocks off the shelves carefully and how to put the blocks back without knocking the buildings down. Show children how proud you are when they are careful around blocks. Show them how to take a building down carefully.

- Have some block play outdoors. If blocks can't be stored outside, take them out in a box and let children play on a rug. A wagon is a good way to get blocks outdoors. Have the children help take the blocks out and put them back on the shelves.

Materials and Notes

Dramatic Play

activity boxes

hats, purses

dolls

small furniture

pots, pans, tea set

water for washing

- Have many things to help Threes make believe: dishes, pots, pans, dolls, doll blankets, beds and carriages, dress-up clothes, and work hats.

- Try to have two or three of the same things so children can play side by side instead of fighting.

- Make sure that what you have in the play area is kept clean and is safe to use; shorten clothes and disinfect shoes.

- Make pretend play more fun by putting out different activity boxes and changing the playhouse into a store or a hospital for a few days.

- Whenever you can, look at books and pictures with the children to give them more information about what they are pretending to be.

- Encourage both boys and girls to enjoy all kinds of pretend play.

- Ask parents for help with collecting things to use for pretend play. One parent might help shorten dress-up clothes. Another might have painters' hats for painters' play or an old hose for the gas station activity box.

- See Dramatic Play Area Ideas on page 217.

Activity Checklist

Dramatic Play

Dramatic play for Threes includes pretend play with dolls, stuffed animals, housekeeping toys, community helper props, and other things children use when they act out what they see happening every day. Adults can help Threes get new information for play by providing field trips, reading books, and providing props for work roles in addition to housekeeping. Threes enjoy make-believe play on their own, but sometimes need adult help to solve problems.

Check for each age group	*36 – 42 mo*	*42 – 48 mo*
1. Dramatic play props are available daily, both indoors and outdoors.	—	—
2. A variety of materials are available for play, including housekeeping things, props for job/community helper play, and fantasy.	—	—
3. Housekeeping area with organized materials on a low shelf and some child-sized furniture is available for child's independent use.	—	—
4. Materials are sturdy, safe, and clean.	—	—
5. Dolls are different races, male and female.	—	—
6. Additional toys and props are stored but handy so that they can be used often.	—	—
7. Clear, large pictures showing family scenes and women and men of different races and ages in work roles are hung where children can see them.	—	—
8. Adult helps children get ideas for play by adding props, reading stories, and taking children on fieldtrips.	—	—
9. Adult interacts with children: talks about play, helps to settle an argument, or begins play for child to copy.	—	—
10. Both boys and girls are encouraged to use materials in their own way.	—	—

221

Threes can

- do simple pretend play
- answer easy questions

Play House

Set up a simple playhouse in a corner of the room. (See Dramatic Play Area Ideas on page 217.) Include <u>small furniture</u>, such as a table and chairs, a low, open shelf, a doll bed, and a pretend stove and sink. Add <u>dolls, pots and pans, and an unbreakable tea set</u>. To help Threes at clean-up time, put <u>picture labels of toys</u> on the shelf and on other places where things go.

Let your Threes play freely in this playhouse. Ask easy questions to help the children talk about their play.

What are you cooking, Kevin?
Breakfast for baby?
What's baby going to eat for breakfast?

 indoors   5–15 min   1–4 Threes

222

Threes can

- put on and take off simple clothes

Dress-up Fun

Collect <u>easy-to-put-on men and women's clothes</u> for your Threes to use in dress-up play. Include hats, shoes, dresses, skirts, jackets, pants, and purses. Shorten clothes to make them safe. Let children put on these big people's clothes and pretend in their own way. Have a large, unbreakable mirror nearby for children to use.

You and Louise are all dressed up, Kendra.
Did you button those big buttons yourself?

Make sure that there are enough clothes for all who want to play, but don't put out too many clothes at once. Then you can add new interest to dress-ups by changing the clothes you put out. Be sure to keep all clothes clean. Spray hats and shoes to disinfect. Have children wear socks when using shoes.

 in or out   5–20 min   1–4 Threes

223

Putting Babies to Bed

Put <u>dolls</u> and a <u>doll bed</u> with <u>little blankets</u> in the play house area. For a doll bed, you can use a <u>dishpan</u> or a very sturdy box. Tell a <u>bedtime story</u>, or show some <u>pictures of babies sleeping</u>. Then let your Threes play in the play house. See what they will tell you about their play.

Why is the baby going to bed, Tony?
He's sleepy? I'll be quiet so he can sleep.
Is he getting up now?
That was a short nap!

Threes can

■ do simple pretend play

 indoors 3–10 min 1–4 Threes

224

Telephone Talk

Have <u>several toy telephones</u> in the playhouse. Let the children play with these freely. As the child holds a phone, pick up another and talk with her. Use lots of words she knows, and ask a few questions to help the child talk to you. Encourage Threes to talk to each other on the toy telephones, too.

Hi, Becca. Who do you want to talk with on the phone?
B.J., Becca wants to talk to you on the telephone!

Threes can

■ do simple pretend play
■ play with another child

 indoors 1–4 min 1–2 Threes

225

Threes can

- do simple pretend play
- say words for many things

Kitchen Play

Make a kitchen play activity box. Include kitchen things, such as dull plastic knives, forks and spoons, a potato masher, a strainer, big cooking spoons, cooks' hats and aprons, measuring cups, and a whisk. Put in pictures of people using some of these things, too.

Look at and talk about the pictures and all the things with your Threes. Then hang up the pictures and put the things into the play-house area. Let the children play and have fun.

What are you stirring with, Henry?
Yes, the big spoon.
And you're stirring with the whisk, Juan.

 in or out | 5–15 min | 1–4 Threes

226

Threes can

- copy adult actions
- talk about familiar things

Changing Baby

Make a changing baby activity box with squares of cloth that will make doll-sized diapers, a few newborn-sized rubber pants, and empty baby powder and lotion bottles. Look at all the things in the box with your Threes. See who knows what each thing is and what it's for. Show the children how you diaper a baby doll. Then put the box out for the Threes to use on their own. You may have to help a little by putting masking tape on diapers to hold them on.

My baby is crying.
Oh dear, Sandy. My baby must be wet.
Could you change her for me?

 in or out | 5–15 min | 1–4 Threes

227

Threes can

- copy adult actions
- enjoy water play

Laundry Day

Tie a <u>rope</u> about two feet high between two trees or two chairs outside. Put <u>buckets of soapy water</u> out in the middle of the play area along with some <u>clean rags</u> or small <u>items of clothing</u>. Let the children pretend to wash and then hang things up on the line to dry. Show the children how to wring out the clothes. Also help them use <u>clothespins</u>. Make sure the children wear <u>waterproof aprons</u> if they need to stay dry.

Carl, you're washing the doll's dress.
It's so nice and clean.
Now what will you do with it?

 outdoors | 5–15 min | 1–6 Threes

228

Threes can

- do simple pretend play

Sandbox Kitchen

On a nice day, check to see that the sandbox is clean. Then bring out a box of <u>pots, pans, unbreakable dishes, and spoons</u>. Make sure there is a <u>board to place things on</u> in the sandbox. Let the children play house in the sandbox. If the sand is damp, show them how to make a cake by patting damp sand into a pan, turning the pan over onto the board, and carefully removing the pan.

Kevin is mixing things in a pot.
What are you cooking, Kevin?

After play is over, have the children help you wash the things and put them back in the box.

 outdoors | 10–15 min | 1–6 Threes

229

Threes can

- help tell a story
- do simple pretend play

Story Act-Out

Read or tell a <u>very familiar story</u> that your Threes will be able to act out. Figure out the different parts children could play. Don't worry if you have more than one child for each part. Let everyone act out the parts they want. Then tell the story as the children act. Give some direction, but not too much. Most of all, have lots of fun.

The first little pig built his house of straw.
Now, let's all be first little pigs and pretend to build our houses over here.

 in or out | 10–15 min | 1–15 Threes

230

Threes can

- copy adult work

Cleaning Day

On a nice day, take out some <u>small brooms, rags, sponges, and a bucket of water</u>. Show the children how to dust and wash equipment, walls, sidewalks, fences, or outdoor furniture, and then let them play freely with the materials.

Tricia, you are really cleaning that slide.
You can dry it with this old towel.

Try this indoors without the water. Or, if you are willing to clean up a wet mess, add water too.

 in or out | 3–15 min | 1–7 Threes

231

Threes can

- pretend about familiar things

Playhouse Bedroom

Set up a bedroom in the playhouse area or in another part of the room. Put <u>pillows, blankets, and a small mattress or an extra cot</u> in the play bedroom. Add some <u>dolls, doll blankets, and dishpans for doll beds</u>. Read a <u>story</u> like *Goodnight Moon,* or collect <u>pictures of people sleeping, reading, or dressing in front of a mirror</u> to help the children remember and talk about bedrooms.

Ask the parents to take pictures of the children's bedrooms, their beds, toys, and closets. Make a bedroom book with these pictures and put it in the book area.

 indoors   5–15 min   1–4 Threes

232

Threes can

- pretend about familiar things

Shower Time

Put a <u>cardboard box big enough for a child to stand in</u> into the playhouse corner. Add clean <u>shower caps</u>, <u>an old towel</u>, some <u>clean, empty shampoo bottles</u>, and a <u>wooden block that the children can use as a bar of soap</u>. Talk with the children about how all these things are used at shower or bath time. Then let them make-believe in the house with the shower as part of their play.

Did you take a shower, Aretha?
Which do you take at home, a shower or bath?

 indoors   2–7 min   1–2 Threes

233

Threes can

- do simple pretend play

Baby's Bath Time

Take some <u>washable dolls</u> outdoors. Also take out some <u>dishpans</u> with <u>warm soapy water</u> and some <u>washcloths</u>. Let the three-year-old undress a doll, and then give him a cloth to bathe the baby. Give him a towel to dry the baby doll, too. Ask questions to help the child talk about what he's doing. If you have two children using the same dishpan, see that each one has a doll and a washcloth. Remember, waterproof aprons help keep children dry.

Leshana, you're washing the baby's leg.
Wash her knees, ears, and tummy.
What will you do when you're done washing baby?

 outdoors | 3–10 min | 1–4 Threes

234

Threes can

- copy adult work

Washing Dishes

Take <u>dishpans</u> full of <u>play dishes</u> outdoors. Put some <u>water, small sponges, and dishsoap</u> into the dishpans. Let a few children at a time wash the dishes. After the dishes are washed, the children can dry them with <u>towels</u>.

Talk about who washes dishes at home and who washes dishes at school. Take a trip to the kitchen to see how dishes are washed there. If there is a dishwasher, you can talk about that, too. Collect <u>pictures</u> of different ways to wash dishes so that you can talk about dishwashing at a story time. On another day, have Threes help you wash washable toys that need cleaning. Be sure they are dry before putting them away.

 outdoors | 5–15 min | 1–4 Threes

235

Threes can

- copy adult work

Garbage Truck

Read the children a <u>book that has pictures of a garbage collector's truck</u>. Talk about what garbage collectors do. Then show them how they can make a garbage truck to clean up the yard. Put a <u>cardboard box</u> into a <u>small wagon</u> and have the children help clean up the yard. Have them wear <u>gloves</u> to be garbage collectors, and have them wash their hands after the job is done.

You're doing a very good job picking up.
The yard is getting very clean.

When the children clean up after a snack or meal, tell them they are doing clean-up work like garbage collectors.

 outdoors 5–10 min 1–4 Threes

236

Threes can

- tell how to use some familiar things
- copy adult work

Gardener Play

Collect toys your Threes can use to pretend to be gardeners—<u>toy lawn mowers, safe plastic gardening tools, a watering can, empty seed packets, and a toy wheelbarrow</u>. Read a <u>short story</u> to the children that shows people using these things to garden. Then talk about the gardening toys the children can play with. See if they know what to do with the different things.

Yes, that looks like a shovel, Darryl.
But see how small it is? It's called a trowel.
What do you think you can do with it?

Bring all the toys outside for the children to use in pretend play. Digging will be easiest in the sandbox.

 in or out 5–15 min 1–5 Threes

237

Threes can

- do simple pretend play with other children

Grocery Store

Make a little grocery store for your Threes to use in their pretend play. Put 10 to 15 clean, empty, familiar food containers on a low shelf. Add a shopping cart, a wagon, some small grocery bags, and plastic fruits and vegetables. Put two toy cash registers on a little table for a "check-out" place. Let the children play with these things in their own special three-year-old way. Talk about the things different children do in their grocery store play.

Are you buying food to cook, Betsy?
And what are you doing, William?

 in or out   3–20 min   1–5 Threes

238

Threes can

- do simple pretend play with other children

Gas Station

Put together in an activity box the things your Threes will need to play gas station—pieces of hose, 1 to 2 yards long, with nozzles attached; sturdy plastic fix-it tools, and mechanic's hats. With the children, look at a book that shows things that happen at a gas station. Ask questions to help your Threes say what they know about gas stations.

What else happens at the gas station, Tanya?

Secure the ends of hoses to the fence outside to show the children where they can bring riding toys to be fixed or filled up. Add the other things and let the children play.

 outdoors   3–20 min   1–6 Threes

239

Threes can

- copy adult work

Carpenters

Read a <u>story about carpenters</u>. Collect <u>things children can use as they pretend to be carpenters</u>. Set up a carpenter shop outdoors with two small hammers, some large pieces of 2″ styrofoam, and some roofing nails with large, flat heads. Add a toy saw, drill, and screwdriver.

Also make carpenters' tool belts so that children can carry the tools with them to the place they are fixing. Let the children pretend to be carpenters. Talk about what they are pretending to build and repair.

Watch carefully if nails or other sharp things are used for this play.

 in or out | 5–15 min | 1–4 Threes

240

Threes can

- pretend play with other children

Take a Trip

Read a <u>story</u> or show a <u>picture about taking a trip by car, bus or train</u>. Ask if anyone has ever taken such a trip, and ask him to talk about it. Suggest that you can help the children make a play car, bus, or train. Use <u>small chairs or cardboard blocks</u> for seats. Add a <u>steering wheel</u> if you have one.

Tell the children they can pack for the trip, and let them use the <u>purses and tote bags</u> in the dress-up area. Have the children take turns being the driver. You ride on the bus, too.

Where are you going, Lin?
Heather, what did you take along?

 in or out | 1–2 min | 1–7 Ones

241

Threes can

- understand the use of some familiar things
- pretend play

Playing Doctors

Put out a box of <u>doctor things</u> for the Threes to play with. Use only safe things, such as a toy or real <u>stethoscope</u>, a <u>flashlight</u>, and <u>band-aids</u>. Do not put in bottles of candy pills because you do not want children ever to take medicine alone. Show them how to use the doctor things with dolls from the playhouse. Talk about going to the doctor and what happens there.

What is the doctor looking for when he asks you to open your mouth and looks in?
Can you hear anything through the stethoscope?

For more play ideas, read a <u>book</u> about going to the doctor to the children.

 in or out　 5–15 min　 1–4 Threes

242

Threes can

- manage large buttons and snaps

Dressing Dolls

Make <u>simple doll clothes that are very easy to put on</u>. Ask parents for help with this. Have clothes that are loose or that fasten with one large button or big snaps. Keep these in a dishpan on a low shelf for Threes to use. Sit with the children when it's time to dress babies. When the <u>dolls</u> are dressed, don't be surprised if they get undressed again very quickly.

Randy, I think this baby is cold!
Would you like to dress her?

 in or out　 5–10 min　 1–5 Threes

243

Masks

Save <u>masks from Halloween costumes</u> to put into a masks make-believe <u>box</u>. Make sure the masks aren't scary ones. Bring the masks out a few months after Halloween time. See if the children know what any of the mask faces are.

What animal has a face like this?
That's right, Jonah. It's a rabbit's face.

Let the children pretend with masks on. Have an <u>unbreakable mirror</u> nearby so children can see how they look. When the play is done, put the masks box away to save for another day.

Try painting faces for pretend play, too. Use face paints or special Halloween make-up that washes off easily.

Threes can

- pretend play with other children

 in or out | 5–20 min | 1–15 Threes

244

Sandbox Beach

Put <u>children's unbreakable sunglasses, sun hats, old beach towels, beach balls, and clean, water-filled suntan lotion bottles</u> into a <u>box</u>. Talk about going to the beach with your Threes. Ask questions to see what they know about the beach and all the things in the box.

Look at a <u>book about the beach</u>, too. Then let the children pretend to be at the beach, outside in warm weather in the sandbox, or inside on a cold, rainy day when it's nice to pretend that the weather is sunny.

Threes can

- pretend about familiar things

 in or out | 5–20 min | 1–6 Threes

245

Threes can

- understand the use of some familiar things
- pretend play

Going to the Dentist

Make a <u>dentist box</u> with some <u>unbreakable hand mirrors</u>, a <u>book about the dentist, and pictures of tooth brushing</u>. Sit with the children and talk about the dentist and what he or she does. Let the children look at your teeth. Have them look at their own teeth in the mirrors. If the children have toothbrushes, have them brush their teeth and see if their teeth are clean after they brush. When they brush, have them look in the sink to see if anything brushed out of their teeth.

You are keeping your teeth clean and healthy, Nadia.
They look nice and white.

Let children pretend to be dentists for dolls and toy animals, too.

 indoors　　 2–10 min　　 1–4 Threes

246

Threes can

- pretend about familiar things

Fishing in a Rowboat

Make a short fishing pole by tying a <u>magnet</u> to a <u>string</u> about 18″ long. Then tie the other end of the string to a 12″ stick. Make three or four of these. Cut out some 6–10″ <u>paper fish</u>. Put a <u>metal paper clip</u> on each fish for a mouth. Have a few <u>big cardboard boxes</u> that the children can use as boats. Put the fish on the floor next to the boxes.

　Show the children how to get into the boats and fish by catching the fish with the magnets on the fishing lines. Then let them play fishing in their own way.

　Have <u>pictures of people fishing</u> to talk about with the children.

 indoors　　 3–15 min　　 1–4 Threes

247

Threes can

■ pretend about familiar things

Painters

Make a painter's activity <u>box</u>, with <u>painters' hats, big brushes, paint rollers with pans, and buckets</u>. Look at <u>pictures of people painting</u> houses, furniture, or fences. Talk about painting with the children. Take the activity box outdoors, and let the Threes use water for paint and pretend to be painters.

You're painting with a big brush, Gina.
What's Terry using to paint?

 outdoors 3–20 min 1–5 Threes

248

Threes can

■ pretend about familiar things

Firefighters

Read a <u>book</u> about firefighters to your Threes. Take a fieldtrip to a fire station, too. Then put out a firefighter activity box for your Threes to use in make-believe play. Have in the box some <u>short pieces of hose, firefighter hats, a light toy plastic hammer</u> to use as an ax, some <u>firefighter badges</u> made of <u>aluminum foil</u> over <u>cardboard</u>, and a <u>bell</u>. The children can use a <u>wagon</u> as the fire truck and put out pretend fires on the playground.

Ring the fire bell, Maruta! The big climber is on fire!

Talk about fire safety with your Threes and remind them that real fires are dangerous.

 outdoors 3–20 min 1–10 Threes

249

Threes can

- pretend play with other children

Zoo Keepers

Talk with your Threes about all the things people who work at the zoo do as part of their job. Show <u>pictures</u> or look at a picture book, too. Help the children set up a zoo. Some children can pretend to be animals and some can be zoo keepers. Give the keepers some ideas for things to do with the animals, such as cleaning the cages, feeding the animals, teaching an animal to do a trick, and moving animals from cage to cage. Then let the children play in their own way.

What a roar! I think the lion is hungry!

 in or out 5–20 min 1–15 Threes

250

Threes can

- pretend play with other children

Post Office

Collect <u>used envelopes</u> and <u>lots of unopened junk mail</u>. Ask parents to help you. Put these into a post office activity box with <u>bags</u> that can be used for mail bags, smaller <u>boxes</u> to sort mail, and <u>free stamps</u> that come in "junk" mail. Talk with the children about the post office and what its workers do.

Let the children pretend play with the things in the post office box. See if they will put stamps on envelopes, deliver mail to different people in the room, and open the "letters" they get. Make sure to use post office words, such as *address, deliver,* and *cancel.*

On a special day when cards are sent, such as Mother's Day or Valentine's Day, have the children use the real post office to mail a card home.

 in or out 2–10 min 1–5 Threes

Dramatic Play Area Ideas

- Make the dramatic play area easy to use.

  Don't put too much out at once, but have enough so children do not fight over toys.

  Have enough open shelves to separate different kinds of things: dishes one place, dress-up clothes and hats another place.

  Don't use a big box or toy chest to keep things in because children can't find things easily.

  Have pictures of toys or other play things on shelves and other storage places to help children at clean-up time. Name things for them to find and put away.

- Make dress-ups fun and safe.

  Have dress-up clothes for girls and boys that are easy to put on and not too long.

  Put loops on dress-up clothes so that children can hang them on low, safe hooks.

  Wash dress-ups often and use plastic hats that are easy to clean.

  Have children wear socks with dress-up shoes and spray shoes often with disinfectant.

  Be sure dress-up shoes are safe: heels not too high, laces tied or removed.

- Have dramatic play outdoors as well as indoors.

  Put a play stove and sink outdoors where the children can use sand and water. Have one indoors, too.

  Use hats outdoors to act out different jobs: painter, firefighter, police.

  Bathe baby dolls, wash doll clothes and dishes outdoors.

- Bring in new ideas for dramatic play.

  Read stories; then put out what children need to act out the stories.

  Use pictures or take walking trips for new ideas.

  Set up different play places—a kitchen, bedroom, store, garage.

  Talk about different jobs children have seen adults do and give them what they need to play.

  Give children a chance to practice self-help skills as they play, such as pouring, washing tables, and sweeping.

- Talk to children and get them to tell you about their play.

  Dramatic play lets you give children new words and new ideas. A story before or after dramatic play often works well.

  Praise children for the things they are learning to do.

  Talk about taking turns, sharing, playing near and with others.

  Use words such as "make-believe" and "pretend" so that children start to understand the difference between real and make-believe.

Materials and Notes

Music

rhyme picture books

record or tape player
records or tapes

wind-up music boxes

musical instruments
home-made and bought

- Plan music times in your daily schedule, but also add informal music to many other things you do with Threes.
- Encourage Threes to sing with the group, but don't force them to. Let a child watch or do another activity when the rest of you sing.
- Relax and enjoy the Threes' music, even if it gets noisy. If the noise is "too much" inside, take the music outside.
- Turn off the record or tape player when a music activity is over. Threes will listen better to music if it is not a part of general background noise.
- If you can't sing, chant or use records and tapes. Your Threes will love your singing, even if you don't think your voice is good.
- Put up the words to new songs where you can see them when you sing until you know all the words by heart.
- Share songs with parents. Threes like to hear the same songs over and over.
- See Music Area Ideas and Songs and Rhymes at the end of this section.

Activity Checklist

Music

Music for Threes includes songs and chants, moving to rhythms, making music with musical toys or instruments, and listening to music made by others. Three-year-olds enjoy all kinds of music experiences: rhythmic movement, singing or chanting, musical instruments. They want to move to music in their own way and can make their own sounds by using everyday objects and simple musical instruments. They remember words and melodies to many songs and can add their own words to them, too.

Check for each age group	*36 – 42 mo*	*42 – 48 mo*
1. Adult sings or chants with children daily, during both planned and informal times.	——	——
2. New songs are introduced regularly and old favorites are repeated so that children can learn them.	——	——
3. Adult makes songs personal by using children's names and by singing about daily events.	——	——
4. Children are encouraged, but not forced to take part in music activities in small groups.	——	——
5. Movement to music is included daily.	——	——
6. Dance props are available (hats, wrist bells, ankle bells).	——	——
7. Adult avoids unnecessary background noise. Radio, records, or tapes are on only when they are being used for children's activities.	——	——
8. Different types of music are used with children (special children's songs, classical records, ethnic music). Volume is adjusted so that children can listen comfortably.	——	——
9. A music area is set up frequently with simple sound-making toys and musical instruments that children can use by themselves.	——	——
10. Adult helps make children aware of sounds and rhythms by planning activities with sounds and talking about them.	——	——

251

Threes can

- play easy music instruments

Music Area Tour

Set up a <u>music area</u> for your Threes. (You'll find Music Area Ideas at the end of this section.) Show children how to take out, use, and put away the things in the area by acting out what to do. Talk about the things in the area and how to use them carefully. Ask questions to see how much your Threes already know.

What do I do when I want to make music?
Yes, good! I choose an instrument.
What did I choose? The bells?
Now I'm done with them, so what do I do?
That's right, I put them back here in the dishpan.

Let the children make music in their own way. Stay near to gently remind them how to use the things in the area.

 indoors | 5–10 min | 1–5 Threes

252

Threes can

- talk about familiar pictures

Music Pictures

In the music area hang <u>pictures of people singing, dancing, or playing music</u>. Make sure the pictures are down low where your Threes can reach and touch them. Look at the pictures with your Threes. Talk about them in many ways. Ask questions to see what the children can tell you about the pictures.

What is the girl doing in the picture?
Yes, she's playing a piano. Do we have a piano here?
Yes, we have a toy piano.
How is our piano different from the one she's playing?

 indoors | 1–5 min | 1–4 Threes

253

Threes can

- sing songs

Tape Children's Singing

Use a <u>tape recorder</u> while your Threes sing. Then play back the tape for them and watch the delight on their faces. Save the tape to play again later. See if the children will sing along with it.

Do you remember this song? Listen.
Do you know who is singing?

On another day, give each child a chance to sing alone or with a friend. Record what they sing. Play it back for them. Later, play it for everyone to listen to.

 in or out 2–10 min # 1–15 Threes

254

Threes can

- copy some sounds made by others

I Sing, You Sing

Sing little sounds to your Threes in different ways. Sing them in high, low, and medium voices. Sing them fast or slowly. See if your Threes can copy the way you sing.

Listen to me sing. Can you sing what I sing?
Ba, ba, ba, ba, ba.
I sang that low and slow.
Listen again. Ba, ba, ba, ba, ba.
Now you try.

Some of your Threes may not copy you exactly. Enjoy whatever they sing back to you.

 in or out 2–5 min # 1–15 Threes

255

Threes can

- play easy music instruments

Play to Music

Give your three-year-olds easy-to-play musical instruments, such as drums or wrist bells. Then put on a record or tape for them to play along with. Try many kinds of music and see if the children play in different ways. Play the record or tape softly.

Here comes the music. Do you hear it?
Now. Play your drums.

Try classical, soul, rock, or any other record you might have. Be sure to turn the music off after you have finished the activity.

 in or out | 5–10 min | 1–15 Threes

256

Threes can

- match simple sounds

Guess the Instrument

Put two musical instruments on a table in front of the three-year-old. Sit across from the child. Have instruments that match those on the table on your lap where the child can't see them. Let the child try out her two instruments to hear how they sound. Then play one of your instruments so that the child can hear it but not see which one it is. See if she can guess which one you played.

Which instrument makes this sound, Nina? That's right!
See, here's mine! Let's play them together.

Begin with instruments that make very different sounds, such as a bell and clacking sticks. When that's too easy, use instruments that sound more like each other.

 in or out | 2–5 min | # 1–2 Threes

257

Threes can

- sing simple songs

Sing Baby to Sleep

Join your Threes as they play with <u>dolls</u>. Rock a baby doll and sing a simple "go to sleep" song like "Rock A Bye Baby." See if your Threes will sing along with you. Smile and look into the children's eyes as you sing quietly together.

My baby's so tired! I will sing her to sleep. Can you help me sing, Jason? If you want, you can sing and rock your baby too.

Later, listen as your Threes play with dolls. See if they sing their babies to sleep on their own.

 in or out | 2–3 min | # 1–4 Threes

258

Threes can

- understand many action words

Action Word Songs

Sing a song about actions to the tune of "This Is the Way We Wash Our Clothes." (See Songs and Rhymes at the end of this section.) Put in lots of different action words that your Threes can try to copy. See if they can do the actions when they hear the words you sing. If they don't know what the word means, do the action so that they can copy what you do.

This is the way we jump up and down. Jump up and down, jump up and down. This is the way we jump up and down so early in the morning.

Try these actions:

stand on tiptoes	hop on two feet
stand on one foot	hop on one foot
jump back	reach to the sky
jump to the side	

 in or out | 3–10 min | # 1–15 Threes

259

Threes can

■ sing simple songs

Cozy Singing Time

Have a special, warm, cozy singing time with just one or two children. Sing a favorite song with them. See if they can sing back to you. Give them a little help if they need it, but they may want to do it all by themselves. Hug them for sharing a song with you. Try to do this with every child, fitting it in whenever you get a chance.

Come here, Ronny. Cuddle with me a little.
Let's sing a song. Do you know a song to sing?

 in or out 2–4 min 1–2 Threes

260

Threes can

■ say and do fingerplays

Fingerplay Songs

Sing or chant fingerplays that have fun hand movements for your Threes. Do them over and over so that your Threes will learn the words and actions. When you think the children know the fingerplays well, have them sing or do the actions without you. Show them how happy you are with their fingerplays, even if they are not perfect. Try some of these:

"Two Little Blackbirds"
"In A Cabin In The Woods"
"Open, Shut Them"
"Little Turtle"

Sing or chant songs that have other kinds of actions, too. Try "I'm A Little Teapot," or "There Was A Duke of York." (See Songs and Rhymes, page 243 and Counting Songs, page 303.)

 in or out 5–10 min 1–15 Threes

261

Threes can

- play easy circle games

Simple Circle Game Songs

Make a circle with some three-year-olds. Begin with a small circle of four or five children. As they get better at staying in a circle, you can add more children.

Do easy circle games at first, such as "Ring Around the Rosey" or "Swing your Hands." Later, add other songs, such as "Put Your Right Hand In," "The Farmer in the Dell," or "London Bridge Is Falling Down."

Soon your Threes will tell you which circle games they want to play.

Let Threes come and go from the circle as they wish.

 in or out   5–10 min   4–15 Threes

262

Threes can

- copy sounds
- play easy musical instruments

Ringers or Clackers?

Put into a dishpan some musical instruments that make ringing sounds (melody bell, cow bell, triangle, tambourine, wrist bells) and some that make clacking sounds (rhythm sticks, clave tone block with mallet, castanets). Tell your Threes you want to sort the instruments into two piles—one of "ringers" and one of "clackers." Have the Threes help you try the instruments one at a time and choose which pile they go in. Ask questions to see if the children know what each instrument is called and what sound it makes.

Yes, that's a cow bell. Jeremy.
Can you make a sound like the cow bells make?
It makes a ringing noise, so I'll put it with these other ringers.

 in or out   5–15 min   1–5 Threes

263

Threes can

■ move to music

Dance Your Own Way

Choose music on <u>records or tapes</u> that your Threes will enjoy moving to. Be sure to have music that will bring out different kinds of movement—fast and slow, music with a hard beat, music with a soft beat, and others.

Tell your Threes to move the way the music tells them. Then play one piece for a minute or two as the children dance. Show the children how much you enjoy the ways they dance. Talk about the music with those who just want to watch.

Make sure there is plenty of space for dancing. Have children lie down to relax while you change the music.

 in or out   3–10 min   1–15 Threes

264

Threes can

■ sing words to familiar songs

Sing with a Music Box Toy

Choose a <u>wind-up music box</u> with a tune you know the words to. Wind it up and sing along as it plays. Have the children sing along with you, if they wish. See if a child can wind up the music box and let it play. Encourage all children to sing along.

Place the music box in the music area for the children to use on their own. See if they sing along without your help.

 in or out   2–4 min   1–15 Threes

265

Threes can

- move to music
- recognize familiar animals

Animal Music Games

Choose music on <u>records or tapes</u> that reminds you of animals your Threes know. Before the music starts, tell your Threes what animal they can pretend to be. Then you and the children can talk about and show some of the movements they might do. Play the music for a minute or two. Let the children move as they wish. Be sure they have plenty of room.

At another time, try having the children tell you different animals they can be with the same music, or change the music and keep the animal the same.

 in or out 3–10 min 1–15 Threes

266

Threes can

- move to music

Dance with Props

Give your Threes props, such as <u>long scarves, paper streamers, or cheerleading pompons</u> to dance with. Show them how these move or swirl in different ways. Play <u>music</u> and let the children dance with the props.

Try props on different parts of the children's bodies: streamers on wrists, waists, knees, and even as head bands. Try a long scarf around a child's head and another around his wrist. As usual, watch children carefully when you use long ribbons or scarves that might trip or choke them.

Try other props such as dress-up clothes, noise-making toys, or dolls to dance with, too.

 in or out 3–10 min 1–15 Threes

267

Threes can

■ play easy instruments

■ follow some directions

Musical Instruments—Stop and Go

Give your Threes <u>musical instruments</u> to play as they listen to a record that you can stop and start. See if you can make a game of playing only when the music is on, and stopping when it stops. It's easier if you have the children put their instruments down when the music stops.

Do you all have an instrument to play?
Put your instrument down on the floor where I can see it.
When the music plays, I want you to play.
When it stops, I want you to put your instrument down.
Do you think you can do that? I bet you can!

Be patient with your Threes who are excited and want to keep playing. Most of all, enjoy the music together.

 in or out 3–8 min 1–15 Threes

268

Threes can

■ point to their own body parts

■ sing easy songs

"Body Parts" Songs

Sing a song or chant a rhyme that names parts of the body. Have your Threes help you sing while they point to their own body parts. Try making up a rhyme of your own, such as this one that you can sing to the tune of "Row, Row, Row Your Boat."

Nose, nose where's your nose?
Pat your nose right now.
Nose, nose where's your nose?
Pat your nose right now.

When children know the easiest body parts, try others:

eyebrow	neck
elbow	chest
ankle	waist
heel	

 in or out 3–5 min 1–15 Threes

269

Threes can

- enjoy picture books
- sing easy songs

Sing with Books

Look at <u>nursery rhyme picture books</u> with your Threes. Sing with the children any of the rhymes that have tunes you know. Later, see if the children can sing any of the rhymes without your help.

Who is in this picture? Yes, Elsie, it's Jack and Jill.
You know the Jack and Jill song, don't you?
You sing and I'll listen.

 in or out   4–10 min   1–15 Threes

270

Threes can

- sing easy songs
- recognize many pictures

Songs with Pictures

Collect <u>pictures</u> that go with the words to familiar songs. Make picture cards by gluing the pictures to <u>sturdy cardboard</u>. Cover with <u>clear contact paper</u>. Before you sing, hold up the pictures and talk about them. Then hold them up again as you come to the words in the song. Try this to help children remember the words to "The Farmer in the Dell," "Old MacDonald," "Little Turtle," or others.

Hang the pictures in the music area where the children can see and touch them, or put the pictures in a sturdy box or dishpan on a shelf in the music area. See if your Threes will sing on their own using the pictures.

 indoors   4–7 min   1–15 Threes

271

Threes can

- sing easy songs
- recognize some opposites

Fast/Slow Singing

Choose a familiar song your Threes enjoy. Try singing the song slowly. Talk about how the song was sung. Then try singing the song fast. Talk about that too. Be ready for lots of giggles when you sing fast.

Let's sing "Mary Had a Little Lamb."
Let's sing it as slowly as we can.
Listen, I'll show you how.
That was slow singing, wasn't it?
It made me sleepy to sing so slowly.
Can you sing like that?

Play records of fast and slow music. Talk about each kind.

 in or out | 4–7 min | 1–15 Threes

272

Threes can

- recognize people's names
- sing easy songs

Songs with Names

When singing songs that have people's names in them, change the names so you use the names of the children in your group.

Let's sing about Justin this time.
Help me sing and use Justin's name!

Don't forget to use your own name once in a while, or names of other favorite adults your Threes know.

 in or out | 2–10 min | 1–15 Threes

273

Threes can

- count a little
- copy adult's actions

Clap and Count

Have your Threes watch and listen as you clap your hands in rhythm. Then see if they can clap and count out the rhythm as you do.

Listen and watch. I'm going to clap and count.
One, two. One, two. One, two.
Can you clap and count the way I'm doing?

Enjoy this game with the children. Show them how much you like the way they try to copy you.

 in or out | 3–7 min | # 1–15 Threes

274

Threes can

- tell easy sound differences
- match simple sounds

Matching Sounds

Cover empty juice cans or plastic jars with colored contact paper so that they all look the same. Then fill two sets of cans with things that make sounds, such as rice, sand, bells, wooden beads, or pebbles. Tape the lids on securely. Let your Threes shake all the cans and listen. Then pick up one can. Shake it. Give the child two other cans to shake. Make sure that one of them matches the one you are shaking. See if the child can find the one whose sound matches yours.

Listen, Katsuji. Which one sounds like this one?
I'll shake it again. Do you hear the sand in the can?

Begin with cans that make very different sounds. See if two children will play this game without you, once they know how.

 in or out | 3–10 min | # 1–2 Threes

275

Threes can

- follow some directions

Making Shakers

Collect lots of juice cans or plastic jars with lids for your threes to fill to make their own shakers. Put out different things the children can choose to put into their cans, such as rice, dried beans, sand, stones, or pebbles.

Let the children take turns filling their cans in their own ways. Remind the children to leave lots of space so the things inside can move to make noise. Secure all lids with strong tape and put each child's name on the shakers they make.

Use the cans at singing time that day. Help the children talk about how they made their shakers, what they put in them, and how they sound.

 in or out 5–10 min 1–5 Threes

276

Threes can

- sing easy songs

What Comes Next?

Sing one line of a song your Threes know well. Then ask them to sing the next line, or even to finish the song for you.

Can you help me sing a song? Listen, I'll start.
Twinkle, twinkle, little star . . .

Also give children a chance to choose words to use in different songs. For example, when singing "Old MacDonald," let the children name the animals to sing about and tell what sounds the animals make.

 in or out 2–5 min 1–15 Threes

277

Threes can

- copy some easy actions
- match easy sounds

Copycat Rhythm Game

Hit <u>two wooden blocks</u> together in a very simple rhythm. Give <u>two more blocks</u> to a three-year-old. See if he can copy the rhythm you made.

Listen, Peter. Listen to the blocks.
Can you make your blocks sound like that?

Try this with a slow or fast one-two, one-two rhythm. Then try it with a slow one-two-three, one-two-three rhythm. Be happy with any try the three-year-old makes at copying the sounds you make.

 in or out   2–4 min   1–2 Threes

278

Threes can

- recognize some opposites
- follow some directions

Loud/Soft Sounds

Talk with your Threes about noises that are loud and noises that are soft. Have the children try out loud and soft voices. Talk about when each should be used. Play a tape or record of loud music, then soft music. Play a <u>musical instrument</u> so it is loud, then soft. Let the children tell you which sounds they hear. See if they can name some other loud and soft noises they know. Later, give each child a musical instrument to play. Have them play the instruments so they are loud, then soft.

When do you like to hear loud music?
Yes, loud music can be fun at a birthday party, Sherry.
Let's play a little loud birthday party music.

 in or out   2–7 min   1–15 Threes

279

Threes can

■ play easy musical instruments

Many Drums

Collect <u>many different kinds of drums</u> for your Threes to try out. Include homemade drums made from oatmeal boxes, or coffee cans with lids, as well as different drums you can buy. Talk about the different ways they can be played, the sounds they make, and how they look. See if your Threes can find other things that sound like drums, too.

Can this bucket be a drum, Katerina?
Let's turn it upside down and thump on it.

 in or out   5–15 min   1–15 Threes

280

Threes can

■ move to rhythm

March to Music

Show your Threes how to march around the room to <u>music</u> with a strong beat. Don't worry if your Threes do not make a straight line to march or if they don't move their feet in time to the music. Let them have fun marching in their own ways.

Let's march to this music. Isn't it fun?
Lift those feet up high.

Try these ideas:

march with drums, bells or other instruments

do an action while moving to the music, such as clapping, tapping your head, or jumping

march around a chair or table

 in or out   5–15 min   1–15 Threes

281

Play Your Kazoo

Make kazoos with four or five Threes at a time. Cover one end of an empty paper towel or toilet paper toll with tissue paper. Secure with tape. Let the children color or put stickers on the rolls and choose the color of tissue paper they wish to use. Put each child's name on his kazoo.

Show the children how to toot into their kazoos. See if they can play a song they know well on their new musical instruments.

Threes can

- follow some directions
- play easy musical instruments

 in or out | 10–15 min | 1–5 Threes

282

Dance with a Partner

Help a few of your Threes choose a partner. Have the couples look at each other. Chant a little song that tells them ways they can move together. As the children get used to working with partners, add more couples to the group.

Clap, clap, clap your hands
Clap your hands together.
Shake, shake, shake your hands
Shake your hands together.
Smile, smile, smile, smile
Smile to each other.

Try other actions the children can do as partners.

Threes can

- play with another child
- copy actions

 in or out | 4–10 min | # 4–8 Threes

283

Threes can

■ watch themselves in a mirror

■ move to music

Mirror Dance

Have a few three-year-olds stand in front of a <u>large, unbreakable mirror</u>. Put on a happy, lively <u>record</u> and see if they will start dancing. Point out the children in the mirror so that they will look at themselves and their friends as they dance.

Look, Dante, you're dancing.
Do you see yourself in the mirror?
I like the way you are moving.

 indoors   3–7 min **#** 1–3 Threes

284

Threes can

■ sing easy songs

What Song Am I Humming?

Choose some songs your Threes know very well. Hum one of them to the children. Tell them you are humming. Ask if they know what song you are humming. See if your Threes can sing the words to the song with you after you hum it for them.

Listen, I'm going to hum a song.
It's a song you know well. That's right, Raul.
That was "Twinkle, Twinkle, Little Star."
Can you sing the words with me?

 in or out   2–10 min **#** 1–15 Threes

285

Threes can

- sing easy songs

What Song Should We Sing?

Help your Threes choose songs to sing that go with things you are talking about. Notice when it might be time to sing a certain song, and then help your children figure out what the song would be.

What did we see outside on the fence?
Yes, Randy. We saw a spider making a web.
We know a song about a spider.
Do you remember the name of the song?

 in or out | 1–3 min | 1–15 Threes

286

Threes can

- sing easy songs

Holiday Songs

At holiday times, teach the children a song or rhyme to go with the holiday. Make sure to learn songs for the different holidays celebrated by all children in your group. Ask your public librarian or parents to help you with this. Or look for records and tapes with holiday songs. For example, at Halloween sing or chant "Five Little Pumpkins." Don't be surprised if the children want to sing these songs all year, especially "Jingle Bells."

 in or out | 2–7 min | 1–15 Threes

287

Threes can

■ enjoy music

Songs for Resting

Sing or play songs to your three-year-olds about sleeping both before and after naptime. Sing or play them softly since the children may not be quite awake. Put children's names in the songs whenever you can.

> *Are you sleeping, are you sleeping, little Marie? ("Are You Sleeping")*
> *Sleepy Danny, will you get up, will you get up, will you get up? ("Lazy Mary")*
> *Rock-A-Bye Travis, in the tree top. ("Rock-a-bye Baby")*

Ask your Threes if there are any favorite sleepy-time songs you could play or sing to them.

 indoors 2–10 min 1–15 Threes

288

Threes can

■ recognize some opposites
■ move to music

Make It Dance

Give children <u>stuffed animals or puppets</u> that they can move to music. Play short parts of different kinds of music, and see how the children move their animals or puppets to each. Help your Threes talk about each kind of music.

> *What did your teddy bear think of that music, Vanessa?*
> *He didn't like it! Why didn't he like it?*
> *Yes, it was slow, wasn't it?*

 in or out 3–7 min 1–15 Threes

289

Threes can

- enjoy music
- follow some directions

Singing Visitors

Invite a parent or other adult to come in to sing with the children. The visit might be more special if the person brings a musical instrument to play. Plan the visit with the guest before she comes. Then she will know what music the children enjoy and how much time to spend. Stay with the visitor and help if needed.

Be sure to talk about the visitor with the children before she arrives. Show how excited and happy you are that she is coming. Take part in the singing, too. Invite people who are interested in dancing with the children to visit, too.

 in or out 10–20 min 1–15 Threes

290

Threes can

- use many words

Explore a New Instrument

Show the children a <u>new musical instrument</u>. Ask questions to help the children tell you as much as they can about the instrument. Show them how it sounds, and let each child try it out. Talk about the way to use and care for the instrument.

Look at this musical instrument.
It's called a kalimba, or thumb piano.
What do you think it's made of?

If the instrument is one that can break easily, keep it out of reach and bring it out when you can watch carefully. Otherwise, add it to the other instruments in the music area.

 in or out 5–10 min 1–15 Threes

291

Threes can

- help clean up
- follow easy directions

Clean-up Song

Sing this song at clean-up time to the tune of "London Bridge."

Let's clean up the toys right now, toys right now, toys right now.
Let's clean up the toys right now. We are finished with play.

Warn children that clean-up time is coming. Give each child a small clean-up job to do. Be as exact as you can so that the Threes know what to do. Break larger jobs into two or more parts and sing easy directions.

Joey, you clean up the blocks, clean up the blocks, clean up the blocks. Joey, you clean up the blocks, and put them on the shelf.

 in or out   5–10 min   **#** 1–15 Threes

292

Threes can

- make easy comparisons
- move to music

What Does the Instrument Say?

Have one child play a rhythm instrument for his friends. When he is done, see if the friends can sing or chant to show the way the music sounded to them. Have another child play the instrument, and have the children copy its sound again. Talk about whether it sounded the same as it did when the first child played.

Does the drum sound the same as it did when Charlie played it? Yes, Jeanette, you played the drum loudly and Charlie played softly.

 in or out   4–10 min   **#** 2–5 Threes

Music Area Ideas

- If you have room for a permanent music area, put *sturdy* musical instruments and toys neatly on shelves. Use picture labels to help Threes remember where things are to be put away. Keep smaller musical instruments in a labeled box or dishpan. If your music area must share space with other toys, keep the instruments in an activity box and bring them out when you want the children to use them.

- Choose a small, quiet corner for a permanent music area. Use low shelves or other sturdy furniture to keep music noises in and other noises out. A carpet on the floor and big soft pillows will cut down on noise, too.

- Have two or more of the best-loved musical instruments or toys. This will cut down on fights.

- Put out only a few musical instruments to begin with. Show children how to use these. Add new things often. Always show and tell your Threes about all of the things you add.

- Buy or make musical instruments and toys such as the following:

    wrist bells, melody bells, cow bells, bells on sticks

    many kinds of drums, with or without sticks

    many kinds of shakers

    sturdy music boxes (wind-up or pull strings)

    jack-in-the-box or other crank music toys

    sturdy toy piano

    xylophone with mallet

    cymbals (large or finger size)

    clackers, clave tone blocks, castanets, or rhythm sticks

    kalimba (thumb piano)

    scraping instruments with sticks, such as guiros

    tambourines

    sand paper blocks

- If you use harmonicas, whistles, horns, recorders, kazoos, or other mouth instruments, make sure to wash them with soap and air dry after each use. Keep these in a separate box. Also be sure that instruments have no loose or broken parts that could cut or choke a child.

- Use the record player, tape recorder, or other delicate music equipment only when you are there to watch closely. These last longer when kept out of three-year-olds' reach.

- Have many toys that make noise. Threes still enjoy some "baby" toys, such as rattles, chime toys, bell toys, or jack-in-the-boxes. Put some of these out, too.

- Change toys and instruments in the music area often. When you add a new musical toy, show it to all your Threes. Talk about what the toy is called, how to use it, how to care for it, and where to put it away. If the toy is a favorite, try to have two or more that are the same.

- Keep children from being crowded in the music area. Give them plenty of choices of other interesting things to do if they can't fit in right away. Make sure children do get a turn after a short wait. Or have music for a larger group outside of the area if there is lots of interest.

- Help Threes keep the area neat and organized. Make sure the area is cleaned up after each day's use.

- Have movement activities in a large enough area so that Threes will not bump into one another. Give them a chance to calm down with a song after they dance.

- Try music outdoors. This will give you lots of space for movement or dance. If you can't have music outdoors, move furniture and other equipment aside to make a bigger space.

- Add dance props for movement and dance. Try musical instruments, dress-ups, hula hoops, and long streamers.

Songs and Rhymes

(See also Counting Songs, page 303.)

A Hunting We Will Go

A hunting we will go, a hunting we will go.
Hi-ho the merrio, a hunting we will go.

Are You Sleeping

Are you sleeping, are you sleeping,
Brother John, Brother John?
Morning bells are ringing,
Morning bells are ringing,
Ding, ding, dong.
Ding, ding, dong.

Clap, Clap, Clap Your Hands

Clap, clap, clap your hands,
Clap your hands together.
Clap, clap, clap your hands,
Clap your hands right now.
Additional verses: (2) Touch your nose (3) Tap your knees (4) Pat your
*   head*

Did You Ever See a Lassie (or Laddie)

Did you ever see a lassie, a lassie, a lassie?
Did you ever see a lassie go this way and that?
Go this way and that way, go this way and that way.
Did you ever see a lassie go this way and that?

The Eensy Weensy Spider

The eensy weensy spider went up the water spout.
Down came the rain and washed the spider out.
Out came the sun and dried up all the rain
And the eensy weensy spider went up the spout again.

The Farmer in the Dell

The farmer in the dell, the farmer in the dell,
Hi Ho the Derry O, The farmer in the dell.
The farmer takes a wife . . .
The wife takes a child . . .
The child takes a nurse . . .
The nurse takes a dog . . .
The dog takes a cat . . .
The cat takes a mouse . . .
The mouse takes the cheese . . .
The cheese stands alone . . .

Head and Shoulders, Knees and Toes

Head and shoulders, knees and toes, knees and toes.
Head and shoulders, knees and toes, knees and toes.
Eyes and ears and mouth and nose.
Head and shoulders, knees and toes, knees and toes.

Here We Go 'Round the Mulberry Bush

Here we go 'round the mulberry bush, the mulberry bush, the mulberry
*   bush,*
Here we go 'round the mulberry bush, so early in the morning.

Hey Diddle Diddle

Hey diddle diddle the cat and the fiddle.
The cow jumped over the moon.
The little dog laughed to see such fun.
And the dish ran away with the spoon.

Hickory Dickory Dock

Hickory, dickory, dock!
The mouse ran up the clock.
The clock struck one,
The mouse ran down.
Hickory, dickory, dock!

Hush Little Baby

Hush, little baby, don't say a word, Momma's gonna buy you a
*   mocking bird.*
If that mocking bird won't sing, Momma's gonna buy you a diamond
*   ring.*
If that diamond ring turns brass, Momma's gonna buy you a looking
*   glass.*
If that looking glass gets broke, Momma's gonna buy you a billy goat.
If that billy goat won't pull, Momma's gonna buy you a cart and bull.
If that cart and bull turn over, Momma's gonna buy you a dog named
*   Rover.*
If that dog named Rover won't bark, Momma's gonna buy you a horse
*   and cart.*
If that horse and cart fall down, you'll still be the sweetest little baby in
*   town.*

I Am Walking

I am walking, walking, walking, I am walking, walking, walking,
I am walking, walking, walking, I am walking, walking, walking,
Now I stop.

If You're Happy and You Know It

If you're happy and you know it, clap your hands. (clap, clap)
If you're happy and you know it, clap your hands. (clap, clap)
If you're happy and you know it then your face will surely show it.
If you're happy and you know it, clap your hands. (clap, clap)
Additional verses: (2) Stamp your feet (3) Nod your head (4) Pat your knees (5) Wave good-bye

I'm A Little Teapot

I'm a little teapot short and stout.
Here is my handle, here is my spout.
When I get all steamed up, hear me shout,
"Just tip me over and pour me out."

In a Cabin, In the Woods

In a cabin, in the woods
Little old man by the window stood
Saw a rabbit hopping by,
Knocking at his door.
"Help me, Help me!" the rabbit said,
"Or the hunter will shoot me dead!"
Little rabbit, come inside;
Safely you'll abide.

Jack and Jill

Jack and Jill went up the hill to fetch a pail of water.
Jack fell down and broke his crown and Jill came tumbling after.

Jack Be Nimble

Jack be nimble.
Jack be quick.
Jack jump over the candlestick.

Lazy Mary

Lazy Mary will you get up, will you get up, will you get up?
Lazy Mary will you get up, will you get up this morning?

Little Duckie Duddle

Little Duckie Duddle
Went wading in a puddle,
Went wading in a puddle quite small.
Said he, "It doesn't matter
How much I splash and splatter,
I'm only a duckie, after all. Quack, Quack."

Little Green Frog

Ah—ump went the little green frog one day.
Ah—ump went the little green frog.
Ah—ump went the little green frog one day
And his eyes went blink, blink, blink.

Little Jack Horner

Little Jack Horner sat in a corner,
Eating his Christmas pie.
He stuck in his thumb and pulled out a plum,
And said, "What a good boy am I."

Little Miss Muffet

Little Miss Muffet
Sat on a tuffet
Eating her curds and whey.
Along came a spider
And sat down beside her
And frightened Miss Muffet away.

Little Turtle*

There was a little turtle
He lived in a box.
He swam in a puddle,
And he climbed on the rocks.
He snapped at a mosquito,
He snapped at a flea,
He snapped at a minnow
And he snapped at me.
He caught the mosquito.
He caught the flea.
He caught the minnow.
But he didn't catch me.

London Bridge

London bridge is falling down, falling down, falling down,
London bridge is falling down, my fair lady.

Mary Had a Little Lamb

Mary had a little lamb,
Little lamb, little lamb,
Mary had a little lamb
Whose fleece was white as snow.

Creative Activities

Muffin Man

Do you know the muffin man, the muffin man, the muffin man?
Do you know the muffin man who lives on Drury Lane?

Oats, Peas, Beans

Oats, peas, beans and barley grow;
Oats, peas, beans and barley grow;
Do you or I or anyone know
How oats, peas, beans and barley grow?

Old MacDonald

Old MacDonald had a farm
E-I - E-I - O
And on his farm he had a cow
E-I - E-I - O
With a moo moo here
And a moo moo there
Here a moo, there a moo
Everywhere a moo moo
Old MacDonald had a farm
E-I - E-I - O.
(Additional verses with other animals)

Old King Cole

Old King Cole was a merry old soul,
And a merry old soul was he.
He called for his pipe and he called for his bowl,
And he called for his fiddlers three.

Open, Shut Them

Open, shut them, open, shut them, give a little clap.
Open, shut them, open, shut them, lay them in your lap.
Creep them, creep them, creep them, creep them right up to your chin.
Open wide your little mouth, but do not let them in.

Pat-A-Cake

Pat-a-cake, pat-a-cake baker's man,
Bake me a cake as fast as you can.
Pat it and prick it and mark it with "B,"
And put it in the oven for baby and me.

Pop Goes the Weasel

All around the cobbler's bench the monkey chased the weasel.
The monkey thought 'twas all in fun.
Pop goes the weasel.

Peas Porridge Hot

Peas porridge hot, peas porridge cold,
Peas porridge in the pot, nine days old.
Some like it hot, some like it cold,
Some like it in the pot nine days old.

Put Your Right Hand In (Hokey Pokey)

Put your right hand in.
Put your right hand out.
Put your right hand in
And you shake it all about.
You do the Hokey Pokey and you turn yourself around
That's what it's all about.
(Continue with left hand, right foot, left foot, whole self.)
Add between verses, if you wish:
Here we go looby loo, here we go looby light
Here we go looby loo, all on a Saturday night.

Ring Around the Rosy

Ring around the rosy,
A pocket full of posies.
Ashes, ashes,
We all fall down.

Rock-A-Bye Baby

Rock-a-bye baby, in the tree top,
When the wind blows, the cradle will rock,
When the bough breaks, the cradle will fall.
And down will come baby, cradle and all.

Row, Row, Row, Your Boat

Row, row, row, your boat
Gently down the stream.
Merrily, merrily, merrily, merrily
Life is but a dream.

Rub-a-Dub-Dub

Rub-a-dub-dub, three men in a tub,
And who do you think they be?
The butcher, the baker, the candlestick maker.
Turn them out, knaves all three.

See Saw, Margery Daw

See saw, Margery Daw, Johnny shall have a new master;
He shall have but a penny a day because he can't work any faster.

Sing A Song of Sixpence

Sing a song of sixpence a pocket full of rye.
Four and twenty blackbirds baked in a pie.
When the pie was opened the birds began to sing,
Wasn't that a dainty dish to set before the king?

Swing Our Hands

Swing our hands, swing our hands, swing our hands together.
Swing our hands, swing our hands, in our circle now.
Tap our toes, tap our toes, tap our toes together
Tap our toes, tap our toes, in our circle now.
*(Continue with shake our heads, move our hips, bend our legs, and
    others)*

Take Me Riding in Your Airplane

Take me riding in your airplane
Take me riding in your airplane
Take me riding in your airplane
I want to go riding in your airplane.
*(Add motions to the song. Continue with bumpety bus, motorcycle,
    bicycle, rowboat, rocket ship, and others.)*

Teddy Bear

Teddy bear, teddy bear, turn around.
Teddy bear, teddy bear, touch the ground,
Teddy bear, teddy bear, show your shoe,
Teddy bear, teddy bear, that will do!

There was a Duke of York

There was a Duke of York.
He had ten thousand men.
He marched them up the hill.
And then he marched them down again.
When you're up, you're up.
And when you're down, you're down.
And when you're only half way up
You're neither up nor down.

This is the Way

This is the way we wash our clothes, wash our clothes, wash our clothes.
This is the way we wash our clothes, so early in the morning.
*Other verses: hang up our clothes, iron our clothes, fold our clothes, put
    on our clothes*

This Little Piggy

This little piggy went to market and this little piggy stayed home,
This little piggy had roast beef and this little piggy had none,
And this little piggy went "wee, wee, wee, wee," all the way home.

Twinkle, Twinkle, Little Star

Twinkle, twinkle, little star, how I wonder what you are.
Up above the world so high, like a diamond in the sky,
Twinkle, twinkle, little star, how I wonder what you are.

Wheels on the Bus

The wheels on the bus go round and round, round and round, round and round.
The wheels on the bus go round and round all through the town.
Additional verses: (2) Baby goes wah wah wah; (3) Lights go blink blink blink; (4) Driver says move on back; (5) Money goes clink clink clink; (6) People go up and down; (7) Wipers go swish, swish, swish

Where Is Thumbkin

Where is thumbkin? Where is thumbkin? Here I am, here I am.
How are you today sir? Very well I thank you. Run away, run away.

Where Oh Where Is Pretty Little Susie?

Where oh where is pretty little Susie?
Where oh where is pretty little Susie?
Where oh where is pretty little Susie?
Way down yonder in the pawpaw patch.

Yankee Doodle

Oh, Yankee Doodle went to town a riding on a pony,
He stuck a feather in his cap and called it macaroni.
Yankee Doodle keep it up; Yandee Doodle Dandy,
Mind the music and the step and with the girls be handy.

Your Own Creative Activities

Write your own activities in these blank boxes. You will find more information on writing your own activities in the Planning section, page 38.

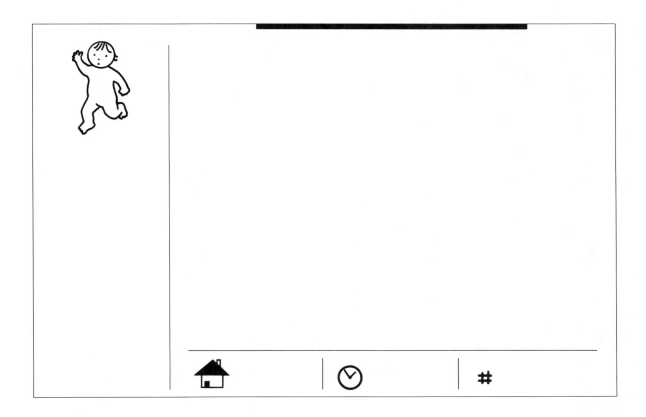

Creative Activities

Index

of Creative Activities

Action Word Songs 258
Animal Cages 205
Animal Music Games 265
Art Area Tour 157
Art Gallery 161
Baby's Bath Time · 233
Big Blocks Train, Bus or Plane 200
Big Boxes as Outdoor Blocks 208
Block Furniture 210
Block Talk 220
Blocks and Boats 214
Blocks in Sand 213
Body Parts Songs 268
Bringing Blocks Outdoors 202
Build a Little Town 212
Build with One Block Shape 216
Build Your Own House 219
Building a Big House 204
Cardboard Blocks with Boards
    Outside 217
Carpenters 239
Chalk Art 168
Changing Baby 226
Clap and Count 273
Clean Up Song 291
Cleaning Day 230
Copy Cat Rhythm Game 277
Cozy Singing Time 259
Crayon Art 159
Crayon Rubbings 189
Cutting Paper Strips 169
Dance With a Partner 282
Dance With Props 266
Dance Your Own Way 263
Dolls With Blocks 199
Dress-Up Fun 222
Dressing Dolls 242
Explore a New Instrument 290
Fast/Slow Singing 271
Finger Play Songs 260
Fingerpaint Prints 188
Fingerpaint on a Tray 160
Fire Fighters 248
Fishing In a Rowboat 246
Gadget Prints 176
Garbage Truck 235

Gardener Play 236
Gas Station 238
Going to the Dentist 245
Great Big Pictures 183
Grocery Store 237
Guess the Instrument 256
Hanging Pictures to Buy 163
Holiday Songs 286
How Many Blocks? 218
I Sing, You Sing 254
In, On, Or Next To? 209
Kitchen Play 225
Laundry Day 227
Lots of Bridges 201
Loud/Soft Sounds 278
Make It Dance 288
Making Shakers 275
Many Drums 279
March to Music 280
Masks Make-Believe 243
Matching Sounds 274
Mirror Dance 283
Mural Fingerpainting 171
Music Area Tour 251
Music Instruments—Stop
    and Go 267
Music Pictures 252
My Art Book 158
Other Toys for Building 207
Painters 247
Painting Little Pictures 173
Paper Plate Masks 179
Paper Scraps Collage 167
Pencil Pictures 175
Picture Stories 187
Picture Talks 165
Play House 221
Play to Music 255
Play Your Kazoo 281
Play Dough Fun 166
Playhouse Bedroom 231
Playing Doctor 241
Post Office 250
Putting Babies to Bed 223
Ringers or Clackers? 262
Road Building 197

Same and Different Blocks 206
Sand and Glue Pictures 185
Sand Casting 190
Sand Drawings 180
Sandbox Beach 244
Sandbox Kitchen 228
Sewing Designs 174
Shower Time 232
Showing Art Work 181
Simple Circle Game Songs 261
Sing Baby to Sleep 257
Sing with Books 269
Sing with a Music Box Toy 264
Singing Visitors 289
Songs for Resting 287
Songs with Names 272
Songs with Pictures 270
Sorting Game at Clean-Up
    Time 195
Spaces to Build 193
Stacking Fun Things 203
Sticker Pictures 170
Story Act Out 229
Stringing Things 172
Take a Trip 240
Taking Turns with Blocks 192
Talk About Block Shapes 194
Tall and Short Towers 196
Tape Children's Singing 253
Telephone Talk 224
Tempera Painting 162
Texture Collage 182
Thin Markers 177
Tour of the Block Area 191
Toy Trains 198
Using Tape 186
Washing Dishes 234
Water Color Paintings 184
Water Color Markers 164
What Comes Next? 276
What Does the Instrument Say? 292
What Song Should We Sing? 285
What Song Am I Humming? 284
What Stacks, What Doesn't? 215
Which Block? Game 211
Yarn and Ribbon Pictures 178
Zoo Keepers 249

Here's Why

*E*xperiences with real things continue to be important to Threes in the development of thinking and feeling. The senses—hearing, sight, smell, taste, and touch—are their main ways of experiencing the world. As children grow, they form ideas to help them understand all the information coming in from their senses. They also learn the words that go with those ideas, to use in thinking and communication.

Ideas about number, shape, size, and color come gradually throughout the preschool years. Starting very early in life, children need many real experiences as a basis for these ideas. They also need adults who talk to them about what they see, hear, and feel. Threes are ready to learn many facts about color, size, shape, and number, so take the time to talk to them about what is around them.

Real things in the world around us are fun to watch and learn about. They move, disappear, change, and are always surprising because they do things on their own. Being outside some time every day, where there is so much to see and freedom to move around, is important for Threes. Good early experiences outdoors can help a child become interested in nature and feel safe in rougher, more natural places.

In this section there are many activities to help Threes use their senses to learn about the world around them. There are also activities that give them chances to play with different shapes, sizes, and colors, and use different numbers of things. These activities will help you share with Threes some of what they will need to know to become good thinkers, as they have fun playing with real things.

Materials and Notes

Nature

sturdy magnifying glass

sand and water

homemade bird feeder

leaf-match game

magnets

lots of safe containers

- Threes learn best about nature through their senses. Give Threes plenty of chances to explore nature in their own way. Ask questions to help them talk about what they know.

- Make sure to keep things safe. You should be sure that the plants, seeds, mushrooms, animals, or insects your Threes touch are not poisonous and will not harm a child. If you are not sure, find out before allowing your Threes to get close.

- Threes ask lots of questions about nature. Try to answer these as simply as you can. Help Threes use their senses to find out answers. Don't be afraid to admit that you do not know an answer. Show Threes how you look in books or ask others to find information.

- Ask parents for help with your nature activities. They can help you supervise fieldtrips, find information you need, and bring in new, interesting things. They can also continue at home the nature activities you have started.

- See Nature Area Ideas, Tips for Nature Walks, Making Matching Games, and Ideas for Making Bird Feeders, pages 275–278.

Activity Checklist

Nature

Nature for Threes includes experiences in exploring natural things both indoors and out, learning words for natural things, and beginning what can be a lifelong appreciation and respect for nature. Collecting natural "treasures," going on nature walks, learning about animals and plants, helping to care for pets, and playing in sand and water are only a few of the nature activities Threes can do, as they gain skills in carrying out activities independently.

Check for each age group	*36–42 mo*	*42–48 mo*
1. Children have a daily outdoor time, weather permitting.	—	—
2. Adult regularly points out and talks about natural outdoor things, such as flowers, birds, insects, plants, animals, the weather.	—	—
3. Adult shows appreciation and respect for nature when with children (shows curiosity and interest rather than disgust about insects, spider webs, worms; has positive attitude about going outside in different kinds of weather).	—	—
4. Adult encourages children to explore safe, natural things with their senses.	—	—
5. Adult asks children easy questions about natural things to encourage talking and thinking things through.	—	—
6. Sand and water play are available indoors and out (water play frequently; sand daily).	—	—
7. A variety of toys is available for sand and water play.	—	—
8. Some natural things are displayed indoors.	—	—
9. Pictures and picture books of familiar natural things are displayed where children can see and touch them.	—	—
10. A special nature area is set up where children and adults can display collections and natural things of interest.	—	—
11. Safe "science experiment" materials are provided, such as magnets, sink and float games, magnifying glasses.	—	—

293

Threes can

- use many words
- keep things in their places

Nature Area

Make a <u>nature area</u> where you and your Threes can put many safe, natural things to look at and find out about. Use a window sill, a small table, or the top of a low bookcase for this. Make sure there is a place nearby where you can put up <u>pictures</u>, too.

Talk about this area with your Threes. Help them notice and talk about the many things they see there. Remind them to handle things carefully and to leave things in the area. (See Nature Area Ideas, page 275.)

Change what you have in the area often.

 indoors 1–10 min 1–5 Threes

294

Threes can

- match simple pictures

Weather Pictures

Find or make <u>pictures that show different kinds of weather</u>. Cover them with <u>clear contact paper</u> if you wish. Include sunny, windy, cloudy, foggy, rainy, and snowy pictures.

Look at the pictures with the children. Ask questions to help them talk about each. See if they can choose a picture that is most like the weather for that day.

Do this outside, or have the children look out a window or door. Bring the pictures out again on different kinds of days. Talk about the different kinds of weather they have really seen and weather they have seen only in pictures.

 in or out 3–8 min 1–15 Threes

295

Threes can

■ play with sand

Sand Play

Set up a <u>sand table</u> for your Threes. If you do not have a sand table, use a <u>sturdy dishpan or other large container</u> for one or two children at a time. Add different-sized <u>unbreakable jars, margarine tubs, cups, funnels, digging tools, and short pieces of hose.</u> Add different toys often. Talk to your Threes about a "no throwing sand" rule before they play. Gently but firmly remind children who forget the rule.

Place the sand table on a floor that can be cleaned easily. Put a <u>mat</u> or large <u>towel</u> under the table to catch the sand that spills. Have a <u>broom</u> and <u>dustpan</u> nearby for quick clean-up. A sandbox with a cover to keep it clean works well for outdoor sand play.

 in or out 5–20 min 1–4 Threes

296

Threes can

■ play with water

Water Play

Set up a water play table for your Threes. If you do not have a <u>water table</u>, try a <u>sturdy dishpan, baby's bathtub, wash tub, or other large container</u> for one or two children at a time. Place it where the Threes can easily reach it and where it will not be tipped over. Add <u>cups, funnels, spoons, things that sink or float, dolls to wash, and other toys.</u>

Let the children play in the water in their own way. Encourage them to keep the water in the table, but expect and be ready for splashes. Roll up long sleeves. Have <u>waterproof aprons</u> ready. A <u>shower curtain</u>, big <u>towel</u>, or plastic <u>mat</u> under the table helps. Keep a <u>mop</u> and old towels nearby to clean up spills. Change the water every day or more often if it becomes dirty.

 in or out 5–20 min 1–4 Threes

297

Threes can

- play with sand and water

Wet Sand/Dry Sand

Give your Threes a fun change by mixing <u>sand</u> and <u>water</u> together for play. Do this in a <u>dishpan</u> if you don't want to get lots of sand wet. Have your Threes help add one to the other. Talk about what they see and feel as you add the water to the sand. Give them play <u>dishes</u>, <u>cookie cutters</u> to use as molds, and <u>cups</u> to make sand pies.

That wet sand sticks to your hands, doesn't it, Gina?
And when you make a sand hill, it stays better than when you use dry sand.

Wet sand takes days to dry out. Talk about how it is drying every day.

 in or out 5–20 min 1–2 Threes

298

Threes can

- tell some things that make up a group

Flower Hunt

Look at Tips for Nature Walks and Fieldtrips on page 275. Then take your Threes on a short flower hunt in the play yard or around the block. Before you go, talk about the flowers they might see. Show some <u>pictures</u>, name the <u>flowers</u>, and talk about how each looks. Tell the children whether they can pick any of the flowers they will see.

On the walk, see if the children know the names or colors of the flowers.

Do you know this flower's name, Thelma? Yes. It's a dandelion. When it gets older it will turn into a ball of fluffy seeds.

Always be on the lookout for bees when looking at flowers, and make the children aware of bees too, without frightening them.

 outdoors 5–15 min 1–5 Threes

299

Flower Picture Matching Game

Look at How to Make a Matching Game for Threes on page 277. Then make a <u>flower matching game</u> with flower pictures that are very different from each other. Show a child how to hold a picture card next to each picture on the matching board until she finds the one that is the same. Then have her put that card on the matching picture and choose the next flower card. Talk about the flowers as the child works.

That's a red tulip, Ana.
Can you find the red tulip that is the same?
Your mom says she has tulips blooming in her garden.

Threes can

■ match easy pictures

 in or out   3–7 min   1–2 Threes

300

Magnet Fun

Put a <u>large horseshoe magnet</u> into a <u>dishpan</u> with <u>some metal things</u> that will be attracted to the magnet, such as a jar lid, a big bolt, and a pair of children's scissors. Also put in <u>some things that the magnet will not pick up</u>, such as a plastic spoon, a crayon, and a small wooden car. Show your Threes how to pick up things with the magnet. Ask the child to name the things the magnet will or will not pick up.

Let the child walk around with the magnet, inside and out, to see what else the magnet will stick to.

What things do magnets stick to?
What sticks to the magnets?

Threes can

■ explore a new thing
■ talk about what they learn

 in or out   3–10 min   1–2 Threes

301

Threes can

- understand when to wear different clothes

Weather Walks

Take a short weather walk with your Threes. As you walk, help them notice as much as they can about the weather. Take weather walks on cold, hot, windy, calm, foggy, sunny, cloudy, snowy, or rainy days. Try walks before or after rain.

Whatever walk you take, point out how the weather looks, feels, and smells. Talk about the clothes you need for that weather. Your Threes will be interested in many other things besides the weather. Let them enjoy the walk in many ways.

 outdoors | 10–15 min. | 1–15 Threes

302

Threes can

- understand when to wear different clothes
- do easy sorting

Clothes Sort

Collect clothes the children wear for different kinds of weather. Include clean mittens, warm hats, sun hats, swim suits, umbrellas, boots, shorts, heavy jackets, and others. Put the clothes into a big bag and look at them, one at a time, with your Threes. Ask questions to see if the children know the kind of weather each piece of clothing is for. Make piles of each type. For example, have clothes for sunny weather in one pile and clothes for rainy weather in another.

When do we wear boots? Yes, they go in the rainy day pile.

Give more information about each thing.

The boots are made of rubber. They keep our feet dry.

 in or out | 7–12 min | 1–15 Threes

303

Threes can

■ play with sand

What's in the Sand Table?

Instead of sand, try sterilized potting soil, pebbles, gravel, or small stones in your sand table (or sand dishpan). Add sturdy things to fill and empty and digging tools. Talk about what's in the sand table as your Threes play. Talk about how it feels, the sounds it makes, its size, color, and more. But most of all, let your Threes use and enjoy it in their own way.

What is in the sand table, Norman?
Does it make the cups heavy?

 in or out   2–20 min   1–4 Threes

304

Threes can

■ follow simple directions

Bird Feeders

Have your Threes help make bird feeders to put up in the play yard or near a window where the children will be able to see them. (Ideas for making bird feeders are on page 278.) As birds come to feed, help your Threes notice them. Talk about the birds that come. Ask questions to see what your Threes know about the birds.

Look, Rosita. See the bird?
It's a chickadee. What's he doing?

Put up pictures of the birds the children see.

 in or out   10–25 min   1–5 Threes

305

Threes can

- tell some things that make up a group

Nature Collections

Have your Threes help you make different kinds of <u>nature collections</u>. They can help you collect leaves, stones, shells, flowers, feathers, or seeds. Tell the children what you want to collect. Show and talk about a few examples. Then see how the Threes eagerly bring in more things to add. Be sure to have a <u>special place to put your collection</u>.

That's a wonderful stone, Jay.
Let's wash it so we can see it more clearly.
I think it's rose quartz. Where did you find it?

Keep a sturdy, <u>unbreakable magnifying glass</u> with the collection. Show the children how things look bigger through the glass.

 in or out | 5–20 min | 1–15 Threes

306

Threes can

- pour from a small container

Caring for Plants

Have a <u>few safe potted plants</u> where Threes can see them every day. (Ask your public library if you need to know which plants are safe.) Be sure they are in a place where they won't be knocked over. Have the children help you care for them. Put a little <u>water</u> into a <u>small cup or pitcher</u>. Ask one of the children to help you water a plant. Show her how to pour the water onto the soil. If the plant needs more water, give other children a chance to help.

This poor plant looks thirsty, doesn't it, Tina?
Would you like to help me water it?
Good pouring. Now the plant feels better.
Are you thirsty too?
Would you like to drink some water?

 in or out | 2–10 min | 1–5 Threes

307

Threes can

- explore a new thing
- talk a little about what they learn

Magnifying Glasses

Put out several safe magnifying glasses for your Threes to try. Be sure they are very sturdy. Plastic or glass magnifiers with thick wooden frames are best. Show the children how to look through the magnifiers. Let the Threes use them, both indoors and out-doors, to look at many things.

What do you see through the magnifying glass, Beth?

Watch carefully so that children do not look into the sun with magnifying glasses. This can hurt eyes badly.

 in or out | 1–7 min | 1–3 Threes

308

Threes can

- tell some things that make up a group

All About Babies

Collect pictures of many kinds of babies. Include animal babies and human babies. Ask parents to bring in baby pictures of the children. Add these to the pictures you already have.

Then hang all the pictures where the Threes can look closely. Write names on them if you wish. Talk about the many babies. Use the names for different babies, such as kitten, puppy, and calf. See which ones the children can name. Ask your Threes how the babies are different from the parents. Talk about what each baby can or cannot do.

Have animal and people babies visit. Be sure your Threes know that they must be quiet and gentle with babies. Have children in very small groups to look at the babies if necessary.

 indoors | 15–30 min | 1–15 Threes

309

Threes can

- talk about things they see

Slugs and Snails

If you have <u>snails or slugs</u> in your area, set up a <u>see-through plastic container, with a lid</u>, in a safe place. Put it where your Threes can look closely. Then you can carefully look under rocks, logs, or in piles of leaves to find a few slugs or snails to go in the container. Let your Threes feed them <u>fresh lettuce, celery tops, spinach, or other leafy greens</u>. The snails or slugs will need no water if the leaves are juicy.

Keep these pets for a week, cleaning the jars often. Look at and talk about them each day. Then have a goodbye time as you let these pets go in a safe place outside, where they will not hurt garden plants.

 indoors   10–20 min   1–15 Threes

310

Threes can

- talk about things they see and feel

Freeze and Melt

On a warm day, pour <u>water</u> into <u>ice cube trays</u> while your Threes watch. Then have them help you put it in the freezer. Later, put the ice cubes in <u>dishpans</u> for outdoor play. See what the children say about how the ice feels. Talk about freezing and melting water.

On another day, have children help you put juice in the freezer to make popsicles. Help the children talk about how the juice freezes and melts.

If you have ice outside in the winter, bring some in and put it in a bowl. See if your Threes can say what happens to it. Make sure the children do not put the ice cubes in their mouths because of danger of choking. Have crushed ice for eating.

 in or out   10–15 min   1–15 Threes

311

Bug Search

Be on the lookout for <u>bugs</u> you and the children can watch with interest. Look for bugs hiding under rocks or in the grass. Remind the children that bugs are delicate and should not be hurt. It is usually best to just look and not touch so that the bug can go about its interesting business.

Let's watch where the ant goes.
Maybe he'll show us where his hole is.

Be sure you can tell which insects are harmful and stay away from them. Ask your public library for help in finding out about harmful insects.

Threes can

- tell some things that make up a group

 in or out | 2–6 min | 1–5 Threes

312

Looking for Shadows

On a bright sunny day, take your Threes outside on a shadow hunt. Help the children move their arms and legs to see how their shadows move. See if one child can work with another to make their shadows touch. Show them how their shadows will disappear if they move into the shade. Later, say this rhyme with the children.

I have a little friend who comes out when I'm in sun.
He jumps with me and hops with me and then we run, run, run.
Who is my little friend who comes out when I'm in sun?
You know it is my shadow—we have so much fun!

Threes can

- follow easy directions
- enjoy rhymes

 outdoors | 2–8 min | 1–15 Threes

313

Threes can

- recognize familiar things by touch

Nature Feelie Bag

Put a plastic container into a big, clean sock to make a feelie bag. Put a natural thing, such as a shell, an acorn, a feather, or a leaf, into the bag. See if your Threes can reach in and guess what's in the bag. Help them use words to tell about what they are feeling.

Is the thing hard or soft, Nicky?
Is it rough or smooth?

Let children take the thing out of the bag if they don't know what it is. Then let them put it back and feel it again.

 in or out   1–3 min   1–6 Threes

314

Threes can

- learn new words

Name Plant Parts

When looking at flowers, trees, or other plants with your Threes, point to and name the root, stem or trunk, branches, leaves, and flowers. In very simple words, tell what each is for. After you have done this many times, see if the child can tell you about parts of plants.

I like the clover you picked for me, Harriette.
What is this part? Yes, it's the flower.
And look! You pulled up some roots, too!
The roots suck up water for the plant to drink.

Point out simple plant parts in pictures of plants, too.

 in or out   1–7 min   1–4 Threes

315

Threes can

- talk about what they see
- do simple comparing

Grasshopper Pets

Catch a <u>grasshopper or cricket</u>. Put it in a <u>big, see-through plastic container with a top</u>. Have your Threes help feed it by bringing in <u>fresh grass</u> for it to eat. Look at the insect, using a <u>magnifying glass</u>, and talk about its body parts—its strong legs, its mouth, its eyes. Ask questions to help the children compare the insect's body parts with their own. See if the children can jump the way the insect does. Remember to let the pet go free at the end of the day.

See the grasshopper's legs, Sarah?
Can you jump like the grasshopper does?
Does he have hands like yours?

 indoors   3–15 min   1–4 Threes

316

Threes can

- be careful with animals
- follow directions

Petting Time for Pets

Have a petting time for <u>a pet</u> you keep in your room or for one that is visiting. Be sure the pet is a safe, healthy one to have with your Threes. Talk about how pets like to be petted gently. For tiny pets such as gerbils, puppies or kittens, have children practice petting a <u>little toy animal</u> with just one or two fingers. Then let one child at a time pet the real animal as you hold it. Threes can pet bigger animals with more fingers or a whole hand. They can practice this on <u>bigger toy animals</u>.

Warn your Threes not to grab or hit a pet. Have the child sit on a chair and put a towel on his lap so the pet won't scratch when it is held. Watch carefully whenever your Threes and pets get together.

 in or out   2–10 min   1–4 Threes

317

Threes can

- understand many words

Talk About Seasons

Help your Threes notice special things about the seasons in your area. Talk about how the air smells or feels, whether the season is wet or dry, how plants or trees change, and other things the children can find out through their senses.

It's getting darker outside.
See the black clouds covering the sun.
What's going to happen outside? Yes, rain.
I love the summer showers we have.
They cool the air so that we aren't so hot.

 in or out   1–4 min   # 1–15 Threes

318

Threes can

- follow easy directions
- tell what some animals eat

Help to Feed Pets

Let your Threes help feed any pets you have for them to watch and enjoy. Give each child only a small amount of food to feed at one time. For example, put a few bits of fish food into the child's palm instead of giving the child the fish food container. Or hand the child a few lettuce pieces for the rabbit, rather than the whole head of lettuce. Then put the rest of the food out of your three-year-olds' reach.

Talk about what the animal eats and when it is hungry. Talk about what you and the children like to eat, too.

Jane, you did a nice job of putting the carrot pieces into Hoppity's cage. What's he doing to the carrot now?

 in or out   2–5 min   # 1–3 Threes

319

Threes can

- use crayons
- follow directions

Leaf Prints

Collect <u>pretty leaves</u> with your three-year-olds. Have each child choose one with a shape he likes best. Place the leaf the child has chosen on a table. <u>Tape</u> a piece of <u>coloring paper</u> over the leaf, so that the paper will not move. Show the child how to scribble over the leaf with a <u>crayon</u> so that its print is made. A small piece of crayon on its side works best. Talk about the shape of the leaf as it magically appears.

Press harder with the crayon, Jason. Then we will see more of the leaf shape.

 in or out   6–15 min   1–5 Threes

320

Threes can

- do simple matching

Leaf Match Game

Collect <u>four or more very different leaves</u>. Find <u>other leaves that closely match the ones you already have</u> in size, shape, and color. Put all the leaves out for the child to see. Show her how to put each leaf with the one it matches.

This is a maple leaf, Sonya.
Can you put it on top of the other maple leaf?

To make leaves last longer, you can place them on <u>sturdy cardboard cards</u> and cover with <u>clear contact paper</u>.

 in or out   3–7 min   1–2 Threes

321

Threes can

- talk about what they see
- do easy sorting

Sink or Float Sorting Game

Put next to your <u>water table</u> or <u>dishpan</u> a few <u>safe things that sink and that float</u>. Show the Threes how to put these into the water. Talk about whether they sink or float. Help the child take each thing out of the water and put it into either a "sink" or "float" pile.

Oh, Terry! What happened to the rock?
Yes, it went down. It does not float.
It's too heavy, so it sinks.
Let's put it in the pile with other things that sink.

See if your Threes can find some more things they want to try out. Watch to be sure they use things that won't be hurt by water.

 in or out | 5–10 min | 1–2 Threes

322

Threes can

- do easy matching
- follow easy directions

Animal Matching Game

Buy or make an <u>animal matching game</u>. Play the game with three or four children, sitting at a small table. Give one board to each child who will play. Then hold up one <u>picture card</u> at a time for all the players to see. See if the Threes can name the animal.

Ask who has that same picture on his board. Help the children look if necessary. Give the picture card to the child who has the same picture on his board, and let him use it to cover that picture. Continue until all pictures have been covered.

When a few children are good at this game, let them play without you. One child can hold up the pictures.

 in or out | 8–12 min | 1–3 Threes

323

Threes can

■ talk about things they see

Looking Inside a Seed

Have your Threes help you put <u>large, dried lima beans</u> into a <u>bowl of water</u> to soak overnight. Tell the children that the seeds will get bigger as they soak up water, that they will be easy to open up when they are wet, and that when the seeds are opened, the children will be able to see a tiny baby plant hiding inside.

The next day, open beans with the Threes. Point out and talk about the tiny plants' leaves. Look at them with a <u>magnifying glass</u>.

If you wish, you can leave a few beans on a pile of wet paper towels. The plant inside will grow a bit more so that you can see the root and stem.

 indoors | 3–15 min | 1–15 Threes

324

Threes can

■ follow easy directions

Sprouting Seeds

Have some <u>quick-sprouting seeds</u> for each of your Threes to plant in their own <u>paper cups</u>. Try dried beans, radish, alfalfa, or grass seeds. Let the children look closely at the seeds and choose three or four to use in cups they have filled with <u>soil</u>. Talk about the names of the seeds, and remind them that the seeds hold baby plants.

Say what the seeds need to start to grow. Help the children plant the seeds (not too deep), <u>water</u> them with a little water in a cup, and notice when they come up. Move small plants to bigger containers if the children are still interested.

 indoors | 7–12 min | 1–5 Threes

325

Threes can

- understand many words
- remember things they see

Things in the Sky

Talk about the sky when you are outside with your Threes. Help them notice the sun and clouds, and the moon and stars if the children are with you when it's dark. Ask parents to help children see things in the night sky.

The moon is still in the sky this morning, Tracy.
Can you find it?

Collect pictures of things the children see in the sky. Hang them down low where the children can look at and touch them. Talk about all the pictures. Let your Threes make a night sky picture by sticking shiny star stickers onto a black piece of paper. Have them add a circle sticker for the moon, too, if they wish.

 in or out | 2–10 min | 1–15 Threes

326

Threes can

- play with a flannel-board

Sky Flannelboards

Look at How to Make a Flannelboard on page 279. Then make two small flannelboards—one covered with light blue felt for a day sky, the other covered with navy blue or black felt for a night sky. Cut out felt stars, moons, suns, and cloud shapes. Put these out in a dishpan with the boards. Talk about the boards and shapes. Then let your Threes use them in their own creative ways. Ask questions to see what the children say about the shapes they used on the night sky or day sky boards.

The sky you made is different from the sky we see out of our window.
What do you see in the sky now?

 indoors | 2–10 min | 1–2 Threes

327

Threes can

- do simple comparing
- understand *same* and *different*

Animal and People Body Parts

Have your Threes help you gather <u>five or more different stuffed animals</u> to look at. Look at the animals one at a time. Ask your Threes which body parts each animal has that they have too. Then see if they can tell you which body parts the animal has that are different from their own. Help your Threes compare by asking questions.

What's this part of the cat?
Yes, it's the tail. Do you have a tail?

Try this with animal pictures, too.

 in or out 6–12 min 1–15 Threes

328

Threes can

- do simple comparing

Thirsty, Sleepy, Hungry

Gather <u>lots of pictures that show people and animals drinking, sleeping, eating, and playing</u>. Hang these down low where the children can see and touch them. Ask what a person does when he or she is thirsty. Have the children point to pictures that tell the answer. Then ask what animals do when they are thirsty. Have the Threes show the pictures that tell the answer. Ask questions to help your Threes see how people and animals are the same and different in drinking, sleeping, eating, and playing.

What's the kitten drinking, Karla?
Do we drink milk, too?
Do we drink it from a saucer on the floor?

Continue with questions for sleepy, hungry, and playing.

 indoors 5–10 min 1–5 Threes

329

Threes can

■ do easy sorting

Sorting Nature Picture Cards

Make sets of picture cards that show different groups of natural things. For example, make a set of shell pictures, a set of tree pictures, and a set of bird pictures. Mix up two sets and help your Threes sort them.

We have bird pictures and shell pictures here.
Let's put all the birds in one pile and all the shells in another.
Here's the first picture. Is it a bird or a shell?
Yes, it's a bird. Let's put it here in the bird pile.

See if your Threes can sort with little help from you.

 in or out 3–12 min 1–3 Threes

330

Threes can

■ follow directions

Pet Store Trip

Plan a trip to visit a pet store. Talk to the pet store manager to set a good time and share special information. Before you go, talk to your Threes about what they will see. Show pictures of these things.

At the pet store, help the children look for things you talked about. After the trip, see what the Threes remember by asking simple questions. Have the pictures the children looked at before the trip in clear view.

What did you see at the pet store, Carolee?
Fish. Yes, I saw the fish, too.
What were the fish doing?
Right! They were swimming in the water.
What else did you see? That's right, puppies.

If you can take photos on the trip, display them for the children to see and talk about.

 in or out 45–90 min 1–3 Threes

Nature Area Ideas

- For your nature area use a small table, the top of a low bookcase, or a big window sill that the Threes can reach and see.
- Make sure there is plenty of light.
- Have a place to put many pictures down where the children can see.
- Have lots of unbreakable jars, boxes, or tubs ready to put outdoor "treasures" into. Some will need lids with holes punched in them for air.
- Put safe things in the area that interest you and the children. If a child brings in something, add to it with pictures, books, or more examples of the same kind of thing.
- Be sure that no plants are poisonous to children.
- Visit the nature area with children. When you see a child looking or exploring, go over and join in. Or call a child who is not busy at play, to look and talk with you. Make these warm, friendly, interesting times.
- Change or add to the area often. Help the children notice the changes.
- If a child cares greatly about something he or she has brought in, make sure it is protected and sent home again.
- Add nature things to other areas in the room. Have plants, pets, pictures, or mobiles wherever they can safely fit in.
- Keep pets such as gerbils or mice out of children's reach. These pets are fun to watch but can bite small fingers. And children can easily hurt the pets. A sturdy aquarium cage is the best home for these animals.
- Make sure any animals you let children come into contact with are healthy and will not pass on any illness. If any child is scratched or bitten, disinfect the injury and let the parent know what happened.

Tips for Nature Walks and Fieldtrips with Threes

- Take very short trips with Threes.
- Be sure that enough adults are along and that their full attention is on the children at all times. One adult for every three children is best. Have parents help if possible.
- If a child is difficult to handle, have one adult care for that child and another "easy" child.
- Take the same walks over again. Look for different things each time.
- If you drive, make sure each child is seat-belted safely and that there is a second adult in the car with the driver.
- Put a name tag on each child.
- Get permission slips from parents. For walks around the block or to a nearby park, one blanket permission for all outings may be enough.
- Let parents know before taking a trip so they can dress children properly and pick them up at the correct time.

- Make sure to be back on time.

- If your trip will be longer than usual, take along a snack and anything else you might need for the children.

- If you want to take a trip to a pet store, go there yourself first and talk to the shopkeeper. Also buy something for your pet there.

- Some Threes may still enjoy running away from adults when on walks. If this is a problem, take nature walks inside your play yard instead. Talk to the children about how important it is for them to stay with you for safety. Practice walking with partners and adults in a safe place. Then try going out again when your Threes are ready.

- Some ideas for nature walks and trips with Threes are:

  walk around the block

  a pet store

  different kinds of farms (dairy, chicken, pig, etc.)

  a zoo, if not too far away (don't try to see everything)

  a big grassy field

  a forest or woods

  a park with trees and flowers

  a country lane

  a pumpkin patch

  an orchard

  up a big hill

  a corral to visit a pony

  a duck pond to feed ducks

  a little stream

  children's back yards that are nearby

How to Make a Matching Game for Threes

- For younger Threes, use four to six pictures that are very different.
- Older Threes may enjoy working with pictures that are more similar, or they may be able to work with more pictures at one time.

1. Collect or draw matching pairs of pictures. You can find matching pictures in two copies of the same catalog, magazine, newspaper ad, or children's activity book. Make sure that the pictures in each pair are exactly the same.

2. Use two sturdy pieces of cardboard that are the same size. Mark each into six (or more) same-sized squares.
3. Cut one piece of the cardboard along the lines to make six cards. Leave the other piece whole, for the Matching Board.

4. Glue one picture from each pair onto each of the small cards. Glue the other pictures into the squares on the large card.
5. Cover the cards and board with clear contact paper to protect the pictures.

Ideas for Making Bird Feeders

Peanut Butter—Cornmeal Mixture

1. Mix peanut butter with cornmeal until you can roll the mixture into a doughy, not-too-sticky ball. Your Threes can help knead the mixture with their hands. Add bird seed, if you wish. Make sure there is enough cornmeal in the mixture so that the birds don't choke on the peanut butter.

2. Put a big ball of the mixture into a mesh onion bag. Hang the bag outside.

OR

Cut clean, empty 6-oz cardboard frozen juice containers so that they are one inch in height. Punch a hole through the cardboard at the open end. Tie a loop of string through the hole as a hanger. Have your Threes help you press the mixture into the cans. Hang outside.

Peanut Butter and Birdseed on Toast

1. Toast bread lightly. Stale bread collected from children's parents is fine for the birds. Your Threes may want to taste this before bird seed is added. Use fresh toasted bread for children to eat.

2. Have your Threes use dull plastic knives to spread peanut butter on toast.

3. Use a dull darning needle to thread a loop of yarn through one corner of the toast.

4. Have children sprinkle bird seeds onto the sticky peanut butter.

5. Hang the toast outside for birds.

How to Make a Flannelboard

1. Cover a board with a large, wide piece of felt or flannel cloth. For the board, use wood, very sturdy cardboard, or an old bulletin board. A rectangle of 2 by 2½ feet works well, but you can make a larger or smaller board if you wish. You can even make individual flannelboards, 11 inches by 14 inches.

fold edges
to back

Front

2. Fold the cloth over the back of the board, making sure the front is pulled smooth. Sew the ends together, or staple and cover securely with heavy tape.

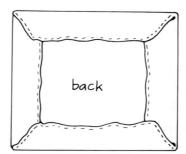

back

3. When you use the board, lean it at an angle against a wall or bookcase. Then the flannel pictures will stay on better. When your Threes use the board, have them place it flat on a table or floor so that the pictures will not fall off.

4. To make pictures, cut out ones you want to use. Cover the front with clear contact paper and glue felt material or sandpaper on the back. Or use pens to draw on felt material. You can buy pictures for use with flannelboards. Check school supply catalogs for prices and ideas.

Materials and Notes

Numbers

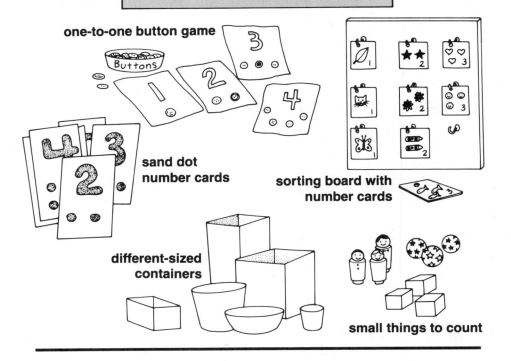

one-to-one button game

Buttons

sand dot number cards

sorting board with number cards

different-sized containers

small things to count

- Count real things whenever your Threes are interested. Don't push the children to memorize numbers. Keep numbers fun and interesting for these little children.

- Some younger Threes may be able to count more than just two or three things. Add more things for them to count as you do any of the number activities in this book.

- Tell parents about some of the counting games you play with the children. Encourage parents to count things with their children at home.

- See How to Make Sand-dot Number Cards and Counting Songs and Rhymes, pages 302–305.

Activity Checklist

Numbers

Number activities for Threes include hearing an adult playfully count things, repeating number rhymes and songs, and hearing quantity and size words used as part of everyday activities. Number activities focus on introducing children to number ideas and words as they occur in the natural setting, so that when they are older, counting and doing mathematics in school will come more easily.

Check for each age group	*36–42 mo*	*42–48 mo*
1. Children help with routines involving counting, such as setting the table.	—	—
2. Adult uses quantity and size words for children when talking about familiar things the children can see, and asks questions to encourage Threes to use these words.	—	—
3. A variety of toys with many pieces, such as beads, pegs, and pull-apart toys, is organized by type and available to children daily.	—	—
4. Adult often counts familiar things with child.	—	—
5. Colorful number pictures and number picture books showing familiar things are placed where child can see and touch them.	—	—
6. Adult regularly looks at and talks about colorful number-picture books with children.	—	—
7. Adult sings or chants number songs and number nursery rhymes with children during both routine care and play times.	—	—
8. Adult asks questions or does activities with child to encourage the child's use of quantity, size, and number words.	—	—
9. Simple number games, such as number sorting and one-to-one matching, are regularly available for children to use with adult supervision if it is necessary.	—	—

331

Threes can

- enjoy action songs and rhymes

Number Songs and Rhymes

Do number songs and rhymes that have fun actions with your Threes every day. (See Counting Songs and Rhymes on page 303.) Use one to begin story time, say another at lunch or snack. Add numbers to some other songs your Threes know well, such as "Put Your Right Hand In" or "If You're Happy and You Know It."

Put one hand in, take one hand out
Put one hand in and shake it all about . . .
If you're happy and you know it shake five fingers . . .

 in or out 1–5 min 1–15 Threes

332

Threes can

- use small pegs
- count two or three things

Pegboard Birthday Cake

Put out small pegs with pegboards in a dishpan. Ask the children to make birthday cakes with candles by putting pegs into the boards. When they have put in as many pegs as they wish, count the pegs to see how old the birthday person is. Point to each peg as you count it. Then pretend to blow out the candles with the child.

You put nine candles on the cake, Lee.
Let's blow them out now.

Try putting one, two, or three pegs into a board. Ask the child to make a cake with the same number of candles you put on your board.

 in or out 2–10 min 1–5 Threes

333

Numbers at Meals

At meal or snack time, allow the Threes to serve themselves <u>easy-to-serve foods</u>, such as apple slices or crackers. Let them serve themselves one, two, or three things at a time. Help them count as they serve.

You may take two apple slices, Dana.
One, two. Good!
And you may take two pieces of cheese, also.

Threes can

- count two or three things
- serve easy foods

 in or out | 5–10 min | 1–15 Threes

334

Number Books

Have lots of <u>picture-number books</u> on the book shelf for your Threes to use. Look at these books with the children, and count the things on the pages with them. Point to each thing as you count. Let the Threes count alone when there are just a few things on a page. Point out the numbers that tell how many.

That's right, Juan. There are two kittens.
This is the number two here.

Threes can

- copy your counting
- count two or three things

 in or out | 4–15 min | 1–15 Threes

335

Threes can

- count two things
- understand same and different

Inside Number Hunt

Ask your Threes to look around the room and find two things that are the same. You can make sure there are some easy things to find by putting pairs of the same things side by side.

Yes, Tina. There are two toy telephones on the shelf. One, two.

Give the children a little help if necessary.

Look here on the window sill.
Do you see two same things here?

Ask children to look for sets of three things, too.

 in or out   3–7 min   1–15 Threes

336

Threes can

- count two or three things

Sand-Dot Number Cards

Make sand-dot number cards. (Directions are on page 302.) Let your Threes look through all the cards with you. Have them feel the numbers and dots as you count. See if they can count the easy numbers on their own.

How many dots are on this card, Dwain?
Yes, one, two. Two dots.
And this card has one, two, three, four, five, six.
That's a lot.

Put the cards in a sturdy box for the children to use on their own.

 in or out   2–5 min   1–3 Threes

337

Threes can

■ copy your counting

Counting Small Toys

Fill three or four margarine tubs with little toys. Try toys such as small toy cars in one tub, teddy bear counters in the next, and little plastic farm animals in another. Let the three-year-old choose a tub of toys to count with you. Have him take out one toy as you say each number. See if he will say each number after you do. Let the child play with the toys for a while. Then count them again to put them away.

Let's see if all the cars are here, Chiang.
Let's count them as we put them in the tub.

 in or out   3–10 min   # 1–2 Threes

338

Threes can

■ count two or three things

Counting with Animal Toys

Have your Threes help you gather a few toy animals to look at. Let each child hold one of the animals. Ask easy number questions about the animals each child is holding.

How many tails? Yes, your horse has one, Peter.
And yours has one, too, Tracy.
How about your frog, Brian? Does it have a tail?
That's right. It has none.
How many eyes?

 in or out   5–10 min   # 1–6 Threes

339

Threes can

- match one-to-one

Blankets for Babies

Put out four small baby dolls in a row. Next to them put a pile of four little baby doll blankets. Ask the child to cover each baby with one blanket. Talk about how many babies and blankets there are.

Oh, Susie! This baby is cold!
Can you put a blanket on her, too?
Does every baby have a blanket now?

Have fun playing other one-to-one matching games with your Threes. Talk about putting one thing into one place. For example, use little toy airplanes with boxes for hangers, or plastic eggs to put into an empty egg carton.

 indoors   3–10 min   1–2 Threes

340

Threes can

- do easy sorting
- count two or three things

Sorting Number Pictures

Make six picture cards that show one thing and six that show two things. Mix the cards up. Look at the cards one at a time with the Threes. Have them tell you how many things are on each card—one or two. Help them sort the cards into boxes—one for the ones and another for the twos.

How many fish are there, Lashawna?
Yes, two. Where should this fish card go?

Leave the cards and boxes on a shelf for the children to use on their own. Later, add six cards that show three things, with another box to sort into.

 in or out   5–10 min   1–3 Threes

341

Threes can

- match one-to-one
- copy your counting

Flannelboard One-to-One Game

Cut out <u>five felt flowers, flower pots and bees</u> for your Threes to use on a <u>flannelboard</u>. (Patterns for these are on page 301.) Ask the child if he can plant one flower in each pot. Then see if he can have one felt bee visit each flower. Let the child have fun moving the bees and flowers around. Make buzzing noises as the bees go from flower to flower. Count the flowers, pots, and bees with the child. Leave these out for the Threes to use on their own.

 in or out | 3–10 min | 1–2 Threes

342

Threes can

- match one-to-one
- copy your counting

One-to-One Table Setting

Have your Threes help you set the table for meals or snacks. You start by putting plastic or paper towel <u>placemats</u> at each place. Then have one child put all the <u>cups</u> out, another do the <u>spoons</u>, and so on. Make sure each child puts one thing onto each placemat. Count for the children as they work. Help them see when they miss a place.

You still have one napkin, Henry.
Look at each placemat.
Is there one with no napkin?

 indoors | 2–5 min | 1–4 Threes

343

Threes can

■ use fingers to show their age

How Old Are You?

Ask your Threes how old they are. See if they can show you by holding up three fingers. Say the numbers for what they are saying with their fingers. Try to get the children to say the words also.

How old are you Antonio? Yes, you are three years old.
Can you say "three years old"?

 in or out   2–4 min   1–15 Threes

344

Threes can

■ play in sand or water
■ say some size words

Measuring Sand or Water

Put out graduated measuring cups and measuring spoons for the Threes to use with sand or water. Let them play freely with these. As they play, talk with them about the sizes of the cups.

Which is the smallest cup, Debby?
Yes, that one is small.
Where's the smallest spoon?
How many of this cup will fill the big cup?
Let's try.

 in or out   3–15 min   1–4 Threes

345

Threes can

- count two or three things

Sharing Food

Have <u>foods at meals or snacks</u> such as apples, bananas, or sandwiches that can be cut into two, three, or four pieces to serve to children. Let the children watch as you cut these up. Count the pieces as you take the food apart and put them back together. Let the children do this, too. Talk about how the pieces are about the same size.

You can each have a piece of banana for snack.
I cut each banana into four pieces.
See the four pieces? They're all about the same size.
Let's count them.

 in or out | 4–8 min | 1–15 Threes

346

Threes can

- copy your counting
- copy actions

Count with Rhythm

Sit with the children and play a rhythm counting game. Count and clap with many different rhythms, slow or fast. See if your Threes can copy what you do. Have them copy the counting you do.

One, two, three, four.
One, two, three, four.
One two, one two, one two, stop!
One two, one two, one two, stop!

Try other movements such as nodding, stamping, or waving.

 in or out | 2–7 min | 1–15 Threes

347

Threes can

- play easy circle games

"Ring Around the Rosey" Count

Play "Ring Around the Rosey" with your Threes. Instead of saying "Ashes, Ashes," count up to a number and then say "All Fall Down." Surprise the children by counting to a low number one time and to a high number the next.

Ring around the rosey,
A pocket full of posies.
One, two, three, four, five, six, seven.
We all fall down!

 in or out 3–7 min 1–7 Threes

348

Threes can

- paste
- count two or three things

Make Number Posters

Cut out <u>pictures</u> so that you have one of one thing, two of another, and so on. For example, have one cat picture, two dog pictures, three babies, four flowers, and so on. Have your Threes help you <u>paste</u> the pictures of each thing to different <u>large pieces of paper</u>. Write the number of things pictured on each paper. As you and the children work together, talk about the numbers and pictures. Hang the posters in a row where your Threes can see and touch them.

How many rabbits are there, Bonnie?
Will you help me count them?

 in or out 10–20 min 1–6 Threes

Activities for Learning from the World Around Them

349

Threes can

- put on and take off lids
- tell one from many

One/Many Listening Game

Collect <u>containers with lids</u>, such as film containers, yogurt cups, or margarine tubs, that the children can't see through. In some of the containers put one thing, such as <u>one button, one paper clip</u>, or <u>one pebble</u>. In the other cups put <u>many of the same things</u>. Have your Threes shake the containers, listen to the sounds, and guess whether they hold one or many things. Let them open the containers to see what's inside, close them up and listen again.

Shake this one, Tyrone.
Does it have one or many things in it?

 in or out 3–10 min 1–3 Threes

350

Threes can

- count two or three things

Outdoor Number Hunt

Take an outdoor walk with your Threes. Ask each child to find three things, such as three pretty rocks, three acorns, or three leaves. Give each child a <u>paper bag or other container</u> to put her three things into. Count out how many things the children have in their bags. Some children may have found more than just the three things you asked for. Count out three of these things. Then show how happy you are to count all the rest.

Oh, Mary! You got three stones and lots more!
Let's count them all!

When you get back indoors, put out all the sets of three things on a table and talk about the number three.

 outdoors 2–20 min 1–15 Threes

351

Threes can

- do simple sorting
- copy your counting

Number Sort Game

Put <u>four plastic spoons</u> and <u>six plastic forks</u> into a <u>box</u>. Put out a <u>picture of a fork and a picture of a spoon</u>. Ask the children to sort the real forks and spoons into the box with the pictures that match. When they are done, help them count how many of each there are. Talk about which has more, the box with forks or the box with spoons. Count up how many forks and spoons there are all together as the children put them back into the box.

Do sorting and counting with many other things the child is familiar with.

 in or out 4–10 min 1–3 Threes

352

Threes can

- copy counting to ten

Count to Ten

Have the children copy as you count to ten many times. Each time you count, do it with a different thing. Count ten fingers, ten toes, ten children, ten blocks, ten chairs, ten dolls, ten books, and more. Have the children try to think of other things you can count to ten.

Let's take off our shoes and see how many toes we have!
Then you can get on your cots for nap.

 in or out 2–10 min 1–15 Threes

353

Threes can

- count two or three things

Answering How Many

Ask your Threes lots of "How Many" questions. Help them count to answer. Ask how many tables there are in the room, how many paint brushes they paint with, how many steps there are on the slide, and how many cubbies there are. See how many each child can count on his own.

How many blocks did you use, Ronny?
You counted them all!

 in or out　 1–3 min　 1–15 Threes

354

Threes can

- put circle pieces together to make a whole

Circle Parts

Cut out <u>four large paper circles</u>. Make them sturdy by covering them with <u>clear contact paper</u>. Cut one in half, one into thirds, one into quarters, and leave the last one whole. Ask your Threes to put the pieces together to make circles like the whole one they see. Talk about halves, thirds, and quarters and how many pieces make up each circle as the children work.

You used one half and two quarters to make a whole circle, Eduardo. Can you make a circle using some other pieces?

Try this with other shapes, too.

 in or out　 3–10 min　 1–3 Threes

355

Threes can

- copy your counting
- understand *most* and *fewest*

How Many Does It Take?

Have <u>five or six different-sized containers</u>, such as large and small margarine tubs and different-sized clean, empty frozen juice cans. Next to these put a <u>dishpan of inch cubes</u>. Let the children fill the containers with the cubes. When they are full, have children help you count how many fit into each. Talk about which container holds the most and which holds the fewest.

How many cubes fit in this little can, Susan? Yes, three. Let's count how many there are in this big one.

 in or out | 3–10 min | 1–4 Threes

356

Threes can

- match one-to-one
- count three or more things

Counting Buttons

Put into a <u>box</u> <u>lots of colorful big buttons</u>. Make <u>five or more 8-by-10-inch cloth mats</u>. On the first mat, write the number 1 and draw one button-sized circle. On the next mat write a 2, with two circles, and so on, until you have five. Spread the mats out on a table or on the floor. Put the buttons near the mats. Show your Threes how to put one button on each circle. Help the children count the buttons they put on all the mats.

Play this game with other things to count, such as poker chips or pretty stones. Instead of cloth mats, try boxes or sheets of cardboard with numbers and circles on them.

 in or out | 5–12 min | 1–3 Threes

357

Threes can

- count two or three things

Number Feelie Bag

Make a <u>feelie bag</u> by putting a <u>plastic margarine tub</u> into a <u>big, clean sock</u>. Put one, two, or three <u>small counting things</u>, such as inch cubes, small balls, or acorns, into the feelie bag. Don't tell your Threes how many are in there. Have one child reach in and try to figure out how many things there are. Let him guess and then count the things as he pulls them out.

That was a surprise, wasn't it, Bob?
There were only two balls.
I bet they rolled around and fooled you!

See what the child does if you surprise him with an empty bag one time. Say the word *none* or *zero* to tell how many there are when the bag is empty.

 in or out　 3–10 min　**#** 1–3 Threes

358

Threes can

- count three or more things
- follow directions

Making Number Books

Help your Threes make their own number books. You can start a book for each child by folding <u>five pieces of paper</u> together in the middle. Then <u>staple</u> the folded edge. Write numbers from one to ten on the inside pages. Put the child's name on the front page. Help the child stick the right number of <u>small stickers</u> onto each page. Give the child only the number of stickers needed for one page at a time.

This is a seven, Karen. Let's count out seven stars.
One, two, three, four, five, six, seven. Good!
Now you can stick them on this page.

Later, look at the books with the children and help them count some more.

 in or out　 10–20 min　**#** 1–4 Threes

Activities for Learning from the World Around Them

359

Threes can

- count three or more things
- follow directions

Count as You Cook

Have each child make his own fruit salad in a cup at snack time. In separate <u>bowls</u>, set out <u>small pieces of fruit</u> such as pineapple chunks, apple slices, banana slices, and raisins. Try picture-word recipe cards next to each bowl to show the Threes how many of each fruit they should take to make their salad. (A sample picture-word recipe for fruit salad is on page 325.) Help each child to count the right amounts.

Look, Roberto. It says two banana slices.
Can you take two slices and put them into your cup?

Let the children eat their salads right away, or make salads earlier, put names on the cups, and all eat together.

 in or out   3–5 min   1–3 Threes

360

Threes can

- count three or more things
- do easy matching

Number-Picture Match Game

Make <u>two sets of number-picture cards</u>. Make one set of five cards that shows from one to five balloons. Make another set that shows from one to five happy faces. Write the number on the cards, too, if you wish. Spread out one set of cards on a table or the floor so that the Threes can easily see and touch them. Then look at the cards in the other set one by one with the children. Help them match the cards to the cards spread out, putting the "ones" together, the "twos" together, and so on.

Yes, Elizabeth. There are two faces on this card.
Can you put it on top of the card with two balloons?

Make sets of cards with other pictures, too.

 in or out   5–10 min   1–2 Threes

Activities for Learning from the World Around Them

361

Number-Picture Sorting Game

Put out a <u>sorting board</u> with a few sets of <u>number-picture cards that show one, two, three or more things</u>. (Directions for making sorting boards are on page 348.) Have the children sort the cards into rows. You can get them started by putting a first card into each pocket. Help the children count and figure out where the rest of the cards go.

How many bears are there, Pete? Yes, there's one.
Which row are the "ones" in?

Let the Threes sort on their own when they're ready, but be sure to notice and be excited about the work they've done.

Threes can

- count three or more things
- do easy sorting

 in or out   5–12 min   1–2 Threes

362

Number Grocery Bags

Put out <u>five sturdy grocery bags</u>. Write a big number on each bag so that they are numbered from one to five. Draw one dot on the bag numbered one, two dots on the bag numbered two, and so on. Fill a <u>toy shopping cart</u> with <u>clean, empty food containers</u> and <u>plastic fruits or vegetables</u>. Show the children how to put one food into the bag marked "one," two foods into the bag marked "two," and continue until all bags have the right number of things in them. Help the children count the dots on the bags and then count as they put the foods in the bags. Then let them play with the foods, grocery cart, and bags on their own.

Threes can

- count three or more things
- do easy matching

 indoors   5–15 min   1–4 Threes

363

Threes can

- use toys with small pieces

Magnetic Numbers

Put out <u>magnetic numbers</u> in a <u>container</u> and a <u>metal board</u> that they will stick to. Let your Threes play freely with these. If they are interested, tell them the names of numbers they touch or move.

That's a three, Annie. You're three years old.

Make sure the small magnets in the numbers you use do not come out easily.

 in or out 2–10 min 1–2 Threes

364

Threes can

- close a space with four blocks

Animals in Cages

Put out a <u>box of small plastic animals</u> with <u>some small blocks</u>. Help the children make cages by putting four or more blocks together. Ask them to put one, two, or three animals in cages they build. Enjoy pretending with the children. Make animal noises, and have animals escape and run around from cage to cage. Talk about how the number of animals in the cages changes.

Oh, oh! My zebra jumped out!
He's running into the elephant cage.
Now there are three animals in the elephant cage!

Try plastic strawberry boxes for cages, too, or use bigger animals with the blocks in the block area.

 in or out 5–20 min 1–4 Threes

365

Threes can

- copy counting to ten

Counting Exercises

On a rainy day when you can't go out or at a time when your Threes are full of energy, do simple exercises with them. As you exercise, help them copy your counting with rhythm.

Let's touch our toes ten times.
Try to count with me.
Now let's jump up and down.
One, two, three, four.
One, two, three, four.

 in or out   3–10 min   # 1–15 Threes

366

Threes can

- understand *far* and *near*
- follow directions

Far/Near Running Game

Have your Threes stand with you at one end of the outside play yard. Ask one child to choose something "far away" in the play yard. When he names it, have all the children run there and then back to you. Talk about how far away the thing was.

Have another child choose a thing that is "near." Have all the children run to that thing and come back. Continue with far and near things. Have the children get to them by walking, hopping, tip-toeing, or rolling. Count how many steps it takes to get to a few of the things.

 outdoors   5–10 min   # 1–15 Threes

367

Threes can

- count two or three things

Hop Once, Hop Twice

Ask your Threes to do one, two, three, or many hops, claps, smiles, or other actions. Have them try to count as they do each one. Add plenty of silly actions so that Threes have fun as they get rid of energy.

Let's squiggle like a worm!
Do two worm squiggles.

Be sure children have plenty of space to move.

 in or out 3–7 min 1–15 Threes

368

Threes can

- understand some time words

Time Talk

Use time words with your Threes. Tell them the time and let them look at a clock or your watch when it's time to do different things.

Do you feel hungry, Stephanie? I do too!
See my watch? It's almost nine o'clock.
At nine o'clock we have snack.

Let the children move the hands on <u>toy clocks</u> in play, or use a <u>timer</u> when children take turns. Talk about the time as children see how these work.

 in or out 1–2 min 1–15 Threes

Felt Flower and
Flower Pot Patterns

How to Make Sand-Dot Number Cards

1. Use ten sturdy cardboard rectangles, about 8 by 10 inches each.
2. Number the cards with big numbers from 1 to 10. Use a wide marker to do this.
3. On each card draw the number of dots that matches the number on the card.
4. Go over the numbers and dots you have made with white glue.
5. Sprinkle fine sand over the glue.
6. Lay the cards flat to let the glue dry. When they are dry, shake the cards gently to let the extra sand fall off.

Activities for Learning from the World Around Them

Counting Songs and Rhymes

Baa Baa Black Sheep

Baa baa black sheep
Have you any wool?
Yes sir, yes sir,
Three bags full.　　　　　(hold up three fingers)
One for the master,　　　　(hold up one finger)
One for the dame,　　　　(hold up two fingers)
And one for the little child　(hold up three fingers)
Who lives down the lane.

The Bee Hive

Here is the bee hive,　　　(put hands together)
Where are the bees?　　　(make a fist)
Hiding out
Where nobody sees.　　　(put hand behind back)
They are coming out now.
They are all alive—　　　(bring hand out)
One, two, three, four, five.　(put up one finger at a time)

Five in the Bed

There were five in the bed
And the little one said,
"Roll over, roll over!"　　(roll one hand over the other)
So they all rolled over
And one fell out.
There were four in the bed
And the little one said, etc.

Five Little Monkeys

Five little monkeys　　　(hold up five fingers)
Jumping on the bed,　　　(jump fingers on palm of other hand)

One fell off　　　　　　(hold up one finger)
And bumped his head.　　(rub head)
They ran for the doctor　　(run fingers across other hand)
And the doctor said,
"No more monkeys jumping on
*   the bed!"*　　　　　(point and shake finger)
(Continue with four, three, two, and one monkey)

Five Little Pumpkins

Five little pumpkins	(hold up five fingers)
Sitting on a gate.	
The first one said,	(hold up one finger)
"Oh my, it's getting late!"	
The second one said,	(hold up two fingers)
"There are witches in the air!"	
The third one said,	(hold up three fingers)
"But we don't care!"	
The fourth one said,	(hold up four fingers)
"Let's have some fun!"	
The fifth one said,	(hold up five fingers)
"Let's run, run, run!"	
Whooooo went the wind,	
And out went the light,	
And the five little pumpkins	
Rolled out of sight.	(roll one hand over the other)

Johnny Works with One Hammer

Johnny works with one hammer	(pretend to hammer with one fist)
One hammer, one hammer, one hammer	
Johnny works with one hammer	
Now he works with two.	(pretend to hammer with two fists)
Continue with:	
two hammers	(use both fists)
three hammers	(use two fists, one foot)
four hammers	(use two fists, two feet)
five hammers	(use two fists, two feet, nod head)
Then he goes to sleep.	(Close eyes, put head on folded hands)

One Little, Two Little, Three Little Children

One little, two little, three little children
Four little, five little, six little children
Seven little, eight little, nine little children
Ten little children right here.
(Sing this, using fingers instead of children)

One, Two, Buckle My Shoe

One, two, buckle my shoe;
Three, four, open the door;
Five, six, pick up sticks;
Seven, eight, lay them straight;
Nine, ten, a big fat hen!

Six Little Ducks

Six little ducks that I once knew	(hold up six fingers)
Fat ones, skinny ones, tall ones too.	
But the first little duck with the feather on his back,	(hold up one finger) (wiggle one finger)
He led the others with a quack, quack, quack.	(open and close fingers to thumb)

Down to the river they did go
Wibble wobble, wibble wobble, to and fro. *(with palms together, move hands back and forth)*
But the first little duck with the feather on his back,
He led the others with a quack, quack, quack. *(open and close fingers to thumb)*

This Old Man

This old man, he played one, he played nick-nack on my thumb,
With a nick-nack paddy-whack, give a dog a bone,
This old man came rolling home.
Additional verses: (2) Shoe; (3) Knee; (4) Door; (5) Hive; (6) Sticks;
    (7) Up in heaven; (8) Gate; (9) Spine; (10) Once again

Three Little Kittens

The three little kittens	The three little kittens
They lost their mittens	They found their mittens
And they began to cry,	And they called out with joy,
"Oh, mother dear,	"Oh, mother dear,
We sadly fear	See here, see here,
Our mittens we have lost."	Our mittens we have found."
"What, lost your mittens?	"What, found your mittens?
You naughty kittens!	You good little kittens!
Then you shall have no pie."	Then you shall have some pie."
"Meow, Meow, we shall have no pie.	"Meow, Meow, we shall have some pie.
Meow, Meow, we shall have no pie."	Meow, Meow, we shall have some pie."

Two Little Blackbirds

Two little blackbirds sitting on a hill.
One named Jack and one named Jill.
Fly away Jack, fly away Jill.
Come back Jack, come back Jill.
Two little blackbirds sitting on a hill.
One named Jack and one named Jill.

Materials and Notes

Five Senses

things to smell

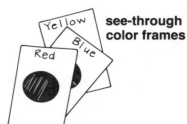

see-through color frames

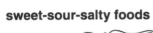

sweet-sour-salty foods

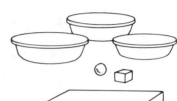

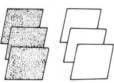

color-shade cards

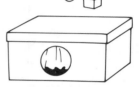

feel-it box

- Give Threes many chances to use all their senses to learn. Help them use many words that tell about what they see, hear, smell, taste, and feel each day.

- Make sure that all things around the children are safe. Then you will not need rules such as "Don't touch," which keep children from learning freely through their senses.

- Talk to parents about some of the senses activities you do so that they can use the ideas at home with their children.

- See Recipes to Cook with Children and the Sample Fruit Salad Recipe, pages 325–326.

Activity Checklist

Five Senses

Although three-year-olds are able to learn some things by listening to adults, using the five senses is still the most natural way for them to learn. They are able to tell you more about what their senses tell them, and are developing the thinking skills needed to understand such concepts as matching sounds, textures or colors.

Check for each age group	*36 – 42 mo*	*42 – 48 mo*
1. Cozy areas and soft things are provided, such as cuddly toys, cushions, rugs.	—	—
2. Indoor noise level is generally low and comfortable. Unnecessary background noise is avoided.	—	—
3. Pictures, mobiles, and other objects are placed where it is easy for children to see them.	—	—
4. Toys of different colors, shapes, textures, or sound qualities are available to children daily.	—	—
5. Foods served to children have little or no added salt or sugar and are not heavily spiced, so that children can enjoy natural flavors and smells.	—	—
6. Children are offered foods with a variety of tastes, colors, and textures.	—	—
7. Games that encourage children to use the senses are available daily (texture or sound matching games, feelie boxes, easy sorting games).	—	—
8. Adult shows children how to use new materials so that children can use them independently.	—	—
9. Senses games are organized by type and stored in sturdy containers.	—	—
10. Adult talks with child about what the child is sensing and asks questions.	—	—

369

Threes can

- enjoy soft cuddly things

Cozy Corner

Set up a cozy corner where your Threes can go to snuggle, play quietly, or look at books. Put lots of fresh, clean <u>pillows and soft toys</u> in this area. Add one or two <u>little blankets</u>, too. Wash these things often. When they are fresh and clean, have the three-year-old smell them. Ask questions to help the children tell how the clean, soft things smell and feel.

Smell the blankets, Marcy.
Joey's dad just washed them and brought them in.
They're nice and clean.
How do they smell?

 indoors 2–7 min 1–4 Threes

370

Threes can

- talk simply about things they smell

Spice Packets

Shake a nice smelling <u>spice</u> (ground cloves, cinnamon) or an <u>extract</u> (vanilla, peppermint) onto eight or ten <u>cotton balls</u>. Put the cotton balls into a square of tightly woven <u>scrap material</u>. Pull the edges together and securely tie the spice packets closed with <u>yarn</u>. Make many of these packets using different smells. Put each packet into a <u>sturdy covered container</u> for your Threes to use. As children take out and smell the packets, talk with them about the different smells.

Oh, what a face you made, Germaine!
May I smell it, please? That's peppermint.
Do you know anything else that smells like that?

Replace old spices with new ones if smells get weak.
  You can also add pictures of things that smell like the spices to play a matching game.

 in or out 2–7 min 1–3 Threes

371

Threes can

- enjoy textures
- talk about how
  things feel

Feelie Books

Buy or make several <u>feelie books</u> to use with your Threes. You can make one by taping or gluing things to feel onto sturdy cardboard pages. Try a feather, a fuzzy cloth, sandpaper, vinyl, and a piece of satin cloth. Punch holes in the pages and loosely tie them together with yarn or string. You can write what each thing is and what children say about how it feels, if you wish. Use these books with the threes. Talk about feeling the pages gently and being careful not to pull things off. Watch the Threes enjoy the ways the things feel. Ask questions to see what they can say about the things.

Put the books out of reach when done, if you need to. Or be ready to replace parts that get lost.

 in or out 4–8 min 1–2 Threes

372

Threes can

- look at things in
  many ways
- learn new words

Upside-Down World

Talk with your Threes about what they see when they look at things upside-down. Be on the lookout for the upside-down times that come so naturally to Threes and talk about them when they happen. Or show a few children how to bend over and look through their legs to see an upside-down world.

Things look different when you're upside-down, don't they, Kevin? The top is on the bottom and the bottom's on the top! What do you see, Norio?

 in or out 1–2 min 1–15 Threes

373

Threes can

■ say names of foods

Smell-Taste Surprises

Put three <u>foods that have strong familiar smells</u> into three <u>plastic containers with lids</u>. Try tuna fish, orange slices, and peanut butter. Have one child at a time close her eyes and smell what's in each container. Talk with the child about what she smells. Let the child open her eyes and look at what she was smelling. See which ones she wants to taste. Talk about the tastes, too.

Do you know what this is?
Do you want to taste a little tuna fish, Jackie?
We had tuna salad for lunch yesterday.

 in or out   3–5 min   1–4 Threes

374

Threes can

■ tell very heavy from very light

Heavy-Light Cans

Collect eight or ten <u>empty juice cans</u>. Fill half with <u>sand</u> or <u>pebbles</u>. Leave the others empty. Seal all the cans tightly with strong <u>tape</u>. Have your Threes pick up the cans and say whether each is heavy or light. Let the children help you sort the cans into a heavy group and a light group. Talk about what you are doing as you do it.

Let's put all the heavy cans here, and all the light ones here.
Is your can heavy or light, Noah?
Yes, it's light. Can you put it here?

Leave the cans in a sturdy box on a low shelf for your Threes to use. Watch to see if they try to sort the cans on their own.

 in or out   5–8 min   1–4 Threes

375

Threes can

- talk about what they see
- enjoy colors

Looking at a Colored World

Frame <u>colored gift-wrap cellophane or see-through plastic sheets</u> for your Threes to look through. For each frame, cut out two 8-by-10-inch <u>cardboard squares</u>. Use an <u>X-acto knife or a single-sided razor blade</u> to cut a hole in the center of each. <u>Glue</u> the colored, see-through cellophane or plastic tightly over the hole of one cardboard frame. Glue the two frames together so that the cellophane is in the middle. Make frames of different colors. Show your Threes how different things look when they are seen through the color frames.

Give Threes chances to look through colored plastic, transparent building toys, cups, or sunglasses, too. Or put colored cellophane on a window for children to look through.

 in or out 2–15 min 1–3 Threes

376

Threes can

- recognize some sounds
- open and close containers

Sound Tubs

Put one small thing into each of five <u>margarine tubs with lids</u>. Use <u>things that will sound different</u> from each other when shaken in the tub. For example, use a bell, block, paper clip, little ball of yarn, and pebble. Show your Threes how to shake the tubs and then look inside to see what made the noise. After a while see if they can guess what's inside by just listening.

Do you remember what made that noise, Dee Dee?
Peek inside to find out.

Put the tubs in a dishpan in a quiet place, for the children to use on their own. Change things in the tubs often.

 in or out 5–10 min 1–3 Threes

377

Threes can

- follow directions
- pour from a pitcher

From Lemon to Lemonade

Help each three-year-old make his own lemonade. First, help each child squeeze one quarter of a <u>lemon</u> into an <u>8-oz cup</u>. Talk about the lemon seeds and have the children take them out. Let the children taste a tiny bit of the lemon juice on one fingertip. Laugh and talk about the sour taste. Have each child add <u>water</u> from a <u>small pitcher</u> to his juice and taste again. Finally, have each child add a <u>teaspoon</u> of <u>sugar</u> and stir. As the children drink, see if they can remember the things they did to make the lemonade. Talk about how the tastes changed.

That was sour, wasn't it!
It was less sour when we added water.
What made it sweet?

 in or out   5–10 min   1–6 Threes

378

Threes can

- enjoy soft tickling

Tickle Things

Use a piece of <u>grass or a feather</u> to tickle a three-year-old's arms, fingers, legs, or toes. Talk about how the soft tickle feels. See if one child can find a tickly thing to tickle a friend. Try tickling with a few different things.

That piece of grass tickled, didn't it, Leo?
Now see how this yarn feels on your arm.

 in or out   2–7 min   1–5 Threes

379

Whispering Directions Game

Play a game in which you whisper fun directions for your Threes to follow. Have them stand facing you and give whispered directions, such as "Pat your head," or "Jump up and down." Help the children remember to quiet down to listen by putting your finger to your lips as a "quiet" sign.

Make sure every child can hear you even though you are whispering.

Threes can

- follow easy directions
- understand some action words

 in or out | 2–5 min | 1–15 Threes

380

Light, Dark, and Medium Colors

Use crayons to make shaded color cards of a few colors. For each color, make a dark shade, a lighter shade, and a very light shade. Show the child one set of cards. See if she can point to the right card when you ask which is light, dark, and in the middle. Have the child help you sort the cards into piles of light, medium, and dark colors.

Let's put all the dark cards here, the light ones here, and the medium ones here, in the middle.

Next time have the children try to put the three shades of the same colors together.

Where are the three red shades?

Threes can

- tell dark and light
- help sort color shades

 in or out | 5–8 min | 1–2 Threes

381

Threes can

- enjoy short stories
- tell about things they know

Scratch and Sniff Books

Look at a "Scratch and Sniff" book with a few of your Threes. As you read the words, let each child scratch and smell the special places on each page. Ask questions to help them say more about the smells.

What's the bunny smelling on this page, Annie?
Yes, it's an apple.
When did we have apples at school, Larry?

 in or out | 5–10 min | 1–3 Threes

382

Threes can

- talk about foods

Changing Food Flavors

At meal or snack times, let children taste foods with no other flavors added. Then offer the same foods with something added that changes the flavor. For example, let children taste plain toast, then taste it with a little butter, and then with sugar and cinnamon as cinnamon toast. Or let children try a plain fish stick and then try one that they dip into ketchup. Talk about all the tastes.

Some other food flavor ideas are:
  oatmeal, plain and with cinnamon
  banana, plain or with peanut butter
  cracker, plain or with cheese
  raw vegetables, plain or with yogurt

 in or out | 6–12 min | 1–15 Threes

383

Threes can

- talk about things they hear, smell, and taste

Popping Corn

<u>Pop corn</u> with your Threes. As you begin, put a few kernels of corn into the <u>pan</u> with <u>oil</u>. Have the children close their eyes and listen. See if they can tell you when they hear the corn pop. Add the rest of the corn. Ask your Threes to tell you when they can smell the popcorn. Have fun eating the popcorn plain and enjoying the good taste.

OK, I poured the corn in.
Let me know when you begin to smell it.

 indoors | 10–20 min | 1–15 Threes

384

Threes can

- put three containers in order, from full to empty

Which Holds Most?

Put out <u>three clear plastic containers</u> of the same size and a <u>dishpan of sand</u>. Have a child help you fill one container full and another half-full. In the last container put just a little sand. Ask the child to show you the containers with the most and the least sand. Ask her to show you the middle one, too. Help her put the containers in order from full to almost empty.

Where's the one with the most sand, Betsy?
That's right. Put it here.

Give the child a chance to fill containers for you to talk about. Try this game with colored water, pebbles, rice, or marbles, too. Use words such as *more* and *less, most* and *least* as you talk.

 in or out | 3–5 min | 1–2 Threes

385

Threes can

■ match same sounds

Melody Bell Match Game

Give the child two <u>melody bells</u> to ring and listen to. Be sure that the sounds the bells make are far apart—one low and one high. Have the child hide his eyes as you ring one of the bells. Then have him ring the bells and tell you which one you rang.

No peeking, Ramon! Just listen. Which bell did I ring?

Add one more bell when a child finds two bells very easy. See if two Threes will play this game together, one ringing bells and one listening.

 in or out 2–5 min 1–2 Threes

386

Threes can

■ tell about how things feel

Feel-It Box

Cut a 3-to-4-inch hole in the end of a <u>large shoe box</u>. <u>Staple</u> or <u>glue</u> a <u>scrap of material</u> on the inside of the box so that it covers the hole like a curtain. Put a <u>familiar toy or other safe thing</u> in the box for a three-year-old to reach in and touch. Make sure the lid is on so that she can't see inside. Ask questions to see if the child can tell a little about what she's feeling. See if she can guess what it is.

How does it feel, Marjorie? Yes, hard.
Can you tell me more about it?
Do you know what it is?

Leave the box out with a few different things for two friends to use together.

 in or out 2–5 min 1–2 Threes

387

Sorting Soft and Hard

Put <u>lots of soft and hard things</u> into a <u>big box</u>. Have the child pull out one thing, feel it, and say whether it's soft or hard. See if the child can sort the hard things into one pile and the soft things into another. Talk about each thing as the child works. Say what each thing is made of.

Threes can

- do simple sorting
- tell soft from hard

What is that, Victor? Yes, it's a block.
Is the block soft or hard?
That's right, it's hard. It's a hard wooden block.
Let's put it here with the other hard things.

Once the children know how to sort on their own, leave the box on a low shelf so that they can work with it when they want.

 in or out | 4–8 min | 1–3 Threes

388

Mixing Juices

Put <u>several kinds of juice</u> into <u>small pitchers</u>. Let your Threes pour a little of each kind into a <u>cup</u> and taste it. Talk about each juice— where it comes from, its color, smell, and taste. Then let the children mix a little of two juices together and taste. Talk about the taste and color. Ask which ones the children like best.

Threes can

- pour well from a small pitcher

Which juices did you mix, Beth?
Grape and apple make a purple drink.
Does it taste good?

Try apple, grape, and cranberry juices together, or orange, grapefruit, and lemonade. Freeze some favorite mixtures to have as popsicles.

 in or out | 5–10 min | 1–5 Threes

389

Threes can

■ tell dark from light

Flashlight Play

Have two or three <u>sturdy flashlights</u> for your Threes to use. Make a <u>dark hide-away place</u> where they can try out the lights. Use a <u>table</u> with a <u>blanket</u> over it, some blankets in the cozy corner for the children to crawl under, or a big <u>box</u> the children can hide in. Let the children decide when they want to have dark and light. Listen to be sure this play is fun and not scary.

It was dark under there, wasn't it, Emma?
Did you like it with the lights off or on?

Collect the flashlights when the play is done so that the batteries last longer.

 in or out 3–20 min 1–3 Threes

390

Threes can

■ learn by smelling and tasting

Nice-Smelling Plants

Have a <u>few safe herb or spice plants</u>, such as mint, basil, marjoram, or chives growing in pots. Let the children smell and taste the leaves of these plants. Show them how they can brush the leaves gently with their fingers to make the leaves smell nice. Be sure the children know that they are not to eat the leaves of other plants in pots.

This is a mint plant, Carmen.
Brush the leaves and smell.
This is a special plant called a spice plant.

 indoors 2–10 min 1–15 Threes

391

Threes can

- recognize what makes familiar sounds

Sounds of Real Things

Use a <u>tape recorder</u> to record sounds of real things the children know. Play the sounds one at a time as the Threes listen. See if the children know what is making each sound.

Try some of these sounds on your tape:

children laughing	a telephone ringing
water running	a cat meowing
wind chimes	thunder
a car horn	a musical instrument

You can make a picture game to go with the tape by collecting <u>pictures that go with the sounds</u>. Put the pictures with the tape for the children to use.

 indoors | 5–12 min | # 1–15 Threes

392

Threes can

- talk about hot and cold

Hot Foods/Cold Foods

Serve meals or snacks with <u>foods of different temperatures</u>. Ask questions to see what the children can say about the foods.

What do you think about this frozen banana, Nathan?
Yes, it is cold!
How do we usually eat bananas?

Try some of these foods:

Cold	Warm
yogurt or fruit juice popsicles	soup
fruit	cocoa
juice or milk	oatmeal

 in or out | 5–10 min | # 1–15 Threes

393

Threes can

- talk a little about what they see, hear, and feel

Surprise Packages

Wrap an <u>unbreakable toy or other familiar thing</u> in many layers of <u>newspaper</u>. <u>Tape</u> each layer closed. Give one of these packages to a child. Have her look at, shake, squeeze, and feel the package to try to guess what's inside. Help her take off one or two layers of newspaper at a time until she figures out what is inside. Ask questions to help her talk about the surprise.

Is the thing hard or soft, Hester?
Is it big or little?

Be sure to have at least one package per child. Have a big bag near to put paper into.

 in or out | 5–7 min | **#** 1–3 Threes

394

Threes can

- say some noises things make

What Makes This Noise?

Collect <u>pictures of familiar things that make noises</u>. Show your Threes the pictures and ask what noise each thing would make.
Try pictures of these:

a hammer	a lion
a baby crying	a telephone
a car	a drum
a bumble bee	a faucet with water running
a mouse	

Talk about which sounds are loud and which are soft, too.

Yes, Barry. The hammer goes bang, bang.
Is that loud or soft?
Can a hammer make a tap, tap, tap noise?

 in or out | 4–10 min | **#** 1–15 Threes

395

Threes can

■ guess things by feeling and listening

Eyes-Closed Walk

Have the child close his eyes or cover them with his hands. Slowly and carefully lead him around the room or play yard while he isn't looking. Have him keep his eyes closed when you get to one place. Let him feel and listen to things nearby and then try to guess where he is.

Here, Seth. Feel this. It's cold and hard and smooth.
Listen carefully, too.
Do you know where we are?

Some children may need to peek a bit to keep from being afraid or just because they're curious. This is fine. Just play the game with them in their own three-year-old way.

 in or out | 2–5 min | **#** 1 child at a time

396

Threes can

■ put three things in order from softest to hardest

Soft, Harder, Hardest Game

Put out a piece of <u>cotton</u>, <u>a sponge</u>, and <u>a block</u> to talk about with your Threes. Let them touch the things and see if they can tell you which is hardest, softest, and in the middle. Help the children put the things in a row in the right order.

Try this with other things, too, such as:

foods—hard carrot, softer pear, softest pudding
outside things—hard stone, softer leaf, softest fluffy dandelion.

 in or out | 2–5 min | **#** 1–5 Threes

397

Threes can

■ follow directions
■ tell loud from soft

Make Sounds Softer

Play a <u>record or tape of music</u> as the Threes listen. Show them how they can make the music sound louder or softer by covering and uncovering their ears with their hands. Talk a little about how not as much sound can go into their ears when they are covered.

Have them cover and uncover their ears as they listen to other noises, too.

 indoors | 2–3 min | **#** 1–15 Threes

398

Threes can

■ tell different tastes

Sweet, Sour, and Salty Tastes

Have a tasting party with your Threes. Choose two or three of these <u>foods</u> and give your Threes a little taste of each. See if the children can say whether each is sweet, sour, or salty. Think up new foods your Threes enjoy that are sweet, sour, or salty. Add them to these lists and try them on another day.

Sweet	Sour	Salty
raisins	yogurt	pretzels
applesauce	lemonade	ham
pudding	grapefruit	saltine crackers
banana bread	dill pickles	cheddar cheese

 in or out | 5–15 min | **#** 1–15 Threes

399

Threes can

- explore with their senses

What's It Made Of?

Put into a <u>box</u> <u>one or two things made of each of these materials:</u> <u>metal, wood, rubber, plastic, cardboard, cloth, clay, and glass.</u>

Have the Threes take out one thing at a time. Ask questions to help them tell you the name of the thing and anything else about the way it looks, feels, or sounds. Talk about what each thing is made of.

Yes, this is a key.
How does the key look? Right, it is shiny.
Is it hard or soft? Is it warm or cold?
Do you know what it's made of?
The key is made of metal.

 in or out | 5–10 min | # 1–15 Threes

400

Threes can

- do easy matching

Matching Textures

Gather <u>material scraps that feel different</u>—rough, smooth, fuzzy, bumpy, slinky, and others. Cut two four-inch squares of each. <u>Glue</u> each one onto a four-inch square of <u>cardboard</u>. You will have two cards of each material. Put these into a <u>dishpan</u>. Look at all the squares with the children. Help them talk about how each feels and looks. See if the Threes can match the cards.

How does that square feel, Mary?
Can you find the other one that's just the same?

Later, use pairs of texture cards that match in texture but not in color, such as a red fuzzy card and a blue one, or a green silky card and a yellow one.

 in or out | 5–10 min | # 1–2 Threes

401

Texture Hunt

Give each child a <u>little paper bag</u> to use on a texture hunt. Have each child hunt for one or two things that are rough, smooth, hard, soft, or other textures they know well. Let the children look for a while. You can help anyone who has trouble. Have the children bring the things they found to show each other. Have them say what texture their things are. Ask questions to find out more about the things the children found. Make a collection of hard things, soft things, and so on.

What did you find, Shawn? Oh yes, a rock.
Is the rock smooth or rough?
Where does it belong?

Threes can

■ recognize and talk about some textures

 in or out   3–10 min   1–15 Threes

402

Cook with Kids

Choose a <u>simple recipe</u> to use as you and your Threes cook. Talk about the <u>foods</u> you are using. Let children taste and smell the foods as they work. Make sure to keep germs from spreading by following sanitation rules: wash hands, use a clean spoon to stir.

You can lick the spoon, Phyllis.
How does that taste?
Then we need to wash the spoon in the dishwasher before we use it again.

See sample recipes and cookbook ideas, pages 325–327.

Threes can

■ follow directions

 indoors   10–20 min   1–15 Threes

Sample Fruit Salad Picture Word Recipe

1. Copy this recipe on large pieces of cardboard to make recipe cards.
2. Put each card in a row on a low table or counter from left to right.
3. Put each bowl of fruit in front of its card.
4. Have each child start on the left and take the right amount of fruit to put into his own cup.

FRUIT SALAD

2 apple slices ①

3 banana slices ②

3 pineapple chunks ③

2 orange sections ④

4 raisins ⑤

Stir and eat ⑥

This recipe is from *Cook and Learn* by Beverly Veitch and Thelma Harms. Menlo Park, CA: Addison-Wesley Publishing Company, 1981.

Recipes to Cook with Children

Vegetable Soup

1. Ask each child to bring a raw vegetable from home.
2. Talk about the vegetables they bring in. Say words that tell how the vegetable looks and feels.
3. Set up an area where the children can *safely* wash, peel and cut up their own vegetables.
4. Dump all of the cut-up fresh vegetables into a crock pot. Add a large can of tomato juice or V-8 juice. Add chicken or beef stock if you have it.
5. Plug the crock pot in and turn it up to medium-high. Talk about the yummy smells you smell all morning as the vegetable soup cooks.
6. Eat your homemade soup with lunch or as a snack.

Applesauce

1. Let each child help clean, peel, core and cut an apple into small pieces. Use many words as you talk about what they are doing.
2. Put all the apple pieces into a large pot or crock pot. Add enough water to cover the apples one fourth of the way. Add a little cinnamon or nutmeg if you wish.
3. Slowly cook the apples all morning until they cook down into applesauce. Talk with your children about how it smells.
4. Eat the applesauce with your lunch.

For more ideas on cooking with children, try:

Cook and Learn by Beverly Veitch and Thelma Harms
> Addison-Wesley Publishing Company
> Jacob Way
> Reading, Massachusetts 01867

Creative Food Experiences for Children by Mary Goodwin and Gerry Pollen
> Center for Science in the Public Interest
> 1755 S. Street N.W.
> Washington, DC 20009

Cool Cooking for Kids by Pat McClenahan and Ida Jaqua
> Fearon-Pitman
> 6 Davis Drive
> Belmont, CA 94002

More than Graham Crackers by Nancy Wannamaker, Kristen Hearn and Sherrill Richarz
> NAEYC
> 1834 Connecticut Avenue, N.W.
> Washington, DC 20009

Materials and Notes

Shape, Size, and Color

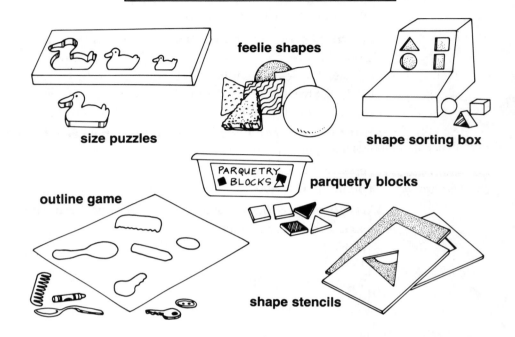

- Make size, shape, and color an everyday part of what you do with Threes. Use size, shape, and color words often, not just as part of a special learning time.

- Have puzzles, shape toys, and nesting toys for Threes to use every day. Keep these stored neatly on low shelves in sturdy containers so that the pieces don't get mixed up or lost.

- Ask parents to help you collect things you need for size, shape, and color activities—scraps of material, big/little things, and others. Ask them to talk with their children about size, shape, and color at home, too.

Activity Checklist

Shape, Size, and Color

Shape, size, and color activities for Threes include activities in which the adult and child point out and enjoy those attributes throughout the day. Many Threes will enjoy games matching sizes, colors, and shapes. Some will be able to do easy sorting. Threes are able to do 5-to-10-piece puzzles and are challenged when you ask them to name two or three colors. Because they can handle more activities independently, there can be several size, shape, and color activities out for them to use every day.

Check for each age group	*36–42 mo*	*42–48 mo*
1. Chances to explore things with obvious variety in shape, size, and color are offered daily in play.	—	—
2. Adult often points out and talks with children about the shape, size, and color of toys and other familiar things the child sees during both play and routine care times.	—	—
3. Pictures and books that show a variety of shapes, sizes, and colors are put where child can easily see and use them.	—	—
4. A variety of age-appropriate shape, size, and color games are available to children throughout the day (games matching size, color, or shape; puzzles; easy sorting games).	—	—
5. Adult shows interested child how to use age-appropriate shape, size, and color games.	—	—
6. Additional materials that require adult supervision are available daily.	—	—
7. Games and other materials are organized by type and stored in sturdy containers.	—	—
8. Games and materials are rotated to provide new interest.	—	—

403

Threes can

- put together two parts to make a whole shape

Put Together Circles and Squares

Cut two big circles and two big squares out of posterboard for each child. Cut one of each in half. Cover with clear contact paper. Talk about the whole shapes with the child. Let her run her fingers around the edges. Then take the shapes apart. See if the child can put them back together again. If a child has trouble with this, have her put each shape together on top of the whole shape.

When the child can do this, add the pieces for a larger or smaller circle and square to the shapes you already have. Then see if the child can put all the shapes together.

 in or out   3–10 min   1–4 Threes

404

Threes can

- tell big from little
- do simple sorting

Big/Little Sorting Game

Put a set of big things with a matching set of little things into a box. For example, include a big brush and a small doll's brush, a big plastic cup and a doll's plastic cup, a big sock and a baby's sock. Next to the box, spread out a large cloth and a smaller one. Help your Threes sort the big things onto the big cloth and the small things onto the small cloth. Show them first how to take one thing from the box and find its big or small match. Then they can decide which of the two things goes on each of the cloths.

Find the other spoon, B.J.
Then you will see which is big and which is little.
Good! Now where does the big spoon go?

 in or out   5–10 min   1–2 Threes

405

Threes can

- match real things to their outlines

Outline Game

Outline <u>eight to ten familiar things</u> on a <u>large piece of posterboard</u>. Cover the posterboard with <u>clear contact paper</u>. Put the things into a <u>sturdy box</u>. Have the three-year-old place each real thing on its outline.

Make several different games, with different things on each. Children who find working with one set very easy may want to do two games at once.

At another time, try outlines of matching big and little things, such as a big key and a small one, a big comb and a small one.

 in or out   5–10 min   1–2 Threes

406

Threes can

- point to a color you name

Color Search

Hold up a <u>card that shows one color</u>. Name the color. Ask your Threes what else they see that is the same color as the one you're holding up. Allow the children to search around the area.

Let each child carry a color card to hold up next to things around the room, if necessary.

Dinah, do you see something blue, like this?
Try looking on the art shelf.
Yes, Brad. That's a blue truck.

 in or out   3–15 min   1–3 Threes

407

Threes can

- match colors
- point to a color you name

Box Color Sort

Color the insides of <u>shallow cardboard boxes</u> so that you have boxes of red, blue, and yellow. Collect <u>small things of these same colors</u>—big beads, teddy bear counters, plastic shapes, or inch cubes. Show your Threes how to sort all the things by color into the colored containers. Tell the children what you are doing, and ask questions to see if they can help. When they know what to do, let them work on their own.

I want to put all the red things into the red box.
Which is the red box, Jean?

Later, add orange, purple, and green boxes with things to sort.

 in or out   3–15 min   1–2 Threes

408

Threes can

- point to colors you name
- recognize clothes names

Clothes Colors

Sit in a circle with your Threes. Look to see who is wearing <u>clothes of different colors</u>. Then ask color questions about clothes and see if your Threes can point out the answers. Hold up a color card for the children to look at if you need to.

Someone is wearing a red shirt today.
Do you see who it is? Yes, it's you, Matthew!
Two of you have on blue jeans. They're very dark blue.
Who is wearing blue jeans?

 in or out   2–6 min   2–15 Threes

409

Threes can

- match colors
- point to a color you name

Cloth Color Card Match Game

Find many different <u>scraps of solid-colored material</u>. Cut out and <u>glue</u> squares of the material to <u>sturdy cardboard cards</u> to make two matching cards of each color. Put the cards into a <u>dishpan</u>. Look at and talk about all the cloth cards with your Threes. Put out one card and see if the child can find the one that matches its color. Let the child match the rest of the cards. Talk about his work when he is done.

You matched all the colors, Donny!
Now can you show Sidney how to match colors?

 in or out   3–10 min   1–3 Threes

410

Threes can

- match colors

Inch Cube Match Game

Put out <u>inch cubes of four colors</u> in a dishpan. Add a few <u>inch cube pattern cards</u>. (You will find inch cube patterns on page 351.) Have the three-year-old choose a card to work with. Show the child how she can match the cubes to the squares of the same color. Talk about the colors as the child works.

Enjoy the more creative ways Threes use the cubes, too.

I see you put the yellow cube on the yellow square, Anette.
And you built a many-colored tower, Darren.
It reminds me of a rainbow.

 in or out   3–10 min   1–3 Threes

411

Threes can

- sort shapes
- do easy sorting

Sorting Feelie Shapes

Cut out five circles, squares, triangles, and rectangles from <u>sturdy cardboard</u>. Use <u>glue</u> to cover one of each shape with <u>sandpaper, fuzzy cloth, satin cloth, bumpy cloth, or vinyl</u>. Trim the edges evenly. Look at, talk about, and feel the shapes with your Threes. Show them how to run their fingers around the edges. Put out <u>four shallow boxes, with one shape drawn on each</u>. Show the children how to sort the shapes into the boxes.

Here's the bumpy square.
Can you find the fuzzy square, Latarsha?

 in or out   5–10 min   1–4 Threes

412

Threes can

- paste
- point to a few colors you name

Circle Designs

Have <u>lots of colorful circle stickers, or construction paper circles</u> for the children to stick on a <u>bigger piece of paper</u> with <u>paste</u>. Let the Threes use the circles to make their own designs. Put out crayons and see what the children add to their designs. Talk about the circle shapes and colors as the children work.

You used lots of circles in your design, Rosa.
Can you show me the yellow one?

Have children make designs with other shapes. Later, use a mixture of shapes, too.

 in or out   5–15 min   1–6 Threes

413

Paint On Shapes

Cut out <u>big paper shapes</u> for your Threes to <u>paint</u> on. Put <u>newspaper</u> under the shapes to keep the easel or table clean. Let the children choose the shapes they wish to use and paint in their own way. Ask questions to help each child talk about the shape and colors he used.

You're painting on the diamond, Joseph.
You've painted a circle here, in the diamond.

When the shapes are dry, you may want to <u>glue</u> them to larger pieces of paper and hang them where the children can see. Be sure each child's name is on his work.

Threes can

■ paint
■ talk about pictures they make

 in or out | 3–12 min | 1–4 Threes

414

Pegboard Match Game

Put out <u>two pegboards</u>, one for large pegs, the other for small pegs. Put ten or more <u>big and small pegs for each board</u> into one <u>container</u>. See if the children can match the pegs to their boards. Talk about big and little sizes as the children work.

Do the big pegs fit into the little holes, Lara?
Do the little ones fit into the big holes?

Threes can

■ tell big from little
■ put pegs in pegboard

 in or out | 3–12 min | # 1–2 Threes

415

Shape, Color, and Size Books

Look at and read <u>picture books about shape, color or size</u> with your Threes. Ask questions to help the children find things you name.

Which is the big dog, Fred? Yes, you're right!
And that's the little one.

Help the children talk about shape, color, and size in other books and pictures, too.

Threes can

- point to some colors and shapes you name
- use size words

 in or out   5–10 min # 1–3 Threes

416

Copying Simple Shapes

Use a <u>crayon or watercolor marker</u> to draw a circle on a <u>piece of paper</u> as the child watches. Talk about the way the line goes all the way around to make a circle. Talk about how the ends of the line meet. Next, see if the child can "be a copycat" and make a circle, too. Show how happy you are with any shape she makes. Then slowly make an "H." Make the two up-and-down lines first. Then add the middle line. Talk about the ways the lines go as you draw. See if the child can copy this shape, too.

Good try, Shannon! It looks like a bridge!

Later, see if the children can copy these shapes in sand or finger-paint.

Threes can

- try to copy a circle and "H" shape

 in or out   2–4 min # 1–2 Threes

417

Threes can

■ see shapes

Shapes in the Room

Point out the shapes of things your Threes see every day. For example, help them notice that balls or wheels are round, and windows and tables are squares or rectangles. Look at some pictures of these familiar things and talk about the shapes some more.

See the wheels on the toy truck?
They're round, aren't they, Akemi?

 in or out   2–5 min   1–15 Threes

418

Threes can

■ sort some shapes

Shape-Sorting Boxes

Put out a few <u>shape-sorting boxes</u> for the Threes to use. Talk about the shapes as the children work with these. Watch carefully to see if any child has trouble. Give that child an easier box to use.

That's a triangle shape, Antonia.
Do you see another triangle to put in?

(Directions for making shape-sorting boxes are on page 347.)

 in or out   3–12 min   1–3 Threes

419

Threes can

- do a 5-to-10-piece puzzle
- use size words

Size Puzzles

Add to your puzzle place some <u>puzzles that have graduated-sized</u> <u>(small, medium and large) pieces of the same picture.</u> Talk about the sizes of the pieces as the children work on these. See if they can point out the biggest and littlest.

You put in the biggest duck, Thomas.
Do you see the smallest?

If a child has trouble doing this kind of puzzle, you can put in the middle pieces and the child can try doing the others.

 in or out 3–9 min 1–3 Threes

420

Threes can

- use size words
- color

Body Outlines

Hang <u>paper from a large roll</u> so that it covers a long wall. Place the paper so it is the right height to outline your Threes' bodies as they stand against the wall. Outline each child, one next to the other. Talk about how tall each child is. Put the children's names on their outlines and let them color their outlines if they wish. When all are done, talk about who is tall, who is shorter, and who is middle-sized.

Are any children the same height?

 indoors 3–5 min 1 child at a time

421

Threes can

- color
- follow directions

Shape Stencils

Make or buy <u>shape stencils</u>. To make these, cut simple shapes into the middle of sturdy pieces of cardboard with an X-acto knife or a single-edged razor blade. The stencil is the frame you have when the shape is removed.

Talk about the stencil shapes with the Threes. Let them run their fingers along the inside edge of the frame. Show your Threes how to place a stencil on a piece of <u>paper</u>, hold it down, and color freely within the shape. Let each child choose a shape to work with and color in his own way.

You're making lots of dots in the square, Beatrice.

 in or out   3–20 min   **#** 1–4 Threes

422

Threes can

- recognize colors

Color Day

Have a special color day with your Threes on which all of you wear and talk about one color. Ask parents to help with this by having them dress their children in that color. Have some extra hats or shirts ready in case parents do not remember. For the one day, you can read or make a book about that color, have something to eat of that color, use that color for art, and have beads or pegs out that are that color. Think of as many fun ideas as you can.

We're having something red today at snack.
Yes, James. You are right! We're having red strawberries!

 in or out   all day   1–15 Threes

423

Threes can

- put together parts of a shape to make a whole

Parquetry Block Play

Put out <u>parquetry blocks</u> for your Threes to use freely. Help them talk about the colors and shapes as they play. Show a child who is interested how to put two shapes together to make a bigger or different shape.

I see you stacked all the diamonds on top of each other, Juan.

Look, Tina, you put two triangles together and made a square!

 in or out 2–15 min 1–3 Threes

424

Threes can

- tell long from short
- follow a path

Long Path/Short Path Game

Use <u>masking tape</u> on the floor to make a long and a short path to a place the children go often. For example, make a long path that goes all around the room from the art table to the sink, and a short path that goes straight to the sink. Have the children try out the paths. Talk about which is long and which is short. Let children choose which path to take as they move from one place to another.

Charlie, you need a little water in this cup. Do you want to follow the long path or the short path to the sink?

Tammy, you need to wash the paint off your hands.

Take the short path to the sink! It starts here.

 indoors 2–7 min 1–5 Threes

425

Threes can

- do easy sorting
- match shapes

Shape-Sorting Board

Put out a <u>sorting board with shape cards</u> to sort. (Directions for making a sorting board with pockets are on page 348.) Help the child get started by talking about how you sort shapes as you do the first few cards.

This is a circle. And here is the row the circles will go in.
I can tell because I see this circle at the top of the row.
Could you put the circle into the first pocket for me, please?
Now here's a triangle.
Where do you think the triangle should go?

 in or out   6–12 min   1–2 Threes

426

Threes can

- tell some things by touch
- point to a shape you name

Shapes Feelie Bag

Make a <u>feelie bag</u> by putting a <u>plastic container</u> into a big, clean sock. Put a <u>flat plastic circle and a square shape</u> into the feelie bag. Ask the child to pull out a shape you name. Show a picture of that shape, if you need to, and talk about how it would feel.

The square has straight sides and pointy corners.
Can you feel the square, Jenny?

When a child can tell the circle from other shapes easily, try a triangle with other shapes. Let two or three friends practice this game together.

 in or out   1–4 min   1–3 Threes

427

Threes can

- match a shape to its picture
- follow directions

Bead Patterns

Make or buy <u>simple bead pattern cards</u> to use with the <u>stringing beads</u>. (See Sample Bead Patterns on page 352.) Show an interested child how to look at the pattern and place the matching beads on the card. Encourage the child to begin at the left of the bead pattern and work towards the right, but don't force this.

When the child has the beads he needs on the card, let him string all the beads in order. Help him hold the beads on the string next to the picture on the card to see if they make the same pattern.

Begin with a few very easy patterns. Offer harder ones for a child who is especially interested and able.

 in or out   3–15 min   1–2 Threes

428

Threes can

- do easy sorting

Color-Sorting Board

Make a <u>set of color picture cards</u> (green things, blue things, and red things) for your Threes to sort on a <u>sorting board</u>. If you wish, you can copy and color in the sample pictures on page 350. In the first place in each row on the board, put a card with a colored rectangle. Then help a child sort through the rest of the cards, putting each in the row whose color it matches. Ask questions to help the child figure out how sorting works.

What's this picture, Tracy?
Yes, a frog. It's a green frog.
Can you show me where the green pictures go?

 in or out   5–20 min   1–3 Threes

429

Threes can

- put three things in order by size

Big to Little

Put out a <u>set of three nesting blocks</u> in a row, from biggest to smallest. Talk about which is big, middle-sized and smallest. Then mix up the blocks. Ask the child to put them in order again.

That's right, Henry. That's the biggest.
Now put the middle-sized block next to it.

Try this with other things:

empty cans

toy cars

plastic jars

teddy bears

Add more things when the children can put three things in order easily.

 indoors 3–10 min # 1–2 Threes

430

Threes can

- follow directions

Shape Potato Prints

Cut a few <u>potatoes</u> in half. Carefully cut the outline of a simple shape into the flat center of each potato half. Make the outline about ½-inch deep. Then slice into the outside of the potato and cut up to where the shape begins. Be careful not to cut the shape off. Cut the outside of the potato away until just the shape is left sticking out. Show the Threes how to press these potato shapes on a <u>tempera-paint-soaked sponge</u>. Then have them press the shape on <u>paper</u> to make a print. Talk about the shape designs the children make.

 in or out 5–20 min # 1–15 Threes

431

Threes can

- name two or three colors
- throw a ball

Color Beanbag Toss

Cover three or four large cardboard boxes with colored contact paper, or paint them. Use colors your Threes can match well. Make beanbags to match the box colors. Have the child stand two or three steps away from the boxes and toss each beanbag into the box of the same color. See which colors they can name as they play.

What color beanbag are you holding now, Michael? Which box will you throw it into?

 in or out   3–12 min   1–3 Threes

432

Threes can

- point to a color you name
- do easy matching

Pattern Match Game

Use scraps of cloth with pretty designs to make a set of pattern-matching cards. Use checks, plaids, stripes, and prints that are all quite different from each other. For each card glue a square of material to a larger sturdy cardboard square. Make two cards of each material. Show the Threes how to spread out the cards and place the same ones on top of each other. Ask questions and talk about the designs as the children work.

Do you see the card that has red and white lines?
Those lines are called stripes.
Do you see the one that is the same?

 in or out   3–15 min   1–2 Threes

433

Threes can

- match simple bead and block patterns

Parquetry Patterns

Put out simple <u>parquetry pattern cards</u> with the <u>parquetry blocks</u> for the Threes to use. Show the children how to place a block onto a matching place on the cards. Talk about the shapes and colors as they work.

You put the red square on the green square.
Are they the same?

Keep the blocks and cards in a <u>container</u> on a low shelf where the Threes can use them on their own.

There are some sample parquetry patterns on pages 352 and 353.

 in or out | 3–15 min | 1–2 Threes

434

Threes can

- name some colors

Color Surprise Game

Put lots of <u>small toys</u> that are a single color each into a <u>big bag</u>. Let each child take a turn pulling one thing out of the bag. Have all the children say the color of that thing as soon as they see it. Make this fun by being excited and surprised when the children can name the color.

What's Ginny going to pull out?
Are you going to know the color of this one?
My goodness! It is a red car!
You really know that color!

 in or out | 2–10 min | 1–15 Threes

435

Threes can

■ name circle, triangle, and square

Naming Shapes

Put lots of <u>circle, triangle, and square shapes</u> into a <u>feelie bag</u>. Have the children take turns pulling out one shape at a time. See if each child can name the shape he pulls out and put it into a pile of things of that shape. Show how happy you are with how well the children play.

Wow, Jerry. You put the square with the other squares!
And you knew its name!

When children know shapes very well, see if they can name them before looking at them.

 in or out │ 3–10 min │ 1–3 Threes

436

Threes can

■ trace a cross and diamond shape

Tracing Shapes

Use a <u>thin-tipped pen</u> to draw different simple shapes on <u>paper</u>. Draw circles, triangles, squares, rectangles, diamonds, and others. Show the Threes how to use a <u>wide marker</u> to trace over the lines you draw. Talk about the shape as the child works. Talk about the kinds of lines, curves, and points that make up each shape.

That's good, Nancy. Now here comes a corner.
Your square has four corners, doesn't it?

 in or out │ 2–5 min │ 1–5 Threes

Activities for Learning from the World Around Them

Homemade Shape-Sorting Boxes

Shoe Box Shape-Sorter

Choose a few different shapes for each box. Make different boxes for different sets of shapes.

1. Choose two to four small table blocks for your shapes.
2. Outline the shapes you want to use on the lid of a sturdy shoe box.
3. Cut out the shapes in the lid with a sharp knife, an X-acto blade, or single-edge razor blade.
4. Store one or more of each block in the shoe box. Show the child how to take the blocks out, put the lid on the box, and drop the shapes through the right holes.

Margarine Tub Shape-Sorter

1. Use $\frac{1}{2}''$ wood or plastic beads for shapes. Use cubes (square) and spheres (round).
2. Have a margarine tub with a lid for each shape.
3. Outline one shape on the lid of each tub. Use a sharp knife, an X-acto blade, or single-edge razor blade to cut the hole.
4. Put round and square beads into a larger container.
5. Show children how to sort the two shapes into the right tubs.

Coffee Can Sorting Boxes

1. Collect coffee cans with plastic lids to use as sorting boxes. Use cans with no rough edges. Cover with pretty contact paper if you wish.
2. Choose some shapes. Use small plastic or wooden blocks.
3. Outline one, two, or three shapes on each lid. Cut them out with a sharp knife, X-acto blade, or single-edge razor blade.
4. Show children how to drop blocks into the correct holes and how to take off and replace the lid to play again.

Giant Shape-Sorting Box

More than one shape may fit into some of the holes on this homemade box. Don't worry if this is so. Talk about the shapes and where they go as the children have fun using them.

1. You can make large shape blocks (circles, squares, triangles, and rectangles) from the styrofoam used to make winter holiday decorations. These blocks will last longer if you cover them with material. Or you can buy foam shapes through school supply companies.
2. Outline your shapes on the sides of a very large, sturdy cardboard box. Use a knife or X-acto blade to cut the shapes out.
3. Put all the shape blocks into a smaller box next to the big box. Show the children how to match the shape blocks to the holes, drop the blocks in, and get the blocks out to play again.

How to Make Sorting Boards

Sorting Board 1: Wooden with Cup Hooks

1. Get a rectangular board about 18 inches wide by 30 inches long. Make sure it is smooth, with no rough edges.
2. Draw a thick, dark line down the center of the board.
3. Screw in six cup hooks, evenly spaced, in a row on each side. You'll need 12 hooks in all.
4. Small pictures that fit between hooks should be glued to oaktag or cardboard and covered with clear contact paper. Punch a hole in the top of each picture to hang it up.
5. Hang up one picture from each set on the first hook. Let the child hang the rest.

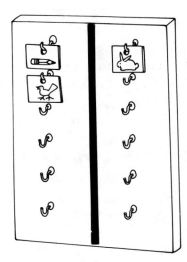

Sorting Board 2: Cloth with Cloth Pockets

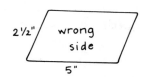
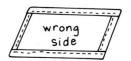

1. Cut out twelve cloth $2\frac{1}{2} \times 5$-inch rectangles. Hem $\frac{1}{4}$ inch on all sides of each.
2. Sew the rectangles onto a sturdy piece of 18″ × 36″ cloth in two rows to make pockets. Be sure to leave the tops (a 5-inch side) of each pocket open. Sew only the two sides and the bottom.
3. Hang this sorting board on a wall, the back of a bookcase, or a closet door.
4. Make sets of cards to fit into the pockets. Be sure that when the card is in the pocket, most of the picture can still be seen.

A shoe bag also works well as a cloth sorting board for bigger pictures.

Sorting Board 3: Cardboard with Pockets

(This board is not as sturdy as Boards 1 and 2)

1. Use 12 sturdy brown envelopes, library card pockets, or envelopes with the flaps turned in and glued down to make them sturdier.
2. Glue the envelopes onto a large posterboard, making six evenly spaced pockets in two lines.
3. Put the sorting board on a low table or floor for children to use. Or try hanging it down low where children can reach it.

Sorting Box

1. Use a grocery box with dividers, such as a box for large soda bottles.
2. Cover the box with colored contact paper, if you want.
3. Use strong tape to make the dividers sturdy.
4. Turn the box on its side so that the dividers become shelves.
5. Put a picture in each space to show children what they will be sorting. Help them get started.

How to Make Picture Card Sets for Sorting Boards

Make six or more cards in each set. (Put out two sets at a time.)

1. Cut cards to fit the pockets or spaces on your sorting board and glue pictures to them.
2. Cover the cards with clear contact paper.
3. If the cards will be hung on cup hooks, punch a hole at the top.
4. Keep each set separate in small zip-lock sandwich bags or hold them together with rubber bands.

Ideas for Easy Picture Cards to Make

flowers	puppies	shapes	fish	babies
boys	houses	(squares,	books	birds
girls	clothes	triangles,	furniture	trees
men	cars	rectangles,	teddy bears	cats
women	airplanes	stars, hearts)	happy faces	boats

Sample Pictures for Color Sorting Board

1. Copy these pictures onto cards that will fit your sorting board.
2. Color the pictures. Give children two or three colors to work on.

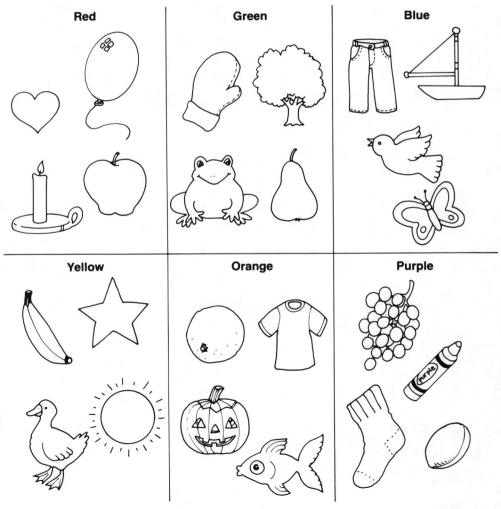

| Red | Green | Blue |
| Yellow | Orange | Purple |

Inch Cube Patterns

1. Copy patterns onto cardboard cards. Use your inch cubes as a guide when you draw.
2. Color the patterns to match the color of cubes you have. Use only two to four colors on a card.
3. Make your own easier or harder patterns for the children you work with.

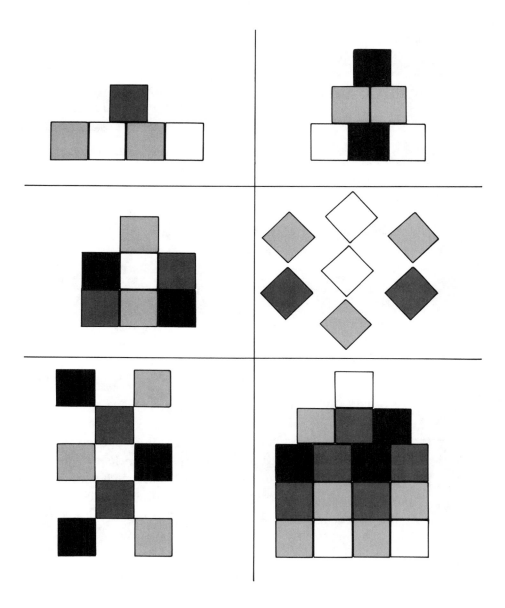

Sample Bead Patterns

1. Copy bead patterns onto cardboard cards. Use the real beads you have as a guide for drawing.
2. Color beads to match the beads you have. Use only two or three colors in one pattern.
3. Show children how to copy the pattern by first putting beads on the cards, then stringing them in the right order.
4. Show children how to string the pattern again.
5. Try making your own patterns, too.

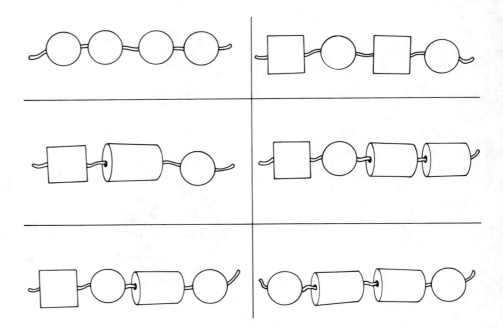

Sample Parquetry Patterns

1. Copy the patterns here and on page 353 onto cardboard cards. Use your own parquetry blocks as a guide as you draw.
2. Color the patterns to match your own parquetry block colors.
3. Show your threes how to place the right block onto the right space.
4. Make up some of your own simple patterns, too.

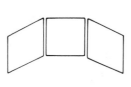 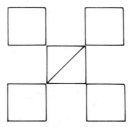 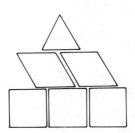

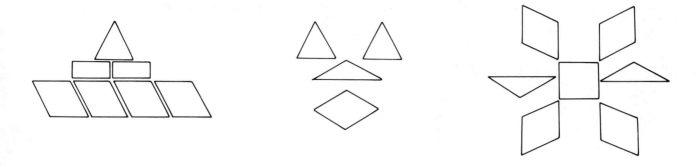

Your Own Activities: Learning from the World Around Them

Write your own activities in these blank boxes. You will find more information on writing your own activities in the Planning section, page 38.

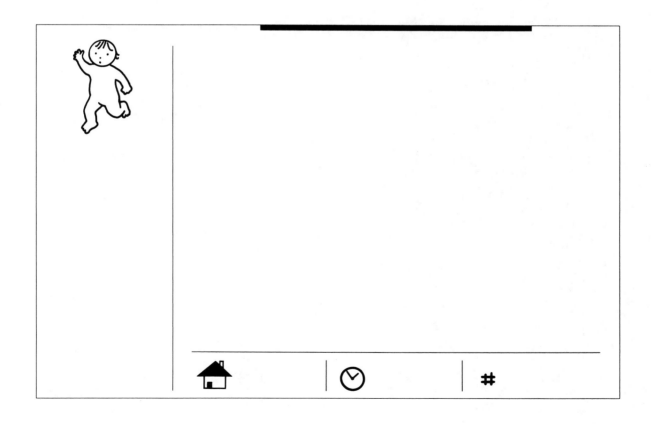

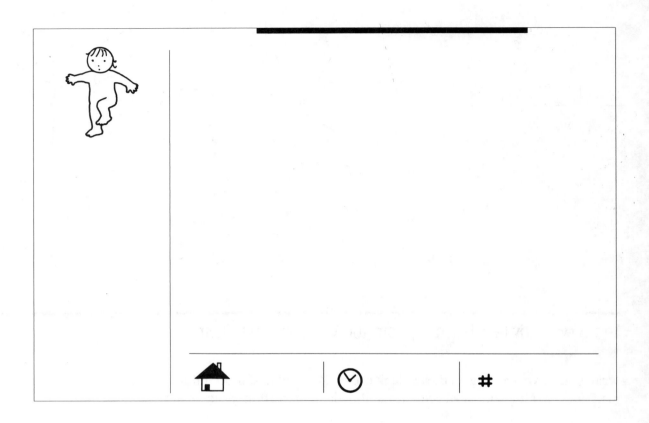

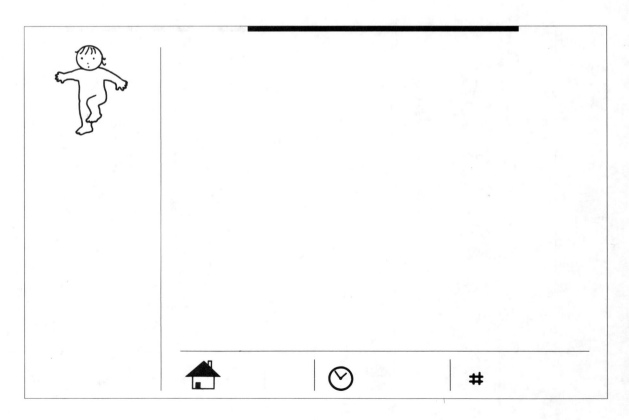